P9-DNS-400

Scrambles Amongst the Alps

IN THE YEARS 1860-'69.

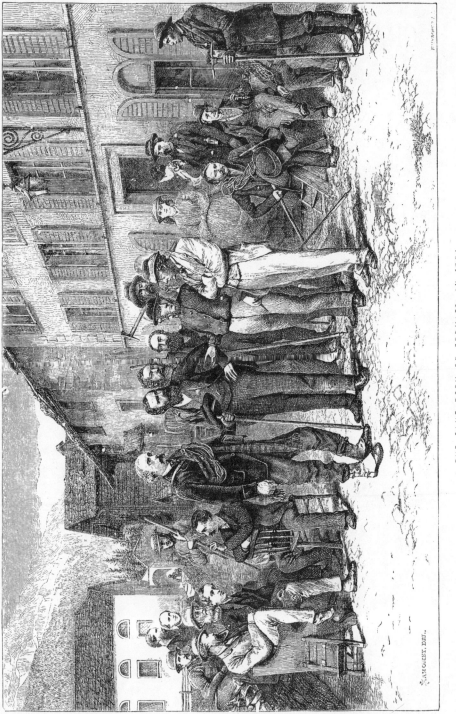

JAMORUY, DEL.

FRONTISPIECE.　　　THE CLUB-ROOM OF ZERMATT, IN 1864.　　　Page 110.

SCRAMBLES AMONGST THE ALPS

IN THE YEARS 1860-'69.

BY

EDWARD WHYMPER.

WITH OVER 100 ILLUSTRATIONS.

Toil and pleasure, in their natures opposite, are yet linked together in a kind
of necessary connection.—Livy.

Ten Speed Press

Cover Design by Brenton Beck
Copyright © 1981 by Ten Speed Press
P O Box 7123
Berkeley, California 94707
All Rights Reserved

ISBN 0-89815-043-4
Library of Congress Catalog Number 81-50250

We wish to thank Nick Clinch for his assistance
in making the publication of this volume possible.

2   3   4   5   —   92   91   90   89   88

PREFACE

In the year 1860, shortly before leaving England for a long Continental tour, a certain eminent London publisher requested me to make for him some sketches of the great Alpine peaks. At this time I had only a literary acquaintance with mountaineering, and had even not seen—much less set foot upon—a mountain. Amongst the peaks which were upon my list was Mont Pelvoux, in Dauphine. The sketches that were required of it were to celebrate the triumph of some Englishmen who intended to make its ascent. They came—they saw—but they did not conquer. By a mere chance I fell in with a very agreeable Frenchman who accompanied this party, and was pressed by him to return to the assault. In 1861 we did so, with my friend Macdonald, and we conquered. This was the origin of my scrambles amongst the Alps.

The ascent of Mont Pelvoux (including the disagreeables) was a very delightful scramble. The mountain air did *not* act as an emetic ; the sky did *not* look black instead of blue ; nor did I feel tempted to throw myself over precipices. I hastened to enlarge my experience, and went to the Matterhorn. I was urged toward Mont Pelvoux by those mysterious impulses which cause men to peer into the unknown. Not only was this mountain reputed to be the highest in France, and on that account was worthy of attention, but it was the dominating point of a most picturesque district of the highest interest, which, to this day, remains almost unexplored. The Matterhorn attracted me simply by its grandeur. It was considered to be the most thoroughly inaccessible of all mountains, even by those who ought to have known better. Stimulated to make fresh exertions by one repulse after another, I returned, year after year, as I had opportunity, more and more determined to find a way up it, or to *prove* it to be really inaccessible.

A considerable portion of this volume is occupied by the history of these attacks on the Matterhorn, and the other excursions that are described have all some connection, more or less remote, with that mountain or with Mont Pelvoux. All are new excursions (that is, excursions made for the first time), unless the contrary is pointed out. Some have been passed over very briefly, and entire ascents or descents have been disposed of in a single line. If they had been worked out at full length, three volumes instead of one would have been required. Generally speaking, the salient points alone have been dwelt upon, and the rest has been left to the imagination. This treatment has saved the reader from much useless repetition.

3

In endeavoring to make the book of some use to those who may wish to go mountain-scrambling, whether in the Alps or elsewhere, undue prominence, perhaps, has been given to our mistakes and failures; and it will doubtless be pointed out that our practice must have been bad if the principles which are laid down are sound, or that the principles must be unsound if the practice was good. It is maintained in an early chapter that the positive, or unavoidable, dangers of mountaineering are very small, yet from subsequent pages it can be shown that very considerable risks were run. The reason is obvious—we were not immaculate. Our blunders are not held up to be admired or to be imitated, but to be avoided.

These scrambles amongst the Alps were holiday excursions, and as such they should be judged. They are spoken of as sport, and nothing more. The pleasure that they gave me cannot, I fear, be transferred to others. The ablest pens have failed, and must always fail, to give a true idea of the grandeur of the Alps. The most minute descriptions of the greatest writers do nothing more than convey impressions that are entirely erroneous—the reader conjures up visions, it may be magnificent ones, but they are infinitely inferior to the reality. I have dealt sparingly in descriptions, and have employed illustrations freely, in the hope that the pencil may perhaps succeed where the pen must inevitably have failed.

The preparation of the illustrations has occupied a large part of my time during the last six years. With the exception of the views upon pp. 18, 19 and 24, the whole of the illustrations have been engraved expressly for the book, and, unless it is otherwise specified, all are from my own sketches. About fifty have been drawn on the wood by Mr. James Mahoney, and I am much indebted to that artist for the care and fidelity with which he has followed my slight memoranda, and for the spirit that he has put into his admirable designs. Most of his drawings will be identified by his monogram. Twenty of the remainder are the work of Mr. Cyrus Johnston, and out of these I would draw especial attention to the view of the Matterhorn facing p. 36, the striated rock upon p. 63, and the bits from the Mer de Glace upon pp. 138, 139. The illustrations have been introduced as illustrations, and very rarely for ornamental purposes. We have subordinated everything in them to accuracy, and it is only fair to the artists who have honored me by their assistance to say that many of their designs would have ranked higher as works of art if they had been subjected to fewer restrictions.

LIST OF ILLUSTRATIONS.

The Drawings were made on the Wood by
H. J. Boot, C. Johnson, J. Mahoney, J. W. North, P. Skelton, W. G. Smith, and C. J. Staniland;
and were Engraved by J. W. and Edward Whymper.

From Photographs. **Designs.*

FULL-PAGE ILLUSTRATIONS.

CONTENTS.

Scrambles Amongst the Alps

IN THE YEARS 1860-'69.

BEACHY HEAD.

CHAPTER I.

ON the 23d of July, 1860, I started for my first tour in the Alps. As we steamed out into the Channel, Beachy Head came into view, and recalled a scramble of many years ago. With the impudence of ignorance, my brother and I, schoolboys both, had tried to scale that great chalk cliff. Not the head itself—where sea-birds circle, and where the flints are ranged so orderly in parallel lines—but at a place more to the east, where the pinnacle called the Devil's Chimney had fallen down. Since that time we have been often in dangers of different kinds, but never have we more nearly broken our necks than upon that occasion.

In Paris I made two ascents. The first to the seventh floor of a house in the Quartier Latin—to an artist friend, who was engaged, at the moment of my entry, in combat with a little Jew. He hurled him with great good-will and with considerable force into some of his crockery, and then recommended me to go up the towers of Notre Dame. Half an hour later I stood on the parapet of the great west front, by the side of the leering fiend which for centuries has looked down upon the great

city. It looked over the Hôtel Dieu to a small and commonplace building, around which there was always a moving crowd. To that building I descended. It was filled with chattering women and eager children, who were struggling to get a good sight of three corpses which were exposed to view. It was the Morgue. I quitted the place disgusted, and overheard two women discussing the spectacle. One of them concluded with, "But that it is droll;" the other answered approvingly, "But that it is droll;" and the Devil of Notre Dame, looking down upon them, seemed to say, "Yes, your climax, the cancan— your end, not uncommonly, that building: it is droll, but that it is droll."

I passed on to Switzerland; saw the sunlight lingering on the giants of the Oberland; heard the echoes from the cow horns in the Lauterbrunnen valley and the avalanches rattling off the Jungfrau; and then crossed the Gemmi into the Valais, resting for a time by the beautiful Oeschinen See, and getting a forcible illustration of glacier-motion in a neighboring valley — the Gasteren Thal. The upper end of this valley is crowned by the Tschingel glacier, which,

as it descends, passes over an abrupt cliff that is in the centre of its course. On each side the continuity of the glacier is maintained, but in the centre it is cleft in twain by the cliff. Lower down it is consolidated again. I scrambled on to this lower portion, advanced toward the cliff, and then stopped to admire the contrast of the brilliant pinnacles of ice with the blue sky. Without a warning, a huge slice of the glacier broke away and fell over the cliff on to the lower portion with a thundering crash. Fragments rolled beyond me, although, fortunately, not in my direction. I fled, and did not stop until off the glacier, but before it was quitted learned another lesson in glacial matters: the terminal moraine, which seemed to be a solid mound, broke away underneath me, and showed that it was only a superficial covering resting on a slope of glassy ice.

On the steep path over the Gemmi there were opportunities for observing the manners and customs of the Swiss mule. It is not perhaps in revenge for

generations of ill-treatment that the mule grinds one's legs against fences and stone walls, and pretends to stumble in awkward places, particularly when coming round corners and on the brinks of precipices; but their evil habit of walking on the outside edges of paths (even in the most unguarded positions) is one that is distinctly the result of association with man. The transport of wood from the mountains into the valleys occupies most of the mules during a considerable portion of the year: the fagots into which the wood is made up project some distance on each side, and it is said that they walk intuitively to the outside of paths having rocks on the other side to avoid the collisions which would otherwise occur. When they carry tourists they behave in a similar manner; and no doubt when the good time for mules arrives, and they no longer carry burdens, they will still continue, by natural selection, to do the same. This habit frequently gives rise to scenes: two mules meet— each wishes to pass on the outside, and neither will give way. It requires considerable persuasion, through the medium of the tail, before such difficulties are arranged.

I visited the baths of Leuk, and saw the queer assemblage of men, women and children, attired in bathing-gowns, chatting, drinking and playing at chess in the water. The company did not seem to be perfectly sure whether it was decorous in such a situation and in such attire for elderly men to chase young females from one corner to another, but it was unanimous in howling at the advent of a stranger who remained covered, and literally yelled when I departed without exhibiting my sketch.

I trudged up the Rhone valley, and turned aside at Visp to go up the Visp Thal, where one would expect to see greater traces of glacial action, if a glacier formerly filled it, as one is said to have done.

I was bound for the valley of Saas, and my work took me high up the Alps on either side, far beyond the limit of trees and the tracks of tourists. The view from the slopes of the Wiessmies, on the eastern side of the valley, five or six thousand feet above the village of Saas, is perhaps the finest of its kind in the Alps. The full height of the three-peaked Mischabel (the highest mountain in Switzerland) is seen at one glance—eleven thousand feet of dense forests, green alps, pinnacles of rock and glittering glaciers. The peaks seemed to me then to be hopelessly inaccessible from this direction.

I descended the valley to the village of Stalden, and then went up the Visp Thal to Zermatt, and stopped there several days. Numerous traces of the formidable earthquake-shocks of five years before still remained, particularly at St. Nicholas, where the inhabitants had been terrified beyond measure at the destruction of their churches and houses. At this place, as well as at Visp, a large part of the population was obliged to live under canvas for several months. It is remarkable that there was hardly a life lost on this occasion, although there were about fifty shocks, some of which were very severe.

At Zermatt I wandered in many directions, but the weather was bad and my work was much retarded. One day, after spending a long time in attempts to sketch near the Hörnli, and in futile endeavors to seize the forms of the peaks as they for a few seconds peered out from above the dense banks of woolly clouds, I determined not to return to Zermatt by the usual path, but to cross the Görner glacier to the Riffel hotel. After a rapid scramble over the polished rocks and snow-beds which skirt the base of the Theodule glacier, and wading through some of the streams which flow from it, at that time much swollen by the late rains, the first difficulty was arrived at, in the shape of a precipice about three hundred feet high. It seemed that there would be no difficulty in crossing the glacier if the cliff could be descended, but higher up and lower down the ice appeared, to my inexperienced eyes, to be impassable for a single person. The general contour of the cliff was nearly perpendicular, but it was a good deal broken up, and there was little difficulty in descending by zigzagging from one mass to another. At length there was a long slab, nearly smooth, fixed at an angle of about forty degrees between two wall-sided pieces of rock : nothing, except the glacier, could be seen below. It was a very awkward place, but being doubtful if return were possible, as I had been dropping from one ledge to another, I passed at length by lying across the slab, putting the shoulder stiffly against one side and the feet against the other, and gradually wriggling down, by first moving the legs and then the back. When the bottom of the slab was gained a friendly crack was seen, into which the point of the bâton could be stuck, and I dropped down to the next piece. It took a long time coming down that little bit of cliff, and for a few seconds it was satisfactory to see the ice close at hand. In another moment a second difficulty presented itself. The glacier swept round an angle of the cliff, and as the ice was not of the nature of treacle or thin putty, it kept away from the little bay on the edge of which I stood. We were not widely separated, but the edge of the ice was higher than the opposite edge of rock ; and worse, the rock was covered with loose earth and stones which had fallen from above. All along the side of the cliff, as far as could be seen in both directions, the ice did not touch it, but there was this marginal crevasse, seven feet wide and of unknown depth.

All this was seen at a glance, and almost at once I concluded that I could not jump the crevasse, and began to try along the cliff lower down, but without success, for the ice rose higher and higher, until at last farther progress was stopped by the cliffs becoming perfectly smooth. With an axe it would have been possible to cut up the side of the ice —without one, I saw there was no alternative but to return and face the jump.

It was getting toward evening, and the solemn stillness of the High Alps was broken only by the sound of rushing water or of falling rocks. If the jump should be successful, well : if not, I fell into that horrible chasm, to be frozen in, or drowned in that gurgling, rushing water. Everything depended on that jump. Again I asked myself,

"Can it be done ?" It *must* be. So, finding my stick was useless, I threw it and the sketch-book to the ice, and first retreating as far as possible, ran forward with all my might, took the leap, barely reached the other side, and fell awkwardly on my knees. Almost at the same moment a shower of stones fell on the spot from which I had jumped.

The glacier was crossed without further trouble, but the Riffel, which was then a very small building, was crammed with tourists, and could not take me in. As the way down was unknown to me, some of the people obligingly suggested getting a man at the chalets, otherwise the path would be certainly lost in the forest. On arriving at the chalets no man could be found, and the lights of Zermatt, shining through the trees, seemed to say, "Never mind a guide, but come along down : we'll show you the way ;" so off I went through the forest, going straight toward them. The path was lost in a moment, and was never recovered : I was tripped up by pine roots, I tumbled over rhododendron bushes, I fell over rocks. The night was pitch-dark, and after a time the lights of Zermatt became obscure or went out altogether. By a series of slides or falls, or evolutions more or less disagreeable, the descent through the forest was at length accomplished, but torrents of a formidable character had still to be passed before one could arrive at Zermatt. I felt my way about for hours, almost hopelessly, by an exhaustive process at last discovering a bridge, and about midnight, covered with dirt and scratches, re-entered the inn which I had quitted in the morning.

Others besides tourists got into difficulties. A day or two afterward, when on the way to my old station near the Hörnli, I met a stout curé who had essayed to cross the Theodule pass. His strength or his wind had failed, and he was being carried down, a helpless bundle and a ridiculous spectacle, on the back of a lanky guide, while the peasants stood by with folded hands, their reverence for the Church almost overcome by their sense of the ludicrous.

I descended the valley, diverging from the path at Randa to mount the slopes

of the Dom (the highest of the Mischabelhörner), in order to see the Weisshorn face to face. The latter mountain is the noblest in Switzerland, and from this direction it looks especially magnificent. On its north there is a large snowy plateau that feeds the glacier of which a portion is seen from Randa, and which on more than one occasion has destroyed that village. From the direction of the Dom—that is, immediately opposite—this Bies glacier seems to descend nearly vertically: it does not do so, although it is very steep. Its size is much less than formerly, and the lower portion, now divided into three tails, clings in a strange, weird-like manner to the cliffs, to which it seems scarcely possible that it can remain attached.

Unwillingly I parted from the sight of this glorious mountain, and went down to Visp. A party of English tourists had passed up the valley a short time before with a mule. The party numbered nine—eight women and a governess. The mule carried their luggage, and was ridden by each in turn. The peasants—themselves not unaccustomed to overload their beasts—were struck with astonishment at the unwonted sight, and made comments, more free than welcome to English ears, on the nonchalance with which young miss sat, calm and collected, on the

miserable beast, while it was struggling under her weight combined with that of the luggage. The story was often repeated; and it tends to sustain some of the hard things which have been said of late about young ladies from the ages of twelve or fourteen to eighteen.

Arriving once more in the Rhone valley, I proceeded to Viesch, and from thence ascended the Æggischhorn, on which unpleasant eminence I lost my way in a fog, and my temper shortly afterward. Then, after crossing the Grimsel in a severe thunderstorm, I passed on to Brienz, Interlachen and Berne, and thence to Fribourg and Morat, Neuchâtel, Martigny and the St.

Bernard. The massive walls of the convent were a welcome sight as I

waded through the snow-beds near the summit of the pass, and pleasant also was the courteous salutation of the brother who bade me enter. He wondered at the weight of my knapsack, and I at the hardness of their bread. The saying that the monks make the toast in the winter that they give to tourists in the following season is not founded on truth: the winter is their most busy time of the year. But it *is* true they have exercised so much hospitality that at times they have not possessed the means to furnish the fuel for heating their chapel in the winter.

Instead of descending to Aosta, I turned aside into the Val Pelline, in order to obtain views of the Dent d'Erin. The night had come on before Biona was gained, and I had to knock long and loud upon the door of the curé's house before it was opened. An old woman with querulous voice and with a large goître answered the summons, and demanded rather sharply what was wanted, but became pacific, almost good-natured, when a five-franc piece was held in her face and she heard that lodging and supper were requested in exchange.

My directions asserted that a passage existed from Prerayen, at the head of this valley, to Breuil, in the Val Tournanche, and the old woman, now convinced of my respectability, busied herself to find a guide. Presently she introduced a native picturesquely attired in high-peaked hat, braided jacket, scarlet waistcoat and indigo pantaloons, who agreed to take me to the village of Val Tournanche. We set off early on the next morning, and got to the summit of the pass without difficulty. It gave me my first experience of considerable slopes of hard, steep snow, and, like all beginners, I endeavored to prop myself up with my stick, and kept it *outside*, instead of holding it between myself and the slope, and leaning upon it, as should have been done. The man enlightened me, but he had, properly, a very small opinion of his employer, and it is probably on that account that, a few minutes after we had passed the summit, he said he would not go any farther and would return to Biona. All argument was useless: he stood still, and to every-

thing that was said answered nothing but that he would go back. Being rather nervous about descending some long snow-slopes which still intervened between us and the head of the valley, I offered more pay, and he went on a little way. Presently there were some cliffs, down which we had to scramble. He called to me to stop, then shouted that he would go back, and beckoned to me to come up. On the contrary, I waited for him to come down, but instead of doing so, in a second or two he turned round, clambered deliberately up the cliff and vanished. I supposed it was only a ruse to extort offers of more money, and waited for half an hour, but he did not appear again. This was rather embarrassing, for he carried off my knapsack. The choice of action lay between chasing him and going on to Breuil, risking the loss of my knapsack. I chose the latter course, and got to Breuil the same evening. The landlord of the inn, suspicious of a person entirely innocent of luggage, was doubtful if he could admit me, and eventually thrust me into a kind of loft, which was already occupied by guides and by hay. In later years we became good friends, and he did not hesitate to give credit and even to advance considerable sums.

My sketches from Breuil were made under difficulties: my materials had been carried off, nothing better than fine sugar-paper could be obtained, and the pencils seemed to contain more silica than plumbago. However, they *were* made, and the pass was again crossed, this time alone. By the following evening the old woman of Biona again produced the faithless guide. The knapsack was recovered after the lapse of several hours, and then I poured forth all the terms of abuse and reproach of which I was master. The man smiled when called a liar, and shrugged his shoulders when referred to as a thief, but drew his knife when spoken of as a pig.

The following night was spent at Cormayeur, and the day after I crossed the Col Ferrex to Orsières, and on the next the Tête Noir to Chamounix. The Emperor Napoleon arrived the same day, and access to the Mer de Glace was refused to tourists; but, by scrambling along the Plan des Aiguilles, I managed to outwit the guards, and to arrive at the Montanvert as the imperial party was leaving, failing to get to the Jardin the same afternoon, but very nearly succeeding in breaking a leg by dislodging great rocks on the moraine of the glacier.

From Chamounix I went to Geneva, and thence by the Mont Cenis to Turin and to the Vaudois valleys. A long and weary day had ended when Paesana was reached. The inn was full, and I was tired and about to go to bed when some village stragglers entered and began to sing. They sang to Garibaldi! The tenor, a ragged fellow, whose clothes were not worth a shilling, took the lead with wonderful expression and feeling. The others kept their places and sang in admirable time. For hours I sat enchanted, and long after I retired the sound of their melody could be heard, relieved at times by the treble of the girl who belonged to the inn.

GARIBALDI!

The next morning I passed the little lakes which are the sources of the Po, on my way into France. The weather was stormy, and misinterpreting the patois of some natives—who in reality pointed out the right way—I missed the track, and found myself under the cliffs of Monte Viso. A gap that was occasionally seen in the ridge connecting it with the mountains to the east tempted me up, and after a battle with a snow-slope of excessive steepness, I reached the summit. The scene was extraordinary, and, in my experience, unique. To the north there was not a particle of mist, and the violent wind coming from that direction blew one back staggering. But on the side of Italy the valleys were completely filled with dense masses of cloud to a certain level; and there—where they felt the influence of the wind—they were cut off as level as the top of a table, the ridges appearing above them.

I raced down to Abries, and went on through the gorge of the Guil to Mont Dauphin. The next day found me at La Bessée, at the junction of the Val Louise with the valley of the Durance, in full view of Mont Pelvoux; and by chance I walked into a cabaret where a Frenchman was breakfasting who a few days before had made an unsuccessful attempt to ascend that mountain with three Englishmen and the guide Michel Croz of Chamounix — a right good fellow, by name Jean Reynaud.

The same night I slept at Briançon, intending to take the courier on the following day to Grenoble, but all places had been secured several days beforehand, so I set out at two P. M. on the next day for a seventy-mile walk. The weather was again bad, and on the summit of the Col de Lautaret I was forced to seek shelter in the wretched little hospice. It was filled with workmen who were employed on the road, and with noxious vapors which proceeded from them. The inclemency of the weather was preferable to the inhospitality of the interior. Outside, it was disagreeable, but grand—inside, it was disagreeable and mean. The walk was continued under a deluge of rain, and I felt the way down, so intense was the darkness, to the village of La Grave, where the people of the inn detained me forcibly. It was perhaps fortunate that they did so, for during that night blocks of rock fell at several places from the cliffs on to the road with such force that they made large holes in the macadam, which looked as if there had been explosions of gunpowder. I resumed the walk at half-past five next morning, and proceeded, under steady rain, through Bourg d'Oysans to Grenoble, arriving at the latter place soon after seven P. M., having accomplished the entire distance from Briançon in about eighteen hours of actual walking.

This was the end of the Alpine portion of my tour of 1860, on which I was introduced to the great peaks, and acquired the passion for mountain-scrambling the development of which is described in the following chapters.

BRIANÇON.

CHAPTER II.
THE ASCENT OF MONT PELVOUX.

THE district of which Mont Pelvoux and the neighboring summits are the culminating points is, both historically and topographically, one of the most interesting in the Alps. As the nursery and the home of the Vaudois, it has claims to permanent attention: the names of Waldo and of Neff will be remembered when men more famous in their time are forgotten, and the memory of the heroic courage and the simple piety of their disciples will endure as long as history lasts.

This district contains the highest summits in France, and some of its finest scenery. It has not perhaps the beauties of Switzerland, but has charms of its own: its cliffs, its torrents and its gorges are unsurpassed, its deep and savage valleys present pictures of gran-

THE DURANCE.

ALÉFROIDE
(12,872)

PIC SANS NOM
(12,815)

MONT PELVOUX
(12,973) (12,923)

MONT PELVOUX AND THE ALÉFROIDE, FROM NEAR MONT DAUPHIN, IN THE VALLEY OF THE DURANCE.

deur, and even sublimity, and it is second to none in the boldness of its mountain forms.

The district includes a mass of valleys which vie with each other in singularity of character and dissimilarity of climate. Some the rays of the sun can never reach, they are so deep and narrow. In others the very antipodes may be found, the temperature more like that of the plains of Italy than of alpine France. This great range of climate has a marked effect on the flora of these valleys: sterility reigns in some, stones take the place of trees, débris and mud replace plants and flowers: in others, in the space of a few miles, one passes vines, apple, pear and cherry trees, the birch, alder, walnut, ash, larch and pine alternating with fields of rye, barley, oats, beans and potatoes.

The valleys are for the most part short and erratic. They are not, apparently, arranged on any definite plan: they are not disposed, as is frequently the case elsewhere, either at right angles to, or parallel with, the highest summits, but they wander hither and thither, taking one direction for a few miles, then doubling back, and then perhaps resuming their original course. Thus long perspectives are rarely to be seen, and it is difficult to form a general idea of the disposition of the peaks.

The highest summits are arranged almost in a horse-shoe form. The highest of all, which occupies a central position, is the Pointe des Écrins; the second in height, the Meije, is on the north; and the Mont Pelvoux, which gives its name to the entire block, stands almost detached by itself on the outside.

At the beginning of July, 1861, I despatched to Reynaud from Havre blankets (which were taxed as "prohibited fabrics"), rope, and other things desirable for the excursion, and set out on the tour of France, but four weeks later, at Nîmes, found myself completely collapsed by the heat, then 94° Fahr. in the shade, so I took a night train at once to Grenoble.

I lost my way in the streets of this picturesque but noisome town, and hav-

ing but a half hour left in which to get a dinner and take a place in the diligence, was not well pleased to hear that an Englishman wished to see me. It turned out to be my friend Macdonald, who confided to me that he was going to try to ascend a mountain called Pelvoux in the course of ten days, but on hearing of my intentions agreed to join us at La Bessée on the 3d of August. In a few moments more I was perched in the banquette *en route* for Bourg d'Oysans, in a miserable vehicle which took nearly eight hours to accomplish less than thirty miles.

At five on a lovely morning I shouldered my knapsack and started for Briançon. Gauzy mists clung to the mountains, but melted away when touched by the sun, and disappeared by jerks (in the manner of views when focused in a magic lantern), revealing the wonderfully bent and folded strata in the limestone cliffs behind the town. Then I entered the Combe de Malval, and heard the Romanche eating its way through that wonderful gorge, and passed on to Le Dauphin, where the first glacier came into view, tailing over the mountain-side on the right. From this place until the summit of the Col de Lautaret was passed, every gap in the mountains showed a glittering glacier or a soaring peak: the finest view was at La Grave, where the Meije rises by a series of tremendous precipices eight thousand feet above the road. The finest distant view of the pass is seen after crossing the col, near Monêtier. A mountain, commonly supposed to be Monte Viso, appears at the end of the vista, shooting into the sky: in the middle distance, but still ten miles off, is Briançon with its interminable forts, and in the foreground, leading down to the Guisane and rising high up the neighboring slopes, are fertile fields, studded with villages and church-spires. The next day I walked over from Briançon to La Bessée, to my worthy friend Jean Reynaud, the surveyor of roads of his district.

All the peaks of Mont Pelvoux are well seen from La Bessée—the highest point as well as that upon which the French engineers erected their cairn in 1828. Neither Reynaud nor any one else knew this. The natives knew only that the engineers had ascended one peak, and had seen from that a still higher point, which they called the Pointe des Arcines or des Écrins. They could not say whether this latter could be seen from La Bessée, nor could they tell the peak upon which the cairn had been erected. We were under the impression that the highest point was concealed by the peaks we saw, and would be gained by passing over them. They knew nothing of the ascent of Monsieur Puiseux, and they confidently asserted that the highest point of Mont Pelvoux had not been attained by any one: it was this point we wished to reach.

Nothing prevented our starting at once but the absence of Macdonald and the want of a bâton. Reynaud suggested a visit to the postmaster, who possessed a bâton of local celebrity. Down we went to the bureau, but it was closed: we hallooed through the slits, but no answer. At last the postmaster was discovered endeavoring (with very fair success) to make himself intoxicated. He was just able to ejaculate, "France! 'tis the first nation in the

MONT PELVOUX FROM ABOVE LA BESSÉE.

world!"—a phrase used by a Frenchman when in the state in which a Briton begins to shout, "We won't go home till morning," national glory being uppermost in the thoughts of one, and home in those of the other. The bâton was produced: it was a branch of a young oak, about five feet long, gnarled and twisted in several directions. "Sir," said the postmaster, as he presented it, "France! 'tis the first—the first nation in the world, by its—" He stuck. "Bâtons," I suggested. "Yes, yes, sir: by its bâtons, by its—its—" and here he could not get on at all. As I looked at this young limb, I thought of my own; but Reynaud, who knew everything about everybody in the village, said there was not a better one; so off we went with it, leaving the official staggering in the road, and muttering, "France! 'tis the first nation in the world!"

The 3d of August came, but Macdonald did not appear, so we started for the Val Louise, our party consisting of Reynaud, myself and a porter, Jean Casimir Giraud, nicknamed "Little

Nails," the shoemaker of the place. An hour and a half's smart walking took us to La Ville de Val Louise, our hearts gladdened by the glorious peaks of Pelvoux shining out without a cloud around them. I renewed acquaintance with the mayor of La Ville. His aspect was original and his manners were gracious, but the odor which proceeded from him was dreadful. The same may be said of most of the inhabitants of these valleys.

Reynaud kindly undertook to look after the commissariat, and I found to my annoyance, when we were about to leave, that I had given tacit consent to a small wine-cask being carried with us, which was a great nuisance from the commencement. It was excessively awkward to handle : one man tried to carry it, and then another, and at last it was slung from one of our bâtons, and was carried by two, which gave our party the appearance of a mechanical diagram to illustrate the uses of levers.

At La Ville the Val Louise splits into two branches — the Val d'Entraigues on the left, and the Vallon d'Alefred (or Ailefroide) on the right: our route was up the latter, and we moved steadily forward to the village of La Pisse, where Pierre Sémiond lived, who was reputed to know more about the Pelvoux than any other man. He looked an honest fellow, but unfortunately he was ill and could not come. He recommended his brother, an aged creature, whose furrowed and wrinkled face hardly seemed to announce the man we wanted ; but, having no choice, we engaged him and again set forth.

Walnut and a great variety of other trees gave shadow to our path and fresh vigor to our limbs, while below, in a sublime gorge, thundered the torrent, whose waters took their rise from the snows we hoped to tread on the morrow.

The mountain could not be seen at La Ville, owing to a high intervening ridge : we were now moving along the foot of this to get to the chalets of Alefred—or, as they are sometimes called, Aléfroide—where the mountain actually commences. From this direction the subordinate but more proximate peaks appear considerably higher than the loftier ones behind, and sometimes completely

IN THE VAL D'ALEFRED.

conceal them. But the whole height of the peak, which in these valleys goes under the name of the "Grand Pelvoux," is seen at one place from its summit to its base—six or seven thousand feet of nearly perpendicular cliffs.

The chalets of Alefred are a cluster of miserable wooden huts at the foot of the Grand Pelvoux, and are close to the junction of the streams which descend from the glacier de Sapenière (or du

Selé) on the left, and the glaciers Blanc and Noir on the right. We rested a minute to purchase some butter and milk, and Sémiond picked up a disreputable-looking lad to assist in carrying, pushing and otherwise moving the wine-cask.

Our route now turned sharply to the left, and all were glad that the day was drawing to a close, so that we had the

THE GRAND PELVOUX DE VAL LOUISE.

shadows from the mountains. A more frightful and desolate valley it is scarcely possible to imagine: it contains miles of boulders, débris, stones, sand and mud—few trees, and they placed so high as to be almost out of sight. Not a soul inhabits it: no birds are in the air, no fish in the waters: the mountain is too steep for the chamois, its slopes too inhospitable for the marmot, the whole too repulsive for the eagle. Not a living thing did we see in this sterile and savage valley during four days, except some few poor goats which had been driven there against their will.

We rested a little at a small spring, and then hastened onward till we nearly arrived at the foot of the Sapenière glacier, when Sémiond said we must turn to the right, up the slopes. This we did, and clambered for half an hour through scattered pines and fallen boulders. Then evening began to close in rapidly, and it was time to look for a resting-place. There was no difficulty in getting one, for all around it was a chaotic assemblage of rocks. We selected the under side of one, which was more than fifty feet long by twenty high, cleared it of rubbish, and then collected wood for a fire.

That camp-fire is a pleasant reminiscence. The wine-cask had got through all its troubles. It was tapped, and the Frenchmen seemed to derive some consolation from its execrable contents. Reynaud chanted scraps of French songs, and each contributed his share of joke, story or verse. The weather was perfect, and our prospects for the morrow were good. My companions' joy culminated when a packet of red fire was thrown into the flames. It hissed and bubbled for a moment or two, and then broke out into a grand flare. The effect of the momentary light was magnificent: all around the mountains were illuminated for a second, and then relapsed into their solemn gloom. One by one our party dropped off to sleep, and at last I got into my blanket-bag. It was hardly necessary, for although we were at a height of at least seven thousand feet, the minimum temperature was above 40° Fahrenheit.

We roused at three, but did not start till half-past four. Giraud had been engaged as far as this rock only, but as he wished to go on, we allowed him to accompany us. We mounted the slopes, and quickly got above the trees, then had a couple of hours' clambering over bits of precipitous rock and banks of débris, and at a quarter to seven got to a narrow glacier—Clos de l'Homme—which streamed out of the plateau on the summit, and nearly reached the glacier de Sapenière. We worked as much as possible to the right, in hope that we should not have to cross it, but were continually driven back, and at last we found that it was necessary to do so. Old Sémiond had a strong objection to the ice, and made explorations on his own account to endeavor to avoid it; but Reynaud and I preferred to cross it, and Giraud stuck to us. It was narrow—in fact, one could throw a stone across it—and was easily mounted on the side, but in the centre swelled into a steep dome, up which we were obliged to cut. Giraud stepped forward and said he should like to try his hand, and having got hold of the axe, would not give it up; and here, as well as afterward when it was necessary to cross the gullies filled with hard snow which abound on the higher part of the mountain, he did all the work, and did it admirably.

Old Sémiond of course came after us when we got across. We then zigzagged up some snow-slopes, and shortly afterward commenced to ascend the interminable array of buttresses which are the great peculiarity of the Pelvoux. They were very steep in many places, but on the whole afforded a good hold, and no climbing should be called difficult which does that. Gullies abounded among them, sometimes of great length and depth. *They* were frequently rotten, and would have been difficult for a single man to pass. The uppermost men were continually abused for dislodging rocks and for harpooning those below with their bâtons. However, without these incidents the climbing would have been dull: they helped to break the monotony.

We went up chimneys and gullies by the hour together, and always seemed to be coming to something, although we never got to it. The outline sketch will help to explain the situation. We stood

at the foot of a great buttress—perhaps about two hundred feet high—and looked up. It did not go to a point as in the diagram, because we could not see the top, although we felt convinced that behind the fringe of pinnacles we did see there was a top, and that it was the edge of the plateau we so

BUTTRESSES OF MONT PELVOUX.

much desired to attain. Up we mounted, and reached the pinnacles; but, lo! another set was seen, and another, and yet more, till we reached the top, and found it was only a buttress, and that we had to descend forty or fifty feet before we could commence to mount again. When this operation had been performed a few dozen times it began to be wearisome, especially as we were in the dark as to our whereabouts. Sémiond, however, encouraged us, and said he knew we were on the right route; so away we went once more.

It was now nearly mid-day, and we seemed no nearer the summit of the Pelvoux than when we started. At last we all joined together and held a council. "Sémiond, old friend, do you know where we are now?" "Oh yes, perfectly, to a yard and a half." "Well, then, how much are we below this plateau?" He affirmed we were not half an hour from the edge of the snow. "Very good: let us proceed." Half an hour passed, and then another, but we were still in the same state: pinnacles, buttresses and gullies were in profusion, but the plateau was not in sight. So we called him again—for he had been staring about latterly as if in doubt—and repeated the question, "How far below are we now?" Well, he thought it might be half an hour more. "But you said that just now: are you sure we are going right?" Yes, he believed we were. Believed!—that would not do. "Are you sure we are going right for the Pic des Arcines?" "Pic des Arcines!" he ejaculated in astonishment, as if he had heard the words for the first time—"Pic des Arcines! No, but for the pyramid, the celebrated pyramid he had helped the great Capitaine Durand," etc.

Here was a fix. We had been talking about it to him for a whole day, and now he confessed he knew nothing about it. I turned to Reynaud, who seemed thunderstruck: "What do you suggest?" He shrugged his shoulders. "Well," we said, after explaining our minds pretty freely to Sémiond, "the sooner we turn back the better, for we have no wish to see your pyramid."

We halted for an hour, and then commenced the descent. It took us nearly seven hours to come down to our rock, but I paid no heed to the distance, and do not remember anything about it. When we got down we made a discovery which affected us as much as the footprint in the sand did Robinson Crusoe: a blue silk veil lay by our fireside. There was but one solution—Macdonald had arrived, but where was he? We soon packed our baggage, and tramped in the dusk, through the stony desert, to Alefred, where we arrived about half-past nine. "Where is the Englishman?" was the first question. He was gone to sleep at La Ville.

We passed that night in a hay-loft, and in the morning, after settling with Sémiond, we posted down to catch Macdonald. We had already determined on the plan of operation, which was to get him to join us, return, and be independent of all guides, simply taking the best man we could get as a porter. I set my heart on Giraud—a good fellow, with no pretence, although in every respect up to the work. But we were disappointed: he was obliged to go to Briançon.

The walk soon became exciting. The natives inquired the result of our expedition, and common civility obliged us to stop. But I was afraid of losing my

man, for it was said he would wait only till ten o'clock, and that time was near at hand. At last I dashed over the bridge—time from Alefred an hour and a quarter—but a cantonnier stopped me, saying that the Englishman had just started for La Bessée. I rushed after him, turned angle after angle of the road, but could not see him: at last, as I came round a corner, he was also just turning another, going very fast. I shouted, and luckily he heard me. We returned, reprovisioned ourselves at La Ville, and the same evening saw us passing our first rock, en route for another. I have said we determined to take no guide, but on passing La Pisse old Sémiond turned out and offered his services. He went well, in spite of his years and disregard of truth. "Why not take him?" said my friend. So we offered him a fifth of his previous pay, and in a few seconds he closed with the offer, but this time came in an inferior position—we were to lead, he to follow. Our second follower was a youth of twenty-seven years, who was not all that could be desired. He drank Reynaud's wine, smoked our cigars, and quietly secreted the provisions when we were nearly starving. Discovery of his proceedings did not at all disconcert him, and he finished up by getting several items added to our bill at La Ville, which, not a little to his disgust, we disallowed.

This night we fixed our camp high above the tree-line, and indulged ourselves in the healthy employment of carrying our fuel up to it. The present rock was not so comfortable as the first, and before we could settle down we were obliged to turn out a large mass which was in the way. It was very obstinate, but moved at length—slowly and gently at first, then faster and faster, at last taking great jumps in the air, striking a stream of fire at every touch, which shone out brightly as it entered the gloomy valley below; and long after it was out of sight we heard it bounding downward, and then settle with a subdued crash on the glacier beneath. As we turned back from this curious sight,

Reynaud asked if we had ever seen a torrent on fire, and told us that in the spring the Durance, swollen by the melting of the snow, sometimes brings down so many rocks that where it passes through a narrow gorge at La Bessée no water whatever is seen, but only boulders rolling over and over, grinding each other into powder, and striking so many sparks that the stream looks as if it were on fire.

We had another merry evening, with nothing to mar it : the weather was perfect, and we lay backward in luxurious repose, looking at the sky spangled with its ten thousand brilliant lights.

> "The ranges stood
> Transfigured in the silver flood.
> Their snows were flashing cold and keen,
> Dead white, save where some sharp ravine
> Took shadow, or the sombre green
> Of hemlocks turned to pitchy black,
> Against the whiteness at their back." *

Macdonald related his experiences over the café noir. He had traveled

R. J. S. MACDONALD.

day and night for several days in order to join us, but had failed to find our first bivouac, and had encamped a few hundred yards from us under another rock, higher up the mountain. The next morning he discerned us going along a ridge at a great height above him, and as it was useless to endeavor to overtake us, he lay down and watched with a heavy heart until we had turned the corner of a buttress and vanished out of sight.

Nothing but the heavy breathing of our already sound-asleep comrades

* J. G. Whittier : *Snow-Bound.*

broke the solemn stillness of the night. It was a silence to be felt. Nothing ! Hark ! what is that dull booming sound above us ? Is that nothing ? There it is again, plainer : on it comes, nearer, clearer : 'tis a crag escaped from the heights above. What a fearful crash ! We jump to our feet. Down it comes with awful fury : what power can withstand its violence ? Dancing leaping, flying, dashing against others, roaring as it descends. Ah, it has passed ! No : there it is again, and we hold our breath as, with resistless force and explosions like artillery, it darts past, with an avalanche of shattered fragments trailing in its rear. 'Tis gone, and we breathe more freely as we hear the finale on the glacier below.

We retired at last, but I was too excited to sleep. At a quarter-past four every man once more shouldered his pack and started. This time we agreed to keep more to the right, to see if it were not possible to get to the plateau without losing any time by crossing the glacier. To describe our route would be to repeat what has been said before. We mounted steadily for an hour and a half, sometimes walking, but more frequently climbing, and then found, after all, that it was necessary to cross the glacier. The part on which we struck came down a very steep slope, and was much crevassed. The word crevassed hardly expresses its appearance : it was a mass of formidable séracs. We found, however, more difficulty in getting on than across it, but, thanks to the rope, it was passed somehow : then the interminable buttresses began again. Hour after hour we proceeded upward, frequently at fault and obliged to descend. The ridge behind us had sunk long ago, and we looked over it and all others till our eyes rested on the majestic Viso. Hour after hour passed, and monotony was the order of the day : when twelve o'clock came we lunched, and contemplated the scene with satisfaction : all the summits in sight, with the single exception of the Viso, had given in, and we looked over an immense expanse—a perfect sea of peaks and snow-fields. Still the pinnacles rose above us, and opinions were freely uttered that we should see no summit of Pelvoux that day. Old Sémiond had become a perfect bore to all: whenever one rested for a moment to look about, he would say, with a complacent chuckle, "Don't be afraid— follow me." We came at last to a very bad piece, rotten and steep, and no

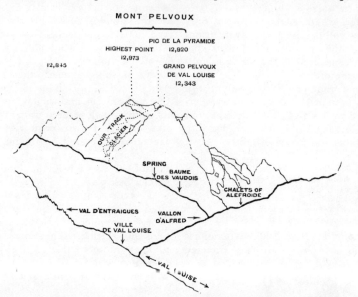

MONT PELVOUX

PIC DE LA PYRAMIDE
HIGHEST POINT   12,920
12,973

12,845   GRAND PELVOUX
DE VAL LOUISE
12,343

OUR TRACK
GLACIER

SPRING
BAUME
DES VAUDOIS

CHALETS OF
ALEFROIDE

VAL D'ENTRAIGUES   VALLON
D'ALFRED
VILLE
DE VAL LOUISE

VAL LOUISE

hold. Here Reynaud and Macdonald confessed to being tired, and talked of going to sleep. A way was discovered out of the difficulty: then some one called out, "Look at the Viso!" and we saw that we almost looked over it. We worked away with redoubled energy, and at length caught sight of the head of the glacier as it streamed out of the plateau. This gave us fresh hopes: we were not deceived, and with a simultaneous shout we greeted the appearance of our long wished-for snows. A large crevasse separated us from them, but a bridge was found: we tied ourselves in line and moved safely over it. Directly we got across there arose before us a fine snow-capped peak. Old Sémiond cried, "The pyramid! I see the pyramid!" "Where, Sémiond, where?" "There, on the top of that peak."

There, sure enough, was the cairn he had helped to erect more than thirty years before. But where was the Pic des Arcines which we were to see? It was nowhere visible, but only a great expanse of snow, bordered by three lower

peaks. Somewhat sadly we moved toward the pyramid, sighing that there was no other to conquer, but hardly had we gone two hundred paces before there rose a superb white cone on the left, which had been hidden before by a slope of snow. We shouted, "The Pic des Arcines!" and inquired of Sémiond if he knew whether that peak had been ascended. As for him, he knew nothing except that the peak before us was called the Pyramid, from the cairn he had, etc., etc., and that it had been ascended since. "All right, then: face about;" and we immediately turned at right angles for the cone, the porter making faint struggles for his beloved pyramid. Our progress was stopped in the sixth of a mile by the edge of the ridge connecting the two peaks, and we perceived that it curled over in a lovely volute. We involuntarily retreated. Sémiond, who was last in the line, took the opportunity to untie himself, and refused to come on, said we were running dangerous risks, and talked vaguely of crevasses. We tied him up again and proceeded. The snow was very soft: we were always knee-deep, and sometimes floundered in up to the waist, but a simultaneous jerk before and behind always released one. By this time we had arrived at the foot of the final peak. The left-hand ridge seemed easier than that upon which we stood, so we curved round to get to it. Some rocks peeped out one hundred and fifty feet below the summit, and up these we crawled, leaving our porter behind, as he said he was afraid. I could not resist the temptation, as we went off, to turn round and beckon him onward, saying, "Don't be afraid—follow me," but he did not answer to the appeal, and never went to the top. The rocks led to a short ridge of ice—our plateau on one side, and a nearly vertical precipice on the other. Macdonald cut up it, and at a quarter to two we stood shaking hands on the loftiest summit of the conquered Pelvoux!

The day still continued everything that could be desired, and far and near countless peaks burst into sight, without a cloud to hide them. The mighty Mont Blanc, full seventy miles away, first caught our eyes, and then, still farther off, the Monte Rosa group; while, rolling away to the east, one unknown range after another succeeded in unveiled splendor, fainter and fainter in tone, but still perfectly defined, till at last the eye was unable to distinguish sky from mountain, and they died away in the far-off horizon. Monte Viso rose up grandly, but it was less than forty miles away, and we looked over it to a hazy mass we knew must be the plains of Piedmont. Southward, a blue mist seemed to indicate the existence of the distant Mediterranean: to the west we looked over to the mountains of Auvergne. Such was the panorama, a view extending in nearly every direction for more than a hundred miles. It was with some difficulty we wrenched our eyes from the more distant objects to contemplate the nearer ones. Mont Dauphin was very conspicuous, but La Bessée was not readily perceived. Besides these, not a human habitation

could be seen: all was rock, snow or ice; and large as we knew were the snow-fields of Dauphiné, we were surprised to find that they very far surpassed our most ardent imagination. Nearly in a line between us and the Viso, immediately to the south of Château Queyras, was a splendid group of mountains of great height. More to the south an unknown peak seemed still higher, while close to us we were astonished to discover that there was a mountain which appeared even higher than that on which we stood. At least this was my opinion: Macdonald thought it not so high, and Reynaud insisted that its height was much about the same as our own.

This mountain was distant a couple of miles or so, and was separated from us by a tremendous abyss, the bottom of which we could not see. On the other side rose this mighty wall-sided peak, too steep for snow, black as night, with sharp ridges and pointed summit. We were in complete ignorance of its whereabouts, for none of us had been on the other side: we imagined that La Bérarde was in the abyss at our feet, but it was in reality beyond the other mountain.

We left the summit at last, and descended to the rocks and to our porter, where I boiled some water, obtained by melting snow. After we had fed and smoked our cigars (lighted without difficulty from a common match), we found it was ten minutes past three, and high time to be off. We dashed, waded and tumbled for twenty-five minutes through the snow, and then began the long descent of the rocks. It was nearly four o'clock, and as it would be dark at eight, it was evident that there was no time to be lost, and we pushed on to the utmost. Nothing remarkable occurred going down. We kept rather closer to the glacier, and crossed at the same point as in the morning. Getting *off* it was like getting *on* it—rather awkward. Old Sémiond had got over, so had Reynaud: Macdonald came next, but as he made a long stretch to get on to a higher mass, he slipped, and would have been in the bowels of a crevasse in a moment had he not been tied.

It was nearly dark by the time we had crossed, but still I hoped that we should be able to pass the night at our rock. Macdonald was not so sanguine, and he was right; for at last we found ourselves quite at fault, and wandered helplessly up and down for an hour, while Reynaud and the porter indulged in a little mutual abuse. The dreary fact that, as we could not get down, we must stay where we were, was now quite apparent.

We were at least ten thousand five hundred feet high, and if it commenced to rain or snow, as the gathering clouds and rising wind seemed to threaten, we might be in a sore plight. We were hungry, having eaten little since three A. M., and a torrent we heard close at hand, but could not discover, aggravated our thirst. Sémiond endeavored to get some water from it, but although he succeeded in doing so, he was wholly unable to return, and we had to solace him by shouting at intervals through the night.

A more detestable locality for a night out of doors it is difficult to imagine. There was no shelter of any kind, it was perfectly exposed to the chilly wind which began to rise, and it was too steep to promenade. Loose, rubbly stones covered the ground, and had to be removed before we could sit with any comfort. This was an advantage, although we hardly thought so at the time, as it gave us some employment, and after an hour's active exercise of that interesting kind I obtained a small strip, about nine feet long, on which it was possible to walk. Reynaud was furious at first, and soundly abused the porter, whose opinion as to the route down had been followed, rather than that of our friend, and at last settled down to a deep dramatic despair, and wrung his hands with frantic gesture, as he exclaimed, "Oh, malheur, malheur! Oh misérables!"

Thunder commenced to growl and lightning to play among the peaks above, and the wind, which had brought the temperature down to nearly freezing-point, began to chill us to the bones. We examined our resources. They were six and half cigars, two boxes of vesuvians, one-third of a pint of brandy-and-water, and half a pint of spirits of wine—rather scant fare for three fellows who had to get through seven hours before daylight. The spirit-lamp was lighted, and the remaining spirits of wine, the brandy and some snow were heated by it. It made a strong liquor, but we only wished for more of it. When that was over, Macdonald endeavored to dry his socks by the lamp, and then the three lay down under my plaid to pretend to sleep. Reynaud's woes were aggravated by toothache: Macdonald somehow managed to close his eyes.

The longest night must end, and ours did at last. We got down to our rock in an hour and a quarter, and found the lad not a little surprised at our absence. He said he had made a gigantic fire to light us down, and shouted with all his might: we neither saw the fire nor heard his shouts. He said we looked a ghastly crew, and no wonder: it was our fourth night out.

We feasted at our cave, and performed some very necessary ablutions. The persons of the natives are infested by certain agile creatures, whose rapidity of motion is only equaled by their numbers and voracity. It is dangerous to approach too near them, and one has to study the wind, so as to get on their weather side: in spite of all such precautions my unfortunate companion and myself were now being rapidly devoured alive. We only expected a temporary lull of our tortures, for the interiors of the inns are like the exteriors of the natives, swarming with this species of animated creation.

It is said that once, when these tormentors were filled with an unanimous desire, an unsuspecting traveler was dragged bodily from his bed! This needs confirmation. One word more, and I have done with this vile subject. We returned from our ablutions, and found the Frenchmen engaged in conversation. "Ah!" said old Sémiond, "as to fleas, I don't pretend to be different to any one else—*I have them.*" This time he certainly spoke the truth.

We got down to La Ville in good time, and luxuriated there for several days: we played many games of bowls with the natives, and were invariably beaten by them. At last it was necessary to part: I walked southward to the Viso, and Macdonald went to Briançon.

After parting from my agreeable companions, I walked by the gorge of the Guil to Abries, and made the acquaintance at that place of an ex-harbormaster of Marseilles—a genial man, who spoke English well. Besides the ex-harbormaster and some fine trout in the neighboring streams, there was little to invite a stay at Abries. The inn— L'Étoile, chez Richard — is a place to be avoided. Richard, it may be observed, possessed the instincts of a robber. At a later date, when forced to

seek shelter in his house, he desired to see my passport, and catching sight of the words John Russell, he entered that name instead of my own in a report to the gendarmerie, uttering an exclamation of joyful surprise at the same time. I foolishly allowed the mistake to pass, and had to pay dearly for it, for he made out a lordly bill, against which all protest was unavailing.

I quitted the abominations of Abries to seek a quiet bundle of hay at Le Chalp, a village some miles nearer to the Viso. On approaching the place the odor of sanctity became distinctly perceptible; and on turning a corner the cause was manifested: there was the priest of the place, surrounded by some of his flock. I advanced humbly, hat in hand, but almost before a word could be said, he broke out with, "Who are you? What are you? What do you want?" I endeavored to explain.

THE BLANKET-BAG.

"You are a deserter—I know you are a deserter: go away, you can't stay here: go to Le Monta, down there—I won't have you here;" and he literally drove me away. The explanation of his strange behavior was that Piedmontese soldiers who were tired of the service had not unfrequently crossed the Col de la Traversette into the valley, and trouble had arisen from harboring them.

However, I did not know this at the time, and was not a little indignant that I, who was marching to the attack, should be taken for a deserter.

So I walked away, and shortly afterward, as it was getting dark, encamped in a lovely hole—a cavity or kind of basin in the earth, with a stream on one side, a rock to windward and some broken pine branches close at hand.

Nothing could be more perfect—rock, hole, wood and water. After making a roaring fire, I nestled in my blanket-bag (an ordinary blanket sewn up, double round the legs, with a piece of elastic ribbon round the open end) and slept, but not for long. I was troubled with dreams of the Inquisition : the tortures were being applied, priests were forcing fleas down my nostrils and into my eyes, and with red-hot pincers were taking out bits of flesh, and then cutting off my ears and tickling the soles of my feet. This was too much : I yelled a great yell, and awoke to find myself covered with innumerable crawling bodies : they were ants. I had camped by an ant-hill, and, after making its inhabitants mad with the fire, had coolly lain down in their midst.

The night was fine, and as I settled down in more comfortable quarters, a brilliant meteor sailed across full 60° of the cloudless sky, leaving a trail of light behind which lasted for several seconds. It was the herald of a splendid spectacle. Stars fell by hundreds, and, not dimmed by intervening vapors, they sparkled with greater brightness than Sirius in our damp climate.

The next morning, after walking up the valley to examine the Viso, I returned to Abries, and engaged a man from a neighboring hamlet for whom the ex-harbormaster had sent—an inveterate smoker, and thirsty in proportion, whose pipe never left his mouth except to allow him to drink. We returned up the valley together, and slept in the hut of a shepherd whose yearly wage was almost as small as that of the herdsman spoken of in *Hyperion* by Longfellow ; and the next morning, in his company, proceeded to the summit of the pass which I had crossed in 1860 ; but we were baffled in our attempt to get near the mountain. A deep notch with precipitous cliffs cut us off from it : the snow-slope, too, which existed in the preceding year on the Piedmontese side of the pass, was now wanting, and we were unable to descend the rocks which lay beneath. A fortnight afterward the mountain was ascended for the first time by Messrs.

Mathews and Jacomb, with the two Crozes of Chamounix. Their attempt was made from the southern side, and the ascent, which was formerly considered a thing totally impossible, has become one of the most common and favorite excursions of the district.

We returned crest-fallen to Abries. The shepherd, whose boots were very much out of repair, slipped upon the steep snow-slopes and performed wonderful but alarming gyrations, which took him to the bottom of the valley more quickly than he could otherwise have descended. He was not much hurt, and was made happy by a few needles and a little thread to repair his abraded garments : the other man, however, considered it willful waste to give him brandy to rub in his cuts, when it could be disposed of in a more ordinary and pleasant manner.

The night of the 14th of August found me at St. Veran, a village made famous by Neff, but in no other respect remarkable, saving that it is supposed to be the highest in Europe. The Protestants *now* form only a miserable minority : in 1861 there were said to be one hundred and twenty of them to seven hundred and eighty Roman Catholics. The poor inn was kept by one of the former, and it gave the impression of great poverty. There was no meat, no bread, no butter, no cheese : almost the only things that could be obtained were eggs. The manners of the natives were primitive : the woman of the inn, without the least sense of impropriety, stayed in the room until I was fairly in bed, and her bill for supper, bed and breakfast amounted to one-and-sevenpence.

In this neighborhood, and indeed all round about the Viso, the chamois still remain in considerable numbers. They said at St. Veran that six had been seen from the village on the day I was there, and the innkeeper declared that he had seen fifty together in the previous week ! I myself saw in this and in the previous season several small companies round about the Viso. It is perhaps as favorable a district as any in the Alps for a sportsman who wishes to hunt the chamois, as the ground over which they wander is by no means of excessive difficulty.

The next day I descended the valley to Ville Vieille, and passed, near the

NATURAL PILLAR NEAR MOLINES (WEATHER ACTION).

by rain. In this case a "block of euphotide or diallage rock protects a friable limestone:" the contrast of this dark cap with the white base, and the singularity of the form, made it a striking object. These natural pillars are among the most remarkable examples of the potent effects produced by the long-continued action of quiet-working forces. They are found in several other places in the Alps, as well as elsewhere.

The village of Ville Vieille boasts of an inn with the sign of the Elephant, which, in the opinion of local amateurs, is a proof that Hannibal passed through the gorge of the Guil. I remember the place because its bread, being only a month old, was unusually soft, and for the first time during ten days it was possible to eat some without first of all chopping it into small pieces and soaking it in hot water, which produced a slimy paste on the outside, but left a hard, untouched kernel.

The same day I crossed the Col Isoard to Briançon. It was the 15th of August, and all the world was *en fête:* sounds of revelry proceeded from the houses of Servières as I passed over the bridge upon which the pyrrhic dance is annually performed, and natives in all degrees

village of Molines, but on the opposite side of the valley, a remarkable natural pillar, in form not unlike a champagne bottle, about seventy feet high, which had been produced by the action of the weather, and in all probability chiefly of inebriation staggered about the paths. It was late before the lights of the great fortress came into sight, but unchallenged I passed through the gates, and once more sought shelter under the roof of the Hôtel de l'Ours.

PART II.

CROSSING MONT CENIS (1861).

CHAPTER III.

THE MONT CENIS—THE FELL RAILWAY.

GUIDE-BOOKS say that the pass of the Mont Cenis is dull. It is long, certainly, but it has a fair proportion of picturesque points, and it is not easy to see how it can be dull to those who have eyes. In the days when it was a rude mountain track, crossed by trains of mules, and when it was better known to smugglers than to tourists, it may have been dull; but when Napoleon's road changed the rough path into one of the finest highways in Europe, mounting in grand curves and by uniform grades, and rendered the trot possible throughout its entire distance, the Mont Cenis became one of the most interesting passes in the Alps. The diligence service which was established was excellent, and there was little or nothing to be gained by traveling in a more expensive manner. The horses were changed as rapidly as on the best lines in the best period of coaching in England, and the diligences themselves were as comfortable as a "milord"

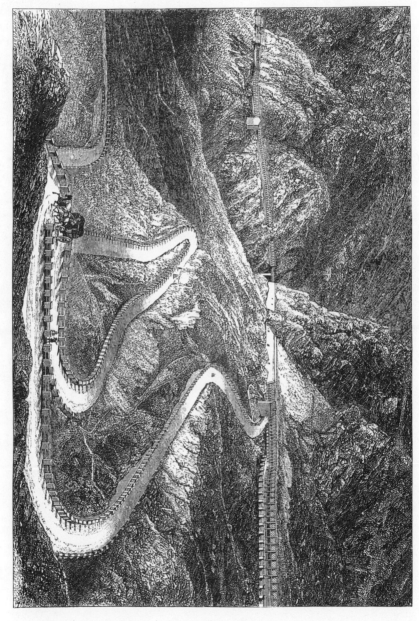

THE MONT CENIS ROAD AND THE FELL RAILWAY NEAR THE SUMMIT OF THE PASS, ON THE ITALIAN SIDE.

could desire. The most exciting portion of the route was undoubtedly that between Lanslebourg and Susa. When the zigzags began teams of mules were hooked on, and the driver and his helpers marched by their side with long whips, which they handled skillfully. Passengers dismounted and stretched their legs by cutting the curves. The pace was slow but steady, and scarcely a halt was made during the rise of two thousand feet. Crack! crack! went the whips as the corners of the zigzags were turned. Great commotion among the mules! They scrambled and went round with a rush, tossing their heads and making music with their bells. The summit was gained, the mules  were detached and trotted back merrily, while we, with fresh horses, were dragged at the gallop over the plain to the other side. The little postilion seated on the leader smacked his whip lustily as he swept round the corners cut through the rock, and threw his head back as the echoes returned, expectant of smiles and of future centimes.

The air was keen and often chilly, but the summit was soon passed, and one quickly descended to warmth again. Once more there was a change. The horses, reduced in number to three, or perhaps two, were the sturdiest and most sure of foot, and they raced down with the precision of old stagers. Woe to the diligence if they stumbled! So thought the conductor, who screwed down the brakes as the corners were approached. The horses, held well in hand, leant inward as the top-heavy vehicle, so suddenly checked, heeled almost over; but in another moment the brake was released, and again they swept down, urged onward by the whip, "hoi" and "ha" of the driver.

All this is changed. The Victor Emmanuel railway superseded a considerable portion of Napoleon's road, and the "Fell" railway the rest, while the great tunnel of the Alps will soon bring about another change.

The Fell railway, which has been open about eighteen months, is a line that well deserves attention. Thirty-eight years ago, Mr. Charles Vignolles, the eminent engineer, and Mr. Ericsson, patented the idea which is now an accomplished fact on the Mont Cenis. Nothing was done with it until Mr. Fell, the projector of the railway which bears his name, took it up, and to him much credit is due for bringing an admirable principle into operation.

The Fell railway follows the great Cenis road very closely, and diverges from it only to avoid villages or houses, or, as at the summit of the pass on the Italian side, to ease the gradients. The line runs from St. Michel to Susa. The distance between these two places is, as the crow flies, almost exactly equivalent to the distance from London to Chatham (30 miles), but by reason of the numerous curves and détours the length of the line is nearly brought up to the distance of London from Brighton (47 miles). From St. Michel to the summit of the pass it rises 4460 feet, or 900 feet more than the highest point of Snowdon is above the level of the sea; and from the summit of the pass to Susa, a distance less than that from London to Kew, it descends no less than 5211 feet!

The railway itself is a marvel. For fifteen miles and three-quarters it has steeper gradients than one in fifteen. In some places it is one in twelve and a half! A straight piece of railway constructed on such a gradient seems to go up a steep hill. One in eighty, or even one in a hundred, produces a very sensible diminution in the pace of a light train drawn by an ordinary locomotive: how, then, is a train to be taken up an incline that is *six* times as steep? It is accomplished by means of a third rail placed midway between the two ordinary ones, and elevated above them.*
The engines are provided with two pairs

---

* This third rail, or, as it is termed, "the centre rail," is laid on all the steep portions of the line and round all except the mildest curves. Thirty miles, in all, of the road have the centre rail.

of horizontal driving-wheels, as well as with the ordinary coupled vertical ones, and the power of the machine is thus enormously increased, the horizontal wheels gripping the centre rail with great tenacity by being brought together, and being almost incapable of slipping like the ordinary wheels when on even a moderate gradient.

The third rail is the ordinary double-headed rail, and is laid horizontally: it is bolted down to wrought-iron chairs three feet apart, which are fixed by common coach-screws to a longitudinal sleeper laid upon the usual transverse ones: the

sleepers are attached to each other by fang-bolts. The dimensions of the dif-

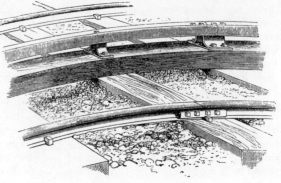

THE CENTRE RAIL ON A CURVE.

ferent parts will be seen by reference to the annexed cross section:

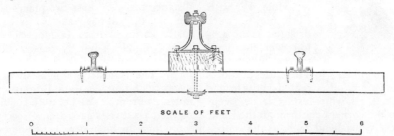

SCALE OF FEET

0   1   2   3   4   5   6

Let us now take a run on the railway, starting from St. Michel. For some distance from that place the gradients are not of an extraordinary character, and a good pace is maintained. The first severe piece is about two miles up, where there is an incline of one in eighteen for more than half a mile; that is to say, the line rises at one step one hundred and sixty-four feet. From thence to Modane the gradients are again moderate (for the Fell railway), and the distance—about ten miles and a half from St. Michel—is accomplished without difficulty in an hour. Modane station is 1128 feet above St. Michel, so that on this *easy* portion of the line there is an average rise of 110 feet per mile, which is equal to a gradient of one in forty-eight—an inclination sufficiently steep to bring an ordinary locomotive very nearly to a halt.

Just after passing Modane station

there is one of the steepest inclines on the line, and it seems preposterous to suppose that any train could ascend it. A stoppage of ten minutes is made at Modane, and on leaving that station the train goes off at the hill with a rush. In a few yards its pace is reduced, and it comes down and down to about four miles an hour, which speed is usually maintained until the incline is passed, without a diminution of the steam-pressure. I say usually, because, if it should happen that there is not sufficient steam, or should the driver happen to make a slip, the train would most likely come back to Modane; for, although the brake-power on the train is much more than sufficient to prevent it running back, the driver could hardly start with the brakes on, and the train would inevitably run back if they were off.

After this incline is passed, the line mounts by comparatively easy gradients toward Fort Lesseillon : it is then at a great height above the Arc, and as one winds round the faces of the cliff out of which the Napoleon road was cut, looking down upon the foaming stream below, without a suspicion of a parapet between the railway and the edge of the precipice, one naturally thinks about what would happen if the engine should leave the rails. The speed, however, that is kept up at this part is very gentle, and there is probably much less risk of an accident than there was in the days of diligences.

The next remarkable point on this line is at Termignon. The valley turns somewhat abruptly to the east, and the course of the railway is not at first perceived. It makes a great bend to the left, then doubles back, and rises in a little more than a mile no less than three hundred and thirty-four feet. This is, perhaps, the most striking piece of the whole line.

Lanslebourg station, 25½ miles from, and 2220 feet above, St. Michel, is arrived at in two hours and a quarter from the latter place. The engines are now changed. Thus far we have been traversing the easy portion of the route, but here the heavy section begins. From Lanslebourg the line rises continuously to the summit of the Mont Cenis pass, and accomplishes an ascent

THE COVERED WAYS ON THE "FELL" RAILWAY (ITALIAN SIDE OF THE MONT CENIS).

of 2240 feet in six miles and a third of distance.

It is curious and interesting to watch the ascent of the trains from Lanslebourg. The puffs of steam are seen rising above the trees, sometimes going in one direction, and sometimes directly the contrary, occasionally concealed by the covered ways—for over two miles out of the six the line is enclosed by planked sides and a corrugated iron roof, to keep out the snow—and then coming out again into daylight. A halt for water has to be made about halfway up ; but the engines are able to start again, and to resume their rate of seven miles an hour, although the gradient is no less than one in fourteen and a half.

The zigzags of the old Cenis road are well known as one of the most remarkable pieces of road-engineering in the Alps. The railway follows them, and runs parallel to the road on the outside throughout its entire distance, with the exception of the turns at the corners, where it is carried a little farther out, to render the curves less sharp. Nevertheless, they are sufficiently sharp (135 feet radius), and would be impracticable without the centre rail.

The run across the top of the pass, from the Summit station to the Grande Croix station—a distance of about five miles—is soon accomplished, and then the tremendous descent to Susa is commenced. This, as seen from the engine,

3

is little less than terrific. A large part
of this section is covered in, and the
curves succeed one another in a manner unknown on any other line. From
the outside the line looks more like a
monstrous serpent than a railway. Inside, one can see but a few yards ahead,
the curves are so sharp, and the rails
are nearly invisible. The engine vi-
brates, oscillates and bounds: it is a
matter of difficulty to hold on. Then,
on emerging into the open air, one looks
down some three or four thousand feet
of precipice and steep mountain-side.
The next moment the engine turns suddenly to the left, and driver and stoker
have to grip firmly to avoid being left
behind; the next, it turns as suddenly
to the right; the next, there is an ac-
cession or diminution of speed from a
change in the gradient. An ordinary
engine, moving at fifty miles an hour,
with a train behind it, is not usually
very steady, but its motion is a trifle
compared with that of a Fell engine
when running down hill.

It may be supposed from this that
traveling over the Fell railway is disagreeable rather than pleasant. It is
not so: the train is steady enough, and
the carriages have remarkably little motion. Outside, they resemble the cars
on the Swiss and American lines: they
are entered at the end, and the seats
are arranged omnibus-fashion, down
the length of the carriage. Each carriage has a guard and two brakes—an
ordinary one and a centre-rail brake:
the handles of these come close together at the platform on one end, and
are easily worked by one man. The
steadiness of the train is chiefly due to
these centre-rail brakes. The flat face
A and the corresponding one on the opposite side are brought together against
the two sides of the centre rail by the
shaft B being turned, and they hold it
as in a vice. This greatly diminishes
the up-and-down motion, and renders
oscillation almost impossible. The
steadiness of the train is still further
maintained by pairs of flanged guide-
wheels under each of the carriages,
which, on a straight piece of line, bare-

ly touch the centre rail, but press upon
it directly there is the least deviation
toward either side.* There is no occa-

CENTRE-RAIL BRAKE.

sion to use the other brakes when the
centre-rail brakes are on: the wheels
of the carriages are not stopped, but
revolve freely, and consequently do not
suffer the deterioration which would
otherwise result.

The steam is shut off and the brakes
are applied a very few minutes after beginning the descent to Susa. The train
might then run down for the entire distance by its own weight. In practice,
it is difficult to apply the proper amount
of retardation: the brakes have frequently to be whistled off, and sometimes it is necessary to steam down
against them. Theoretically, this ought
not of course to occur: it only happens
occasionally, and ordinarily the train
goes down with the steam shut off, and
with the centre-rail brakes screwed up
moderately. When an average train—
that is, two or three carriages and a
luggage-van—is running down at the
maximum speed allowed (fifteen miles
an hour), the brakes can pull it up dead
within seventy yards. The pace is properly kept down to a low point in descending, and doing so, combined with the
knowledge that the brake-power can
easily lessen it, will tend to make the
public look favorably on what might
otherwise be considered a dangerous
innovation. The engines also are provided with the centre-rail brake, on a

* The carriages are not coupled in the ordinary way,
and although there are no buffers, properly speaking,
and in spite of the speed of the train being changed incessantly, there is a freedom from the jarring which is
so common on other lines. The reason is simply that
the carriages are coupled up tightly.

pattern somewhat different from those on the carriages, and the flat sides which press against the rails are renewed *every journey*. It is highly desirable that they should be, for a single run from Lanslebourg to Susa grinds a groove into them about three-eighths of an inch in depth.

Driving the trains over the summit section requires the most constant attention and no small amount of nerve, and the drivers, who are all English, have well earned their money at the end of their run. Their opinion of the line was concisely and forcibly expressed to me by one of them in last August: "Yes, mister, they told us as how the line was very steep, but they didn't say that the engine would be on one curve, when the fourgon was on another, and the carriages was on a third. Them gradients, too, mister, they says they are one in twelve, but I think they are one in *ten, at the least*, and they didn't say as how we was to come down them in that snakewise fashion. It's worse than the G. I. P.,* mister: there a fellow could jump off, but here, in them covered ways, there ain't no place to jump to."

CHAPTER IV.

MY FIRST SCRAMBLE ON THE MATTERHORN.

"What power must have been required to shatter and to sweep away the missing parts of this pyramid; for we do not see it surrounded by heaps of fragments: one only sees other peaks—themselves rooted to the ground—whose sides, equally rent, indicate an immense mass of débris, of which we do not see any trace in the neighborhood. Doubtless this is that débris which, in the form of pebbles, boulders and sand, fills our valleys and our plains."—DE SAUSSURE.

Two summits amongst those in the Alps which yet remained virgin had excited my admiration. One of these had been attacked numberless times by the best mountaineers without success: the cther, surrounded by traditional inaccessibility, was almost untouched. These

* The Great Indian Peninsula Railway, the line with the celebrated Bhore Ghaut incline, sixteen miles long, on an average gradient of one in forty-eight, which is said to have cost £800,000, or about double the entire cost of the Mount Cenis Railway, and six times its cost mile for mile. The Fell railway cost £8000 per mile.

mountains were the Weisshorn and the Matterhorn.

After visiting the great tunnel of the Alps in 1861, I wandered for ten days in the neighboring valleys, intending presently to attempt the ascent of these two peaks. Rumors were floating about that the former had been conquered, and that the latter was shortly to be attacked, and they were confirmed on my arrival at Chatillon, at the entrance of the Val Tournanche. My interest in the Weisshorn abated, but it was raised to the highest pitch on hearing that Professor Tyndall was at Breuil, and intending to try to crown his first victory by another and a still greater one.

Up to this time my experience with guides had not been fortunate, and I was inclined, improperly, to rate them at a low value. They represented to me pointers-out of paths and great consumers of meat and drink, but little more; and, with the recollection of Mont Pelvoux, I should have greatly preferred the company of a couple of my countrymen to any number of guides. In answer to inquiries at Chatillon, a series of men came forward whose faces expressed malice, pride, envy, hatred and roguery of every description, but who seemed to be destitute of all good qualities. The arrival of two gentlemen with a guide, who they represented was the embodiment of every virtue and exactly the man for the Matterhorn, rendered it unnecessary to engage any of the others. My new guide in *physique* was a combination of Chang and Anak; and although in acquiring him I did not obtain exactly what was wanted, his late employers did exactly what *they* wanted, for I obtained the responsibility, without knowledge, of paying his back fare, which must have been a relief at once to their minds and to their purses.

When walking up toward Breuil, we inquired for another man of all the knowing ones, and they, with one voice, proclaimed that Jean-Antoine Carrel, of the village of Val Tournanche, was the cock of his valley. We sought, of course, for Carrel, and found him a well-made, resolute-looking fellow, with a certain defiant air which was rather taking. Yes, he would go. Twenty francs a day, whatever was the result, was his price. I assented. But I must take his comrade. "Why so?" Oh, it was absolutely impossible to get along without another man. As he said this an evil countenance came forth out of the darkness and proclaimed itself the comrade. I demurred, the negotiations broke off, and we went up to Breuil. This place will be frequently mentioned in subsequent chapters, and was in full view of the extraordinary peak the ascent of which we were about to attempt.

It is unnecessary to enter into a minute description of the Matterhorn after all that has been written about that famous mountain. My readers will know that that peak is nearly fifteen thousand feet high, and that it rises abruptly, by a series of cliffs which may properly be termed precipices, a clear five thousand feet above the glaciers which surround its base. They will know, too, that it was the last great Alpine peak which remained unscaled—less on account of the difficulty of doing so than from the terror inspired by its invincible appearance. There seemed to be a *cordon* drawn around it, up to which one might go, but no farther. Within that invisible line jins and affreets were supposed to exist—the Wandering Jew and the spirits of the damned. The superstitious natives in the surrounding valleys (many of whom still firmly believe it to be not only the highest mountain in the Alps, but in the world) spoke of a ruined city on its summit wherein the spirits dwelt; and if you laughed they gravely shook their heads, told you to look yourself to see the castles and the walls, and warned one against a rash approach, lest the infuriate demons from their impregnable heights might hurl down vengeance for one's derision. Such were the traditions of the natives. Stronger minds felt the influence of the wonderful form, and men who ordinarily spoke or wrote like rational beings, when they came under its power seemed to quit their

senses and ranted and rhapsodized, losing for a time all common forms of speech. Even the sober De Saussure was moved to enthusiasm when he saw the mountain, and, inspired by the spectacle, he anticipated the speculations of modern geologists in the striking sentences which are placed at the head of this chapter.

The Matterhorn looks equally imposing from whatever side it is seen: it never seems commonplace, and in this respect, and in regard to the impression it makes upon spectators, it stands almost alone amongst mountains. It has no rivals in the Alps, and but few in the world.

The seven or eight thousand feet which compose the actual peak have several well-marked ridges and numerous others. The most continuous is that which leads toward the north-east: the summit is at its higher, and the little peak called the Hörnli is at its lower, end. Another one that is well pronounced descends from the summit to the ridge called the Furgen Grat. The slope of the mountain that is between these two ridges will be referred to as the eastern face. A third, somewhat less continuous than the others, descends in a south-westerly direction, and the portion of the mountain that is seen from Breuil is confined to that which is comprised between this and the second ridge. This section is not composed, like that between the first and second ridge, of one grand face, but it is broken up into a series of huge precipices, spotted with snow-slopes and streaked with snow-gullies. The other half of the mountain, facing the Z'Mutt glacier, is not capable of equally simple definition. There are precipices apparent but not actual; there are precipices absolutely perpendicular; there are precipices overhanging; there are glaciers and there are hanging glaciers; there are glaciers which tumble great *séracs* over greater cliffs, whose débris, subsequently consolidated, becomes glacier again; there are ridges split by the frost, and washed by the rain and melted snow into towers and spires; while everywhere there are

THE MATTERHORN. FROM NEAR THE SUMMIT OF THE THEODULE PASS.

COL DU LION

THE "SHOULDER"

EAST FACE

DENT BLANCHE

ceaseless sounds of action, telling that the causes are still in operation which have been at work since the world began, reducing the mighty mass to atoms and effecting its degradation.

Most tourists obtain their first view of the mountain either from the valley of Zermatt or from that of Tournanche. From the former direction the base of the mountain is seen at its narrowest,

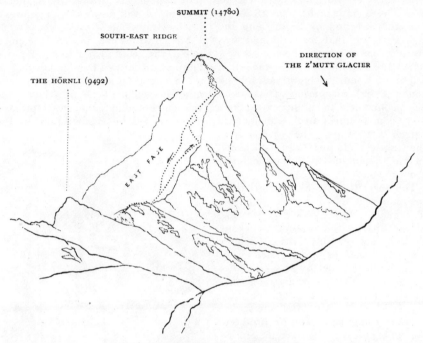

SUMMIT (14780)

SOUTH-EAST RIDGE

DIRECTION OF
THE Z'MUTT GLACIER

THE HÖRNLI (9492)

EAST FACE

THE MATTERHORN FROM THE NORTH-EAST.

and its ridges and faces seem to be of prodigious steepness. The tourist toils up the valley, looking frequently for the great sight which is to reward his pains, without seeing it (for the mountain is first perceived in that direction about a mile to the north of Zermatt), when all at once, as he turns a rocky corner of the path, it comes into view, not, however, where it is expected: the face has to be raised up to look at it— it seems overhead. Although this is the impression, the fact is that the summit of the Matterhorn from this point makes an angle with the eye of less than 16°, while the Dom, from the same place, makes a larger angle, but is passed by unobserved. So little can dependence be placed on unaided vision.

The view of the mountain from Breuil, in the Val Tournanche, is not less strik-ing than that on the other side, but usually it makes less impression, because the spectator grows accustomed to the sight while coming up or down the valley. From this direction the mountain is seen to be broken up into a series of pyramidal, wedge-shaped masses: on the other side it is remarkable for the large, unbroken extent of cliffs that it presents, and for the simplicity of its outline. It was natural to suppose that a way would more readily be found to the summit on a side thus broken up than in any other direction. The eastern face, fronting Zermatt, seemed one smooth, impossible cliff from summit to base: the ghastly precipices which face the Z'Mutt glacier forbade any attempt in that direction. There remained only the side of Val Tournanche, and it will be found that nearly all the earliest attempts to ascend the mountain were made on that side.

The first efforts to ascend the Matterhorn of which I have heard were made by the guides—or rather by the chasseurs—of Val Tournanche. These attempts were made in the years 1858-'59, from the direction of Breuil, and the highest point that was attained was about as far as the place which is now called the "Chimney" (cheminée), a height of about twelve thousand six hundred and fifty feet. Those who were concerned in these expeditions were Jean-Antoine Carrel, Jean Jacques Carrel, Victor Carrel, the Abbé Gorret and Gabrielle Maquignaz. I have been unable to obtain any further details about them.

The next attempt was a remarkable one; and of it, too, there is no published account. It was made by Messrs. Alfred, Charles and Sandbach Parker, of Liverpool, in July, 1860. These gentlemen, *without guides*, endeavored to storm the citadel by attacking the eastern face, that to which reference was just now made as a smooth, impracticable cliff. Mr. Sandbach Parker informs me that he and his brothers went along the ridge between the Hörnli and the peak until they came to the point where the ascending angle is considerably increased. This place is marked on Dufour's map of Switzerland 3298 mètres (10,820 feet). They were then obliged to bear a little to the left to get on to the face of the mountain, and afterward they turned to the right and ascended about seven hundred feet farther, keeping as nearly as was practicable to the crest of the ridge, but occasionally bearing a little to the left; that is, more on to the face of the mountain. The brothers started from Zermatt, and did not sleep out. Clouds, a high wind and want of time were the causes which prevented these daring gentlemen from going farther. Thus their highest point was under twelve thousand feet.

The third attempt upon the mountain was made toward the end of August, 1860, by Mr. Vaughan Hawkins, from the side of the Val Tournanche. A vivid account of his expedition has been published by him in "Vacation Tourists," and it has been referred to several times by Professor Tyndall in the numerous papers he has contributed to Alpine literature. I will dismiss it, therefore, as briefly as possible.

Mr. Hawkins had inspected the mountain in 1859 with the guide J. J. Bennen, and he had formed the opinion that the south-west ridge would lead to the summit. He engaged J. Jacques Carrel, who was concerned in the first attempts, and, accompanied by Bennen (and by Pro-

J. J. BENNEN (1862).

fessor Tyndall, whom he had invited to take part in the expedition), he started for the gap between the little and the great peak.

Bennen was a guide who was beginning to be talked about. During the chief part of his brief career he was in the service of Wellig, the landlord of the inn on the Æggischhorn, and was hired out by him to tourists. Although his experience was limited, he had acquired a good reputation; and his book of certificates, which is lying before me, shows that he was highly esteemed by his employers. A good-looking man, with courteous, gentlemanly manners, skillful and bold, he might by this time have taken a front place amongst guides if he had only been endowed with more prudence. He perished miserably in the spring of 1864 not far from his home, on a mountain called the Haut de Cry, in the Valais.

Mr. Hawkins' party, led by Bennen, climbed the rocks abutting against the Couloir du Lion on its south side, and attained the Col du Lion, although not without difficulty. They then followed the south-west ridge, passed the place at which the earliest explorers had turned back (the Chimney), and ascended about three hundred feet more. Mr. Hawkins and J. J. Carrel then stopped, but Bennen and Professor Tyndall mounted a few feet higher. They retreated, however, in less than half an hour, finding that there was too little time, and, descending to the col by the same route as they had followed on the ascent, proceeded thence to Breuil—down the couloir instead of by the rocks. The point at which Mr. Hawkins stopped is easily identified from his description. Its height is 12,992 feet above the sea. I think that Bennen and Tyndall could not have ascended more than fifty or sixty feet beyond this in the few minutes they were absent from the others, as they were upon one of the most difficult parts of the mountain. This party therefore accomplished an advance of about three hundred and fifty or four hundred feet.

Mr. Hawkins did not, as far as I know, make another attempt; and the next was made by the Messrs. Parker in July, 1861. They again started from Zermatt, followed the route they had struck out on the previous year, and got a little higher than before; but they were defeated by want of time, left Zermatt shortly afterward on account of bad weather, and did not again renew their attempts. Mr. Parker says: "In neither case did we go as high as we could. At the point where we turned we saw our way for a few hundred feet farther, but beyond that the difficulties seemed to increase." I am informed that both attempts should be considered as excursions undertaken with the view of ascertaining whether there was any encouragement to make a more deliberate attack on the north-east side.

My guide and I arrived at Breuil on the 28th of August, 1861, and we found that Professor Tyndall *had* been there a day or two before, but had done nothing. I had seen the mountain from nearly every direction, and it seemed, even to a novice like myself, far too much for a single day. I intended to sleep out upon it as high as possible, and to attempt to reach the summit on the following day. We endeavored to induce another man to accompany us, but without success. Matthias zum Taugwald and other well-known guides were there at the time, but they declined to go on any account. A sturdy old fellow—Peter Taugwalder by name—said he would go. His price? "Two hundred francs." "What! whether we ascend or not?" "Yes—nothing less." The end of the matter was, that all the men who were more or less capable showed a strong disinclination or positively refused to go (their disinclination being very much in proportion to their capacity), or else asked a prohibitive price. This, it may be said once for all, was the reason why so many futile attempts were made upon the Matterhorn. One first-rate guide after another was brought up to the mountain and patted on the back, but all declined the business. The men who went had no heart in the matter, and took the first opportunity to turn back,* for they were, with the exception of one man—to whom reference will be made presently—universally impressed with the belief that the summit was entirely inaccessible.

We resolved to go alone, but, anticipating a cold bivouac, begged the loan of a couple of blankets from the innkeeper. He refused them, giving the curious reason that we had bought a bottle of brandy at Val Tournanche, and had not bought any from him! No brandy, no blankets, appeared to be his rule. We did not require them that

* The guide Bennen must be excepted.

night, as it was passed in the highest cow-shed in the valley, which is about an hour nearer to the mountain than is the hotel. The cowherds, worthy fellows seldom troubled by tourists, hailed our company with delight, and did their best to make us comfortable, brought out their little stores of simple food, and, as we sat with them round the great copper pot which hung over the fire, bade us in husky voice, but with honest intent, to beware of the perils of the haunted cliffs. When night was coming on we saw stealing up the hillside the forms of Jean-Antoine Carrel and the comrade. "Oh ho!" I said, "you have repented?" "Not at all : you deceive yourself." "Why, then, have you come here?" "Because we ourselves are going on the mountain to-morrow." "Oh, then it is *not* necessary to have more than three?" "Not for *us*." I admired their pluck, and had a strong inclination to engage the pair, but finally decided against it. The comrade turned out to be the J. J. Carrel who had been with Mr. Hawkins, and was nearly related to the other man.

JEAN-ANTOINE CARREL (1869).

Both were bold mountaineers, but Jean - Antoine was incomparably the better man of the two, and he is the finest rock-climber I have ever seen. He was the only man who persistently refused to accept defeat, and who continued to believe, in spite of all discouragements, that the great mountain was not inaccessible, and that it could be ascended from the side of his native valley.

The night wore away without any excitement, except from the fleas, a party of whom executed a spirited fandango

on my cheek to the sound of music produced on the drum of my ear by one of their fellows beating with a wisp of hay. The two Carrels crept noiselessly out before daybreak, and went off. We did not leave until nearly seven o'clock, and followed them leisurely, leaving all our properties in the cow-shed, sauntered over the gentian-studded slopes which intervene between the shed and the Glacier du Lion, left cows and their pastures behind, traversed the stony wastes and arrived at the ice. Old, hard beds of snow lay on its right bank (our left hand), and we mounted over them on to the lower portion of the glacier with ease. But as we ascended crevasses became numerous, and we were at last brought to a halt by some which were of very large dimensions ; and as our cutting powers were limited, we sought an easier route, and turned naturally to the lower rocks of the Tête du Lion, which overlook the glacier on its west. Some good scrambling took us in a short time on to the crest of the ridge which descends toward the south ; and thence up to the level of the Col du Lion there was a long natural staircase, on which it was seldom necessary to use the hands. We dubbed the place "The Great Staircase." Then the cliffs of the Tête du Lion, which rise above the couloir, had to be skirted. This part varies considerably in different seasons, and in 1861 we found it difficult, for the fine steady weather of that year had reduced the snow-beds abutting against it to a lower level than usual, and the rocks which were left exposed at the junction of the snow with the cliffs had few ledges or cracks to which we could hold. But by half-past ten o'clock we stood on the col, and looked down upon the magnificent basin out of which the Z'Mutt glacier flows. We decided to pass the night upon the col, for we were charmed with the capabilities of the place, although it was one where liberties could not be taken. On one side a sheer wall overhung the Tiefenmatten glacier — on the other, steep, glassy slopes of hard snow descended to the Glacier du Lion, furrowed by water and by falling stones : on the north there was the great peak of the Matterhorn,* and on the south the cliffs of the Tête du Lion. Throw a bottle down to the

THE COL DU LION, LOOKING TOWARD THE TÊTE DU LION.

Tiefenmatten — no sound returns for more than a dozen seconds.

> " How fearful
> And dizzy 'tis to cast one's eyes so low !"

But no harm could come from that side—neither could it from the other. Nor was it likely that it would from the Tête du Lion, for some jutting ledges conveniently overhung our proposed resting-place. We waited for a while, basked in the sunshine, and watched or listened to the Carrels, who were sometimes seen or heard high above us upon the ridge leading toward the summit; and, leaving at mid-day, we descended to the cow-shed, packed up the tent and other properties, and returned to the col, although heavily laden, be-

* The engraving is made after a sketch taken from the rocks of the Matterhorn, just above the col.

fore six o'clock. This tent was constructed on a pattern suggested by Mr. Francis Galton, and it was not a success. It looked very pretty when set up in London, but it proved thoroughly useless in the Alps. It was made of light canvas, and opened like a book : one end was closed permanently and the other with flaps : it was supported by two alpenstocks, and had the canvas sides prolonged so as to turn in underneath. Numerous cords were sewn to the lower edges, to which stones were to be attached, but the main fastenings were by a cord which passed underneath the ridge and through iron rings screwed into the tops of the alpenstocks, and were secured by pegs. The wind, which playfully careered about the surrounding cliffs, was driven through our gap with the force of a blow-pipe : the flaps of the tent would not keep down, the pegs would not stay in, and it exhibited so marked a desire to go to the top of the Dent Blanche that we thought it prudent to take it down and to sit upon it. When night came on we wrapped ourselves in it, and made our camp as comfortable as the circumstances would allow. The silence was impressive. No living thing was near our solitary bivouac ; the Carrels had turned back and were out of hearing ; the stones had ceased to fall and the trickling water to murmur—

> " The music of whose liquid lip
> Had been to us companionship,
> And in our lonely life had grown
> To have an almost human tone." *

It was bitterly cold. Water froze hard in a bottle under my head. Not surprising, as we were actually on snow, and in a position where the slightest wind was at once felt. For a time we dozed, but about midnight there came from high aloft a tremendous explosion, followed by a second of dead quiet. A great mass of rock had split off and was descending toward us. My guide started up, wrung his hands and exclaimed, "O my God, we are lost !" We heard it coming, mass after mass pouring over the precipices, bounding and

* J. G. Whittier.

rebounding from cliff to cliff, and the great rocks in advance smiting one another. They seemed to be close, although they were probably distant, but some small fragments, which dropped upon us at the same time from the ledges just above, added to the alarm, and my demoralized companion passed the remainder of the night in a state of shudder, ejaculating "Terrible !" and other adjectives.

We put ourselves in motion at daybreak, and commenced the ascent of the south-west ridge. There was no more sauntering with hands in the pockets · each step had to be earned by downright climbing. But it was the most pleasant kind of climbing. The rocks were fast and unencumbered with débris, the cracks were good, although not numerous, and there was nothing to fear except from one's self. So we thought, at least, and shouted to awake echoes from the cliffs. Ah ! there is no response. Not yet : wait a while—everything here is upon a superlative scale : count a dozen and then the echoes will return from the walls of the Dent d'Herens, miles away, in waves of pure and undefiled sound, soft, musical and sweet. Halt a moment to regard the view ! We overlook the Tête du Lion, and nothing except the Dent d'Herens, whose summit is still a thousand feet above us, stands in the way : the ranges of the Graian Alps, an ocean of mountains, are seen at a glance, governed by their three great peaks, the Grivola, Grand Paradis and Tour de St. Pierre. How soft, and yet how sharp, they look in the early morning ! The mid-day mists have not begun to rise—nothing is obscured : even the pointed Viso, all but a hundred miles away, is perfectly defined.

Turn to the east and watch the sun's slanting rays coming across the Monte Rosa snow-fields. Look at the shadowed parts and see how even they, radiant with reflected light, are more brilliant than man knows how to depict. See how, even there, the gentle undulations give shadows within shadows, and how, yet again, where falling stones or ice have left a track, there are shadows upon shadows, each with a light and a dark side, with infinite gradations of matchless tenderness. Then note the sunlight as it steals noiselessly along and reveals countless unsuspected forms —the delicate ripple-lines which mark the concealed crevasse, and the waves of drifted snow, producing each minute more lights and fresh shadows, sparkling on the edges and glittering on the ends of the icicles, shining on the heights and illuminating the depths, until all is aglow and the dazzled eye returns for relief to the sombre crags.

Hardly an hour had passed since we left the col before we arrived at the "Chimney." It proved to be the counterpart of the place to which reference has been before made : a smooth, straight slab of rock was fixed at a considerable angle between two others equally smooth. My companion essayed to go up, and after crumpling his long body into many ridiculous positions, he said that he would not, for he could not do it. With some little trouble I got up it unassisted, and then my guide tied himself on to the end of our rope, and I endeavored to pull him up. But he was so awkward that he did little for himself, and so heavy that he proved too much for me, and after several attempts he untied himself and quietly observed that he should go down. I told him he was a coward, and *he* mentioned his opinion of me. I requested him to go to Breuil, and to say that he had left his "monsieur" on the mountain, and he turned to go, whereupon I had to eat humble pie and ask him to come back ; for although it was not very difficult to go up, and not at all dangerous with a man standing below, it was quite another thing to come down, as the lower edge overhung in a provoking manner. The day was perfect, the sun was

pouring down grateful warmth, the wind had fallen, the way seemed clear, no insuperable obstacle was in sight ; but what could one do alone ? I stood on the top, chafing under this unexpected contretemps, and remained for some time irresolute ; but as it became apparent that the Chimney was swept more frequently than was necessary (it was a natural channel for falling stones), I turned at last, descended with the assistance of my companion, and returned with him to Breuil, where we arrived about mid-day.

The Carrels did not show themselves, but we were told that they had not got to any great height,* and that the "comrade," who for convenience had taken off his shoes and tied them round his waist, had managed to let one of them slip, and had come down with a piece of cord fastened round his naked foot. Notwithstanding this, they had boldly glissaded down the Couloir du Lion, J. J. Carrel having his shoeless foot tied up in a pocket handkerchief.

The Matterhorn was not assailed again in 1861. I left Breuil with the conviction that it was little use for a single tourist to organize an attack upon it, so great was its influence on the morals of the guides, and persuaded that it was desirable at least two should go, to back each other when required ; and departed with my guide over the Col Théodule, longing more than before to make the ascent, and determined to return— if possible with a companion — to lay siege to the mountain until one or the other was vanquished.

* I learned afterward from Jean-Antoine Carrel that they got considerably higher than upon their previous attempts, and about two hundred and fifty or three hundred feet higher than Professor Tyndall in 1860. In 1862 I saw the initials of J.-A. Carrel cut on the rocks at the place where he and his comrade had turned back.

PART III.

AT BREUIL (GIOMEIN). *See page* 55.

CHAPTER V.

RENEWED ATTEMPTS TO ASCEND THE MAT-
TERHORN.

THE year 1862 was still young, and
the Matterhorn, clad in its wintry
garb, bore but little resemblance to the
Matterhorn of the summer, when a new
force came to do battle with the mountain from another direction. Mr. T. S.
Kennedy of Leeds conceived the extraordinary idea that the peak might prove
less impracticable in January than in
June, and arrived at Zermatt in the former month to put his conception to the
test. With stout Peter Perrn and sturdy
Peter Taugwalder he slept in the little
chapel at the Schwarzensee, and on the
next morning, like the Messrs. Parker,

followed the ridge between the peak
called Hörnli and the great mountain.
But they found that snow in winter
obeyed the ordinary laws, and that the
wind and frost were not less unkind
than in summer. "The wind whirled
up the snow and spiculæ of ice into our
faces like needles, and flat pieces of ice
a foot in diameter, carried up from the
glacier below, went flying past. Still
no one seemed to like to be the first to
give in, till a gust fiercer than usual
forced us to shelter for a time behind a
rock. Immediately it was tacitly understood that our expedition must now end,
but we determined to leave some me-
mento of our visit, and, after descending a considerable distance, we found a

suitable place with loose stones of which to build a cairn. In half an hour a tower six feet high was erected, a bottle, with the date, was placed inside, and we retreated as rapidly as possible." This cairn was placed at the spot marked upon Dufour's Map of Switzerland 10,820 feet (3298 metrès), and the highest point attained by Mr. Kennedy was not, I imagine, more than two or three hundred feet above it.

Shortly after this, Professor Tyndall gave, in his little tract—*Mountaineering in* 1861—an account of the reason why he had left Breuil in August, 1861, without doing anything. It seems that he sent his guide Bennen to reconnoitre, and that the latter made the following report to his employer: "Herr, I have examined the mountain carefully, and find it more difficult and dangerous than I had imagined. There is no place upon it where we could well pass the night. We might do so on yonder col upon the snow, but there we should be almost frozen to death, and totally unfit for the work of the next day. On the rocks there is no ledge or cranny which could give us proper harborage; and starting from Breuil, it is certainly impossible to reach the summit in a single day." "I was entirely taken aback," says Tyndall, "by this report. I felt like a man whose grip had given way, and who was dropping through the air. . . . Bennen was evidently dead against any attempt upon the mountain. 'We can, at all events, reach the lower of the two summits,' I remarked. 'Even that is difficult,' he replied; 'but when you have reached it, what then? The peak has neither name nor fame.'"*

I was more surprised than discouraged by this report by Bennen. One-half of

his assertions I knew to be wrong. The col to which he referred was the Col du Lion, upon which he had passed a night less than a week after he had spoken so authoritatively; and I had seen a place not far below the "Chimney"—a place about five hundred feet above the col—where it seemed possible to construct a sleeping-place. Bennen's opinions seem to have undergone a complete change. In 1860 he is described as having been enthusiastic to make an attempt—in 1861 he was dead against one. Nothing dismayed by this, my friend Mr. Reginald Macdonald, our companion on the Pelvoux—to whom so much of our success had been due —agreed to join me in a renewed assault from the south; and although we failed to secure Melchior Anderegg and some other notable guides, we obtained two men of repute—namely, Johann zum Taugwald and Johann Kronig of Zermatt. We met at that place early in July, but stormy weather prevented us even from crossing to the other side of the chain for some time. We crossed the Col Théodule on the 5th, but the weather was thoroughly unsettled: it was raining in the valleys and snowing upon the mountains. Shortly before we gained the summit we were made extremely uncomfortable by hearing mysterious rushing sounds, which sometimes seemed as if a sudden gust of wind was sweeping along the snow, and at others almost like the swishing of a long whip; yet the snow exhibited no signs of motion and the air was perfectly calm. The dense, black storm-clouds made us momentarily expect that our bodies might be used as lightning-conductors, and we were well satisfied to get under shelter of the inn at Breuil without having submitted to any such experience.

We had need of a porter, and by the advice of our landlord descended to the chalets of Breuil in search of one Luc Meynet. We found his house, a mean abode, encumbered with cheese-making apparatus, and tenanted only by some bright-eyed children; but as they said that Uncle Luc would soon be

* *Mountaineering in* 1861, pp. 86, 87. Tyndall and Bennen were mistaken in supposing that the mountain has two summits; it has only one. They seem to have been deceived by the appearance of that part of the south-west ridge which is called "the shoulder" (l'épaule), as seen from Breuil. Viewed from that place, its southern end has certainly, through foreshortening, the semblance of a peak; but when one regards it from the Col Théodule, or from any place in the same direction, the delusion is at once apparent.

home, we waited at the door of the little chalet and watched for him. At last a speck was seen coming round the corner of the patch of pines below

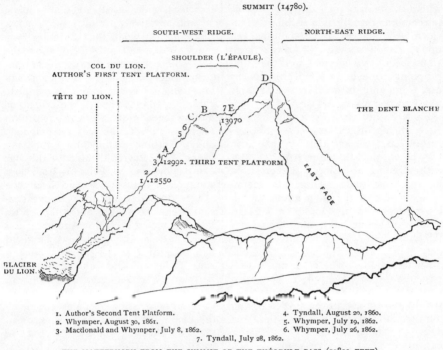

SUMMIT (14780).

SOUTH-WEST RIDGE.   NORTH-EAST RIDGE.

SHOULDER (L'ÉPAULE).
COL DU LION.
AUTHOR'S FIRST TENT PLATFORM.

TÊTE DU LION.

THE DENT BLANCHE

B   7 E
C   13970

A
4
3 12992. THIRD TENT PLATFORM
2
1 12550

EAST FACE

GLACIER
DU LION.

1. Author's Second Tent Platform.   4. Tyndall, August 20, 1860.
2. Whymper, August 30, 1861.   5. Whymper, July 19, 1862.
3. Macdonald and Whymper, July 8, 1862. 6. Whymper, July 26, 1862.
                7. Tyndall, July 28, 1862.

THE MATTERHORN FROM THE SUMMIT OF THE THÉODULE PASS (10899 FEET).

Breuil, and then the children clapped their hands, dropped their toys and ran eagerly forward to meet him. We saw an ungainly, wobbling figure stoop down and catch up the little ones, kiss them on each cheek, and put them into the empty panniers on each side of the mule, and then heard it come on caroling, as if this was not a world of woe; and yet the face of little Luc Meynet, the hunchback of Breuil, bore traces of trouble and sorrow, and there was more than a touch of sadness in his voice when he said that he must look after his brother's children. All his difficulties were, however, at length overcome, and he agreed to join us to carry the tent.

In the past winter I had turned my attention to tents, and that which we had brought with us was the result of experiments to devise one which should be sufficiently portable to be taken over the most difficult ground, and which should combine lightness with stability. Its base was just under six feet square, and a section perpendicular to its length was an equilateral triangle, the sides of which were six feet long. It was intended to accommodate four persons. It was supported by four ash poles six feet and a half long and one inch and a quarter thick, tapering to the top to an inch and an eighth: these were shod with iron points. The order of proceeding in the construction of the tent was as follows: Holes were drilled through the poles about five inches from their tops for the insertion of two wrought-iron bolts, three inches long and one-quarter of an inch thick. The bolts were then inserted, and the two pairs of poles were set out (and fixed up by a cord) to the proper dimensions. The roof was then put on. This was made of the rough, unbleached calico called forfar, which can be obtained in six-feet widths, and it was continued round for about two feet on each side, on to the floor.  The width of the material was the length of the tent, and seams were thus avoided in the roof. The forfar was sewn round each pole, particular care being taken to avoid wrinkles and to get the whole perfectly taut. The flooring was next put in and sewn down to the forfar. This was of the ordinary plaid mackintosh, about nine feet square, the surplus three feet being continued up the sides to prevent draughts. It is as well to have two feet of this surplus on one side, and only one foot on the other, the latter amount being sufficient for the side occupied by the feet. One end was then permanently closed by a triangular piece of forfar, which was sewn down to that which was already

ALPINE TENT.

fixed. The other end was left open, and had two triangular flaps that overlapped each other, and which were fastened up when we were inside by pieces of tape. Lastly, the forfar was nailed down to the poles to prevent the tent getting out of shape. The cord which was used for climbing served for the tent: it was passed over the crossed poles and underneath the ridge of the roof, and the two ends—one fore and the other aft—were easily secured to pieces of rock. Such a tent costs about four guineas, and its weight is about twenty-three pounds; or, if the lightest kind of forfar is used, it need not exceed twenty pounds.

Sunday, the 6th of July, was showery, and snow fell on the Matterhorn, but we started on the following morning with our three men, and pursued my route of the previous year. I was requested to direct the way, as none save myself had been on the mountain before, but I did not distinguish myself on this occasion, and led my companions nearly to the top of the small peak before the mistake was discovered. The party becoming rebellious, a little exploration was made toward our right, and we found that we were upon the top of the cliff overlooking the Col du Lion. The upper part of the small peak is of a very different character to the lower part : the rocks are not so firm, and they are usually covered or intermixed with snow and glazed with ice : the angle too is more severe. While descending a small snow-slope to get on to the right track, Kronig slipped on a streak of ice and went down at a fearful pace. Fortunately, he kept on his legs, and by a great effort succeeded in stopping just before he arrived at some rocks that jutted through the snow, which would infallibly have knocked him over. When we rejoined him a few minutes later we found that he was incapable of standing, much less of moving, with a face corpse-like in hue, and trembling violently. He remained in this condition for more than an hour, and the day was consequently far advanced before we arrived at our camping-place on the col. Profiting by the experience of last year, we did not pitch the tent actually on the snow, but collected a quantity of débris from the neighboring ledges, and after constructing a rough platform of the larger pieces, leveled the whole with the dirt and mud.

Meynet had proved invaluable as a tent-bearer, for, although his legs were more picturesque than symmetrical, and although he seemed to be built, on principle, with no two parts alike, his very deformities proved of service ; and we quickly found he had a spirit of no common order, and that few peasants are more agreeable companions or better climbers than little Luc Meynet, the hunchback of Breuil. He now showed himself not less serviceable as a scavenger, and humbly asked for gristly pieces of meat rejected by the others, or for suspicious eggs, and seemed to consider it a peculiar favor, if not a treat,

to be permitted to drink the coffee-grounds. With the greatest contentment he took the worst place at the door of the tent, and did all the dirty work which was put upon him by the guides, as gratefully as a dog who has been well beaten will receive a stroke.

A strong wind sprang up from the east during the night, and in the morning it was blowing almost a hurricane. The tent behaved nobly, and we remained under its shelter for several hours after the sun had risen, uncertain what it was best to do. A lull tempted us to move, but we had scarcely ascended a hundred feet before the storm burst upon us with increased fury. Advance or return was alike impossible : the ridge was denuded of its débris, and we clutched our hardest when we saw stones as big as a man's fist blown away horizontally into space. We dared not attempt to stand upright, and remained stationary on all fours, glued, as it were, to the rocks. It was intensely cold, for the blast had swept along the main chain of the Pennine Alps and across the great snow-fields around Monte Rosa. Our warmth and courage rapidly evaporated, and at the next lull we retreated to the tent, having to halt several times in that short distance. Taugwald and Kronig then declared that they had had enough, and refused to have anything more to do with the mountain. Meynet also informed us that he would be required down below for important cheese-making operations on the following day. It was therefore needful to return to Breuil, and we arrived there at 2.30 P. M., extremely chagrined at our complete defeat.

Jean - Antoine Carrel, attracted by rumors, had come up to the inn during our absence, and after some negotiations agreed to accompany us, with one of his friends named Pession, on the first fine day. We thought ourselves fortunate, for Carrel clearly considered the mountain a kind of *preserve*, and regarded our late attempt as an act of *poaching*. The wind blew itself out during the night, and we started again, with these two men and a porter, at 8

A. M. on the 9th, with unexceptionable weather. Carrel pleased us by suggesting that we should camp even higher than before; and we accordingly proceeded, without resting at the col, until we overtopped the Tête du Lion. Near the foot of the "Chimney," a little below the crest of the ridge and on its eastern side, we found a protected place; and by building up from ledge to ledge (under the direction of our leader, who was a mason by profession) we at length constructed a platform of sufficient size and of considerable solidity. Its height was about twelve thousand five hundred and fifty feet above the sea; and it exists, I believe, at the present time. We then pushed on, as the day was very fine, and after a short hour's scramble got to the foot of the Great Tower upon the ridge (that is to say, to Mr. Hawkins' farthest point), and afterward returned to our bivouac. We turned out again at 4 A. M., and at 5.15 started upward once more, with fine weather and the thermometer at 28°. Carrel scrambled up the Chimney, and Macdonald and I after him. Pession's turn came, but when he arrived at the top he looked very ill, declared himself to be thoroughly incapable, and said that he must go back. We waited some time, but he did not get better, neither could we learn the nature of his illness. Carrel flatly refused to go on with us alone. We were helpless. Macdonald, ever the coolest of the cool, suggested that we should try what we could do without them, but our better judgment prevailed, and finally we returned together to Breuil. On the next day my friend started for London.

Three times I had essayed the ascent of this mountain, and on each occasion had failed ignominiously. I had not advanced a yard beyond my predecessors. Up to the height of nearly thirteen thousand feet there were no extraordinary difficulties: the way so far might even become "a matter of amusement." Only eighteen hundred feet remained, but they were as yet untrodden, and might present the most formidable obstacles. No man could expect to climb them by himself. A morsel of rock only seven feet high might at any time defeat him if it were perpendicular. Such a place might be possible to two, or a bagatelle to three men. It was evident that a party should consist of three men at least. But where could the other two men be obtained? Carrel was the only man who exhibited any enthusiasm in the matter, and he in 1861 had absolutely refused to go unless the party consisted of at least *four* persons. Want of men made the difficulty, not the mountain.

The weather became bad again, so I went to Zermatt on the chance of picking up a man, and remained there during a week of storms. Not one of the good men, however, could be induced to come, and I returned to Breuil on the 17th, hoping to combine the skill of Carrel with the willingness of Meynet on a new attempt by the same route as before; for the Hörnli ridge, which I had examined in the mean time, seemed to be entirely impracticable. Both men were inclined to go, but their ordinary occupations prevented them from starting at once.

My tent had been left rolled up at the second platform, and whilst waiting for the men it occurred to me that it might have been blown away during the late stormy weather; so I started off on the 18th to see if this were so or not. The way was by this time familiar, and I mounted rapidly, astonishing the friendly herdsmen—who nodded recognition as I flitted past them and the cows—for I was alone, because no man was available. But more deliberation was necessary when the pastures were passed and climbing began, for it was needful to mark each step in case of mist or surprise by night. It is one of the few things which can be said in favor of mountaineering alone (a practice which has little besides to commend it) that it awakens a man's faculties and makes him observe. When one has no arms to help and no head to guide him except his own, he must needs take note even of small things, for he cannot afford to throw away a chance; and

4

so it came to pass upon my solitary scramble, when above the snow-line and beyond the ordinary limits of flowering plants, when peering about noting angles and landmarks, that my eyes fell upon the tiny straggling plants—oftentimes a single flower on a single stalk—pioneers of vegetation, atoms of life in a world of desolation, which had found their way up—who can tell how ?—from far below, and were obtaining bare sustenance from the scanty soil in protected nooks ; and it gave a new interest to the well-known rocks to see what a gallant fight the survivors made (for many must have perished in the attempt) to ascend the great mountain. The gentian, as one might have expected, was there, but it was run close by saxifrages and by *Linaria alpina*, and was beaten by *Thlaspi rotundifolium ;* which latter plant was the highest I was able to secure, although it too was overtopped by a little white flower which I knew not and was unable to reach.

The tent was safe, although snowed up, and I turned to contemplate the view, which, when seen alone and undisturbed, had all the strength and charm of complete novelty. The highest peaks of the Pennine chain were in front — the Breithorn (13,685 feet), the Lyskamm (14,889), and Monte Rosa (15,217) ; then turning to the right, the entire block of mountains which separated the Val Tournanche from the Val d'Ayas was seen at a glance, with its dominating summit, the Grand Tournalin (11,155). Behind were the ranges dividing the Val d'Ayas from the valley of Gressoney, backed by higher summits. More still to the right the eye wandered down the entire length of the Val Tournanche, and then rested upon the Graian Alps with their innumerable peaks, and upon the isolated pyramid of Monte Viso (12,643) in the extreme distance. Next, still turning to the right, came the mountains intervening between the Val Tournanche and the Val Barthélemy : Mont Rouss (a round-topped, snowy summit, which seems so important from Breuil, but which is in reality only a buttress of the higher mountain, the

Château des Dames) had long ago sunk, and the eye passed over it, scarcely heeding its existence, to the Becca Salle (or, as it is printed on the map, Bec de Sale), a miniature Matterhorn, and to other and more important heights. Then the grand mass of the Dent d'Hérens (13,714) stopped the way--a noble mountain, encrusted on its northern slopes with enormous hanging glaciers, which broke away at mid-day in immense slices, and thundered down on to the Tiefenmatten glacier ; and lastly, most splendid of all, came the Dent Blanche (14,318), soaring above the basin of the great Z'Muttgletscher. Such a view is hardly to be matched in the Alps, and *this* view is very rarely seen, as I saw it, perfectly unclouded.

Time sped away unregarded, and the little birds which had built their nests on the neighboring cliffs had begun to chirp their evening hymn before I thought of returning. Half mechanically I turned to the tent, unrolled it and set it up : it contained food enough for several days, and I resolved to stay over the night. I had started from Breuil without provisions or telling Favre, the innkeeper, who was accustomed to my erratic ways, where I was going. I returned to the view. The sun was setting, and its rosy rays, blending with the snowy blue, had thrown a pale, pure violet far as the eye could see ; the valleys were drowned in a purple gloom, while the summits shone with unnatural brightness ; and as I sat in the door of the tent and watched the twilight change to darkness, the earth seemed to become less earthly and almost sublime : the world seemed dead, and I its sole inhabitant. By and by the moon, as it rose, brought the hills again into sight, and by a judicious repression of detail rendered the view yet more magnificent. Something in the south hung like a great glow-worm in the air : it was too large for a star, and too steady for a meteor, and it was long before I could realize the incredible fact that it was the moonlight glittering on the great snow-slope on the north side of Monte Viso, at a distance, as the crow flies, of ninety-eight miles. Shivering, at last I entered the tent and made my coffee. The night was passed comfortably, and the next morning, tempted by the brilliancy of the weather, I proceeded yet higher in search of another place for a platform.

Solitary scrambling over a pretty wide area had shown me that a single individual is subjected to very many difficulties which do not trouble a party of two or three men, and that the disadvantages of being alone are more felt while descending than during the ascent. In order to neutralize these inconveniences, I had devised two little appliances, which were now brought into use for the first time. One was a claw, a kind of grapnel, about five inches long, made of shear steel one-fifth of an inch thick. This was of use in difficult places where there was no hold within arm's length, but where there were cracks or ledges some distance higher. It could be stuck on the end of the alpenstock and dropped into such places, or, on extreme occasions, flung up until it attached itself to something. The edges that laid hold of the rocks were serrated, which tended to make them catch more readily: the other end had a ring to which a rope was fastened. It must not be understood that this was employed for hauling one's self up by for any great distance, but that it was used in ascending, at the most, for only a few yards at a time. In descending, however, it could be prudently used for a greater distance at a time, as the claws could be planted firmly; but it was necessary to keep the rope taut and the pull constantly in the direction of the length of the implement, otherwise it had a tendency to slip away. The second device

was merely a modification of a dodge practiced by all climbers. It is frequently necessary for a single man (or for the last man of a party) during a descent to make a loop in the end of his rope, which he passes over some rocks, and to come down holding the free end. The loop is then jerked off, and the process may be repeated. But as it sometimes happens that there are no rocks at hand which will allow a loose loop to be used, a slip-knot has to be resorted to, and the rope is drawn in tightly. Consequently, it will occur that it is not possible to jerk the loop off, and the rope has to be cut and left behind. To prevent this, I had a wrought-iron ring (two and a quarter inches in diameter and three-eighths of an inch thick) attached to one end of my rope, and a loop could be made in a moment by passing the other end of the rope through the ring, which of course slipped up and held tightly as I descended holding the free end. A strong piece of cord was also attached to the ring, and on arriving at the bottom this was pulled: the ring slid back again, and the loop was whipped off readily. By means of these two simple appliances I was able to ascend and descend rocks which otherwise would have been completely impassable. The combined weight of these two things amounted to less than half a pound.

The rocks of the south-west ridge are by no means difficult for some distance above the Col du Lion. This is true of the rocks up to the level of the Chimney, but they steepen when that is passed, and remaining smooth and with but few fractures, and still continuing to dip outward, present some steps of a very uncertain kind, particularly when they are glazed with ice. At this point (just above the Chimney) the climber is obliged to follow the southern (or Breuil) side of the ridge, but in a few feet more one must turn over to the northern (or Z'Mutt) side, where in most years Nature kindly provides a snow-slope. When this is surmounted, one can again return to the crest of the ridge, and follow it by easy rocks to the foot of the Great Tower. This was the highest point attained by Mr. Hawkins in 1860, and it was also our highest on the 9th of July.

This Great Tower is one of the most striking features of the ridge. It stands out like a turret at the angle of a castle. Behind it a battlemented wall leads upward to the citadel. Seen from the Théodule pass, it looks only an insignificant pinnacle, but as one approaches it (on the ridge), so it seems to rise, and when one is at its base it completely conceals the upper parts of the mountain. I found here a suitable place for the tent, which, although not so well protected as the second platform, possessed the advantage of being three hundred feet higher up; and fascinated by the wildness of the cliffs, and enticed by the perfection of the weather, I went on to see what was behind.

The first step was a difficult one : the ridge became diminished to the least possible width, it was hard to keep one's balance, and just where it was narrowest a more than perpendicular mass barred the way. Nothing fairly within arm's reach could be laid hold of : it was necessary to spring up, and then to haul one's self over the sharp edge by sheer strength. Progression directly upward was then impossible. Enormous and appalling precipices plunged down to the Tiefenmatten glacier on the left, but round the right-hand side it was just possible to go. One hindrance then succeeded another, and much time was consumed in seeking the way. I have a vivid recollection of a gully of more than usual perplexity at the side of the Great Tower, with minute ledges and steep walls ; of the ledges dwindling down, and at last ceasing ; of finding myself, with arms and legs divergent, fixed as if crucified, pressing against the rock, and feeling each rise and fall of my chest as I breathed ; of screwing my head round to look for a hold, and not seeing any, and of jumping sideways on to the other side.

Places such as this gully have their charm so long as a man feels that the difficulties are within his power, but their enchantment vanishes directly they are too much for him, and when he feels this they are dangerous to him. The line which separates the difficult from the dangerous is sometimes a very shadowy one, but it is not an imaginary one. It is a true line, without breadth. It is often easy to pass and very hard to see. It is sometimes passed unconsciously, and the consciousness that it has been passed is felt too late ; but so long as a man undertakes that which is well within his power, he is not likely to pass this line, or consequently to get into any great danger, although he may meet with considerable difficulty. That which is within a man's power varies, of course, according to time, place and circumstance, but as a rule he can tell pretty well when he is arriving at the end of his tether ; and it seems to me, although it is difficult to determine for another, even approximately, the limits to which it is prudent for him to go, that it is tolerably easy to do so for one's self. But (according to my opinion) if the doubtful line is crossed consciously, deliberately, one passes from doing that which is justifiable to doing that which is unjustifiable, because it is imprudent.

I expect that any intelligent critic will inquire, "But do you really mean to assert that dangers in mountaineering arise only from superlative difficulty, and that the perfect mountaineer does not run any risks ?" I am not prepared to go quite so far as this, although there is only one risk to which the scrambler on the Higher Alps is unavoidably subject which does not occur to pedestrians in London's streets. This arises from falling rocks, and I shall endeavor in the course of this work to make the reader understand that it is a *positive* danger, and one against which skill, strength and courage are equally unavailing. It occurs at unexpected times, and may occur in almost any place. The critic may retort, "Your admission of this one danger destroys all the rest of the argument." I agree with him that it would do so if it were a *grave* risk to life. But although it is a real danger, it is not a very serious risk. Not many cases can be quoted of accidents which have happened through falling stones, and I do not know an instance of life having been lost in this way in the High Alps.* I suppose, however, few persons will maintain that it is unjustifiable to do anything, for sport or otherwise, so long as *any* risk is incurred, else it would be unjustifiable to cross Fleet street at mid-day. If it were one's bounden duty to avoid every risk, we should have to pass our lives indoors. I conceive that the pleasures of mountaineering outweigh the risks arising from this particular cause, and that the practice will not be vetoed on its account. Still, I wish to stamp it as a *positive* danger, and as one which may imperil the life of the most perfect mountaineer.

This digression has been caused by an innocent gully which I feared the reader might think was dangerous. It was an untrodden vestibule, which led to a scene so wild that even the most sober description of it must seem an exaggeration. There was a change in the quality of the rock, and there was a change in the appearance of the ridge. The rocks (talcose gneiss) below this spot were singularly firm—it was rarely necessary to test one's hold: the way led over the living rock, and not up rent-off fragments. But here all was decay and ruin. The crest of the ridge was shattered and cleft, and the feet sank in the chips which had drifted down ; while above, huge blocks, hacked and carved by the hand of

*The contrary is the case in regard to the Lower Alps. Amongst others, the case may be mentioned of a lady who (not very long ago) had her skull fractured while sitting at the base of the Mer de Glace.

time, nodded to the sky, looking like the gravestones of giants. Out of curiosity I wandered to a notch in the ridge, between two tottering piles of immense masses which seemed to need but a few pounds on one or the other side to make them fall, so nicely poised that they would literally have rocked in the wind, for they were put in motion by a touch, and based on support so frail that I wondered they did not collapse before my eyes. In the whole range of my Alpine experience I have seen nothing more striking than this desolate, ruined and shattered ridge at the back of the Great Tower. I have seen stranger shapes — rocks which mimic the human form, with monstrous leering faces, and isolated pinnacles sharper and greater than any here—but I have never seen exhibited so impressively the tremendous effects which may be produced by frost, and by the long-continued action of forces whose individual effects are imperceptible.

It is needless to say that it is impossible to climb by the crest of the ridge at this part : still, one is compelled to keep near to it, for there is no other way. Generally speaking, the angles on the Matterhorn are too steep to allow the formation of considerable beds of snow, but here there is a corner which permits it to accumulate, and it is turned to gratefully, for by its assistance one can ascend four times as rapidly as upon the rocks.

The Tower was now almost out of sight, and I looked over the central Pennine Alps to the Grand Combin and to the chain of Mont Blanc. My neighbor, the Dent d'Hérens, still rose above me, although but slightly, and the height which had been attained could be measured by its help. So far, I had no doubts about my capacity to descend that which had been ascended ; but in a short time, on looking ahead, I saw that the cliffs steepened, and I turned back (without pushing on to them and getting into inextricable difficulties), exulting in the thought that they would be passed when we returned together, and that I had without assistance got nearly to the height of the Dent d'Hérens, and considerably higher than any one had been before.* My exultation was a little premature.

About five P. M. I left the tent again, and thought myself as good as at Breuil. The friendly rope and claw had done good service, and had smoothed all the difficulties. I lowered myself through the Chimney, however, by making a fixture of the rope, which I then cut off and left behind, as there was enough and to spare. My axe had proved a great nuisance in coming down, and I left it in the tent. It was not attached to the bâton, but was a separate affair —an old navy boarding-axe. While cutting up the different snow-beds on the ascent, the bâton trailed behind fastened to the rope; and when climbing the axe was carried behind, run through the rope tied round my waist, and was sufficiently out of the way; but in descending, when coming down face outward (as is always best where it is possible), the head or the handle of the weapon caught frequently against the rocks, and several times nearly upset me. So, out of laziness if you will, it was left in the tent. I paid dearly for the imprudence.

The Col du Lion was passed, and fifty yards more would have placed me on the "Great Staircase," down which one can run. But on arriving at an angle of the cliffs of the Tête du Lion, while skirting the upper edge of the snow which abuts against them, I found that the heat of the two past days had nearly obliterated the steps which had been cut when coming up. The rocks happened to be impracticable just at this corner, so nothing could be done except make the steps afresh. The snow was too hard to beat or tread down, and at the angle it was all but ice: half a dozen steps only were required, and then the ledges could be followed again. So I held to the rock

* A remarkable streak of snow (marked "cravate" in the outline of the Matterhorn as seen from the Théodule) runs across the cliff at this part of the mountain. My highest point was somewhat higher than the lowest part of this snow, and was conseqently nearly 13,500 feet above the sea.

with my right hand, and prodded at the snow with the point of my stick until a good step was made, and then, leaning round the angle, did the same for the other side. So far well, but in attempting to pass the corner (to the present moment I cannot tell how it happened) I slipped and fell.

The slope was steep on which this took place, and descended to the top of a gully that led down through two subordinate buttresses toward the Glacier du Lion, which was just seen, a thousand feet below. The gully narrowed and narrowed until there was a mere thread of snow lying between two walls of rock, which came to an abrupt termination at the top of a precipice that intervened between it and the glacier. Imagine a funnel cut in half through its length, placed at an angle of forty-five degrees, with its point below and its concave side uppermost, and you will have a fair idea of the place.

The knapsack brought my head down first, and I pitched into some rocks about a dozen feet below: they caught something and tumbled me off the edge, head over heels, into the gully. The bâton was dashed from my hands, and I whirled downward in a series of bounds, each longer than the last—now over ice, now into rocks—striking my head four or five times, each time with increased force. The last bound sent me spinning through the air, in a leap of fifty or sixty feet, from one side of the gully to the other, and I struck the rocks, luckily, with the whole of my left side. They caught my clothes for a moment, and I fell back on to the snow with motion arrested: my head fortunately came the right side up, and a few frantic catches brought me to a halt in the neck of the gully and on the verge of the precipice. Bâton, hat and veil skimmed by and disappeared, and the crash of the rocks which I had started, as they fell on to the glacier, told how narrow had been the escape from utter destruction. As it was, I fell nearly two hundred feet in seven or eight bounds. Ten feet more would have

"IN ATTEMPTING TO PASS THE CORNER I SLIPPED AND FELL."

taken me in one gigantic leap of eight hundred feet on to the glacier below.

The situation was still sufficiently serious. The rocks could not be left go for a moment, and the blood was spurting out of more than twenty cuts. The most serious ones were in the head, and I vainly tried to close them with one hand while holding on with the other. It was useless: the blood jerked out in blinding jets at each pulsation. At last, in a moment of inspiration, I kicked out a big lump of snow and stuck it as a plaster on my head. The idea was a happy one, and the flow of blood diminished: then, scrambling up, I got, not a moment too soon, to a place of safety and fainted away. The sun was setting when consciousness returned, and it was pitch dark before the Great Staircase was descended; but by a combination of luck and care the whole forty-eight hundred feet of descent to Breuil was accomplished without a slip or once missing the way. I slunk past the cabin of the cowherds, who were talking and laughing inside, utterly ashamed of the state to which I had been brought by my imbecility, and entered the inn stealthily, wishing to escape to my room unnoticed. But Favre met me in the passage, demanded, "Who is it?" screamed with fright when he got a light, and aroused the household. Two dozen heads then held solemn council over mine, with more talk than action. The natives were unanimous in recommending that hot wine (syn. vinegar), mixed with salt, should be rubbed into the cuts. I protested, but they insisted. It was all the doctoring they received. Whether their rapid healing was to be attributed to that simple remedy or to a good state of health, is a question: they closed up remarkably soon, and in a few days I was able to move again.

It was sufficiently dull during this time. I was chiefly occupied in meditating on the vanity of human wishes, and in watching my clothes being washed in the tub which was turned by the stream in the front of the house; and I vowed that if an Englishman should at any time fall sick in the Val Tour-

nanche, he should not feel so solitary as I did at this dreary time.*

The news of the accident brought Jean-Antoine Carrel up to Breuil, and along with the haughty chasseur came one of his relatives, a strong and able young fellow named Cæsar. With these two men and Meynet I made another start on the 23d of July. We got to the tent without any trouble, and on the following day had ascended beyond the Tower, and were picking our way cautiously over the loose rocks behind (where my traces of the week before were well apparent) in lovely weather, when one of those abominable and almost instantaneous changes occurred to which the Matterhorn is so liable on its southern side. Mists were created out of invisible vapors, and in a few minutes snow fell heavily. We stopped, as this part was of excessive difficulty, and, unwilling to retreat, remained on the spot several hours, in hopes that another change would occur; but as it did not, we at length went down to the

* As it seldom happens that one survives such a fall, it may be interesting to record what my sensations were during its occurrence. I was perfectly conscious of what was happening, and felt each blow, but, like a patient under chloroform, experienced no pain. Each blow was, naturally, more severe than that which preceded it, and I distinctly remember thinking, "Well, if the next is harder still, that will be the end!" Like persons who have been rescued from drowning, I remember that the recollection of a multitude of things rushed through my head, many of them trivialities or absurdities which had been forgotten long before; and, more remarkable, this bounding through space did not feel disagreeable. But I think that in no very great distance more consciousness as well as sensation would have been lost, and upon that I base my belief, improbable as it seems, that death by a fall from a great height is as painless an end as can be experienced.

The battering was very rough, yet no bones were broken. The most severe cuts were—one four inches long on the top of the head, and another of three inches on the right temple: this latter bled frightfully. There was a formidable-looking cut, of about the same size as the last, on the palm of the left hand, and every limb was grazed or cut more or less seriously. The tips of the ears were taken off, and a sharp rock cut a circular bit out of the side of the left boot, sock and ankle at one stroke. The loss of blood although so great, did not seem to be permanently injurious. The only serious effect has been the reduction of a naturally retentive memory to a very commonplace one; and although my recollections of more distant occurrences remain unshaken, the events of that particular day would be clean gone but for the few notes which were written down before the accident.

base of the Tower, and commenced to make a third platform, at the height of 12,992 feet above the sea. It still continued to snow, and we took refuge in the tent. Carrel argued that the weather had broken up, and that the mountain would become so glazed with ice as to render any attempt futile; and I, that the change was only temporary, and that the rocks were too hot to allow ice to form upon them. I wished to stay until the weather improved, but my leader would not endure contradiction, grew more positive and insisted that we must go down. We went down, and when we got below the col his opinion was found to be wrong: the cloud was confined to the upper three thousand feet, and outside it there was brilliant weather.

Carrel was not an easy man to manage. He was perfectly aware that he was the cock of the Val Tournanche, and he commanded the other men as by right. He was equally conscious that he was indispensable to me, and took no pains to conceal his knowledge of the fact. If he had been commanded or if he had been entreated to stop, it would have been all the same. But, let me repeat, he was the only first-rate climber I could find who believed that the mountain was not inaccessible. With him I had hopes, but without him none; so he was allowed to do as he would. His will on this occasion was almost incomprehensible. He certainly could not be charged with cowardice, for a bolder man could hardly be found; nor was he turning away on account of difficulty, for nothing to which we had yet come seemed to be difficult to *him;* and his strong personal desire to make the ascent was evident. There was no occasion to come down on account of food, for we had taken, to guard against this very casualty, enough to last for a week; and there was no danger and little or no discomfort in stopping in the tent. It seemed to me that he was spinning out the ascent for his own purposes, and that although he wished very much to be the first man on the top, and did not object to be accompanied

by any one else who had the same wish, he had no intention of letting one succeed too soon—perhaps to give a greater appearance of *éclat* when the thing was accomplished. As he feared no rival, he may have supposed that the more difficulties he made the more valuable he would be estimated, though, to do him justice, he never showed any great hunger for money. His demands were fair, not excessive; but he always stipulated for so much per day, and so, under any circumstances, he did not do badly.

Vexed at having my time thus frittered away, I was still well pleased when he volunteered to start again on the morrow if it was fine. We were to advance the tent to the foot of the Tower, to fix ropes in the most difficult parts beyond, and to make a push for the summit on the following day.

The next morning (Friday, the 25th), when I arose, good little Meynet was ready and waiting, and he said that the two Carrels had gone off some time before, and had left word that they intended marmot-hunting, as the day was favorable for that sport. My holiday had nearly expired, and these men clearly could not be relied upon; so, as a last resort, I proposed to the hunchback to accompany me alone, to see if we could not get higher than before, though of reaching the summit there was little or no hope. He did not hesitate, and in a few hours we stood—for the third time together—upon the Col du Lion, but it was the first time Meynet had seen the view unclouded. The poor little deformed peasant gazed upon it silently and reverently for a time, and then unconsciously fell on one knee in an attitude of adoration, and clasped his hands, exclaiming in ecstasy, "O beautiful mountains!" His actions were as appropriate as his words were natural, and tears bore witness to the reality of his emotion.

Our power was too limited to advance the tent, so we slept at the old station, and, starting very early the next morning, passed the place where we had turned back on the 24th, and subse

A CANNONADE ON THE MATTERHORN. (1862.)

quently my highest point on the 19th. We found the crest of the ridge so treacherous that we took to the cliffs on the right, although most unwillingly. Little by little we fought our way up, but at length we were both spread-eagled on the all-but perpendicular face, unable to advance and barely able to descend. We returned to the ridge. It was almost equally difficult, and infinitely more unstable; and at length, after having pushed our attempts as far as was prudent, I determined to return to Breuil, and to have a light ladder made to assist us to overcome some of the steepest parts. I expected, too, that by this time Carrel would have had enough marmot-hunting, and would deign to accompany us again.

We came down at a great pace, for we were now so familiar with the mountain and with each other's wants that we knew immediately when to give a helping hand and when to let alone. The rocks also were in a better state than I have ever seen them, being almost entirely free from glaze of ice. Meynet was always merriest on the difficult parts, and on the most difficult kept on enunciating the sentiment, "We can only die once," which thought seemed to afford him infinite satisfaction. We arrived at the inn early in the evening, and I found my projects summarily and unexpectedly knocked on the head.

Professor Tyndall had arrived while we were absent, and he had engaged both Cæsar and Jean-Antoine Carrel. Bennen was also with him, together with a powerful and active friend, a Valaisan guide named Anton Walter. They had a ladder already prepared, provisions were being collected, and they intended to start on the following morning (Sunday). This new arrival took me by surprise. Bennen, it will be remembered, refused point-blank to take Professor Tyndall on the Matterhorn in 1861. "He was dead against any attempt on the mountain," says Tyndall. He was now eager to set out. Professor Tyndall has not explained in what way this revolution came about in

his guide. I was equally astonished at the faithlessness of Carrel, and attributed it to pique at our having presumed to do without him. It was useless to compete with the professor and his four men, who were ready to start in a few hours, so I waited to see what would come of their attempt.

Everything seemed to favor it, and they set out on a fine morning in high spirits, leaving me tormented with envy and all uncharitableness. If they succeeded, they carried off the prize for which I had been so long struggling; and if they failed, there was no time to make another attempt, for I was due in a few days more in London. When this came home clearly to me, I resolved to leave Breuil at once, but when packing up found that some necessaries had been left behind in the tent. So I went off about mid-day to recover them, caught the army of the professor before it reached the col, as they were going very slowly, left them there (stopping to take food) and went on to the tent. I was near to it when all at once I heard a noise aloft, and on looking up perceived a stone of at least a foot cube flying straight at my head. I ducked and scrambled under the lee side of a friendly rock, while the stone went by with a loud buzz. It was the advanced guard of a perfect storm of stones, which descended with infernal clatter down the very edge of the ridge, leaving a trail of dust behind, with a strong smell of sulphur that told who had sent them. The men below were on the look-out, but the stones did not come near them, and breaking away on one side went down to the glacier.

I waited at the tent to welcome the professor, and when he arrived went down to Breuil. Early next morning some one ran to me saying that a flag was seen on the summit of the Matterhorn. It was not so, however, although I saw that they had passed the place where we had turned back on the 26th. I had now no doubt of their final success, for they had got beyond the point which Carrel, not less than myself, had always considered to be the most questionable place on the whole mountain. Up to it there was no choice of route— I suppose that at no one point between it and the col was it possible to diverge a dozen paces to the right or left—but beyond it it was otherwise, and we had always agreed in our debates that if it could be passed success was certain.

The accompanying outline from a sketch taken from the door of the inn at Breuil will help to explain. The letter A indicates the position of the Great Tower; C, the "cravate" (the strongly-marked streak of snow referred to in note on page 54, and which we just failed to arrive at on the 26th); B, the

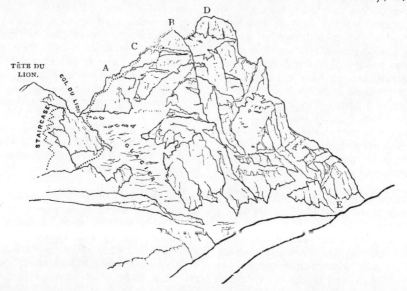

place where we now saw something that looked like a flag. Behind the point B a nearly level ridge leads up to the foot of the final peak, which will be understood by a reference to the outline on page 46, on which the same letters indicate the same places. It was just now said, we considered that if the point C could be passed, success was certain. Tyndall was at B very early in the morning, and I did not doubt that he would reach the summit, although it yet remained problematical whether he would be able to stand on the very highest point. The summit was evidently formed of a long ridge, on which there were two points nearly equally elevated—so equally that one could not say which was the highest—and between the two there seemed to be a deep notch, marked D on the outlines, which might defeat one at the very last moment.

My knapsack was packed, and I had drunk a parting glass of wine with

Favre, who was jubilant at the success which was to make the fortune of his inn, but I could not bring myself to leave until the result was heard, and lingered about, as a foolish lover hovers round the object of his affections even after he has been contemptuously rejected. The sun had set before the men were descried coming over the pastures. There was no spring in their steps: they too were defeated. The Carrels hid their heads, but the others said, as men will do when they have been beaten, that the mountain was horrible, impossible, and so forth. Professor Tyndall told me they had arrived *within a stone's throw of the summit*, and admonished me to have nothing more to do with the mountain. I understood him to say that he should not try again, and ran down to the village of Val Tournanche, almost inclined to believe that the mountain was inaccessible, leaving the tent, ropes and other matters in the hands of Favre, to be placed at the disposal of any person who wished to ascend it—more, I am afraid, out of irony than generosity. There may have been those who be-

lieved that the Matterhorn could be ascended, but anyhow their faith did not bring forth works. No one tried again in 1862.

PART IV.

"BUT WHAT IS THIS?"

CHAPTER VI.

THE VAL TOURNANCHE — THE BREUILJOCH — ZERMATT — ASCENT OF THE GRAND TOURNALIN.

I CROSSED the Channel on the 29th of July, 1863, embarrassed by the possession of two ladders, each twelve feet long, which joined together like those used by firemen, and shut up like parallel rulers. My luggage was highly suggestive of housebreaking, for, besides these, there were several coils of rope and numerous tools of suspicious appearance; and it was reluctantly admitted into France, but it passed through the custom-house with less trouble than I anticipated, after a timely expenditure of a few francs.

I am not in love with the douane. It is the purgatory of travelers, where un-

congenial spirits mingle together for a time before they are separated into rich and poor. The douaniers look upon tourists as their natural enemies: see how eagerly they pounce upon the portmanteaus! One of them has discovered something. He has never seen its like before, and he holds it aloft in the the face of its owner with inquisitorial insolence: "But *what is* this?" The explanation is but half satisfactory "But what is *this?*" says he, laying hold of a little box. "Powder." "But that is forbidden to carry of powder on the railway." "Bah!" says another and older hand, "pass the effects of monsieur;" and our countryman — whose cheeks had begun to redden under the stares of his fellow-travelers— is allowed to depart with his half-worn

tooth-brush, while the discomfited dou-
anier gives a mighty shrug at the strange
habits of those "whose insular position
excludes them from the march of continental ideas."

My real troubles commenced at Susa.
The officials there, more honest and
more obtuse than the Frenchmen, declined at one and the same time to be
bribed or to pass my baggage until a
satisfactory account of it was rendered ;
and as they refused to believe the true
explanation, I was puzzled what to say,
but was presently relieved from the di-
lemma by one of the men, who was
cleverer than his fellows, suggesting
that I was going to Turin to exhibit in
the streets—that I mounted the ladder
and balanced myself on the end of it,
then lighted my pipe and put the point
of the bâton in its bowl, and caused the
bâton to gyrate around my head. The
rope was to keep back the spectators,
and an Englishman in my company
was the agent. "Monsieur is acrobat,
then ?" "Yes, certainly." "Pass the
effects of monsieur the acrobat !"

These ladders were the source of endless trouble. Let us pass over the doubts
of the guardians of the Hôtel d'Europe
(Trombetta) whether a person in the
possession of such questionable articles
should be admitted to their very respectable house, and get to Chatillon, at the
entrance of the Val Tournanche. A
mule was chartered to carry them, and
as they were too long to sling across its
back, they were arranged lengthways,
and one end projected over the animal's head, while the other extended
beyond its tail. A mule when going up
or down hill always moves with a jerky
action, and in consequence of this the
ladders hit my mule severe blows between its ears and its flanks. The
beast, not knowing what strange creature it had on its back, naturally tossed
its head and threw out its legs, and
this, of course, only made the blows that
it received more severe. At last it ran
away, and would have perished by rolling down a precipice if the men had not
caught hold of its tail. The end of the
matter was, that a man had to follow

the mule, holding the end of the ladders, which obliged him to move his
arms up and down incessantly, and to
bow to the hind quarters of the animal
in a way that afforded more amusement
to his comrades than it did to him.

I was once more *en route* for the Matterhorn, for I had heard in the spring
of 1863 the cause of the failure of Professor Tyndall, and learned that the
case was not so hopeless as it appeared
to be at one time. I found that he arrived as far only as the northern end of
"the shoulder." Carrel and all the men
who had been with me knew of the existence of the cleft at this point, and of the
pinnacle which rose between it and the
final peak, and we had frequently talked about the best manner of passing the
place. On this we disagreed, but we
were both of opinion that when we got
to "the shoulder" it would be necessary
to bear gradually to the right or to the
left, to avoid coming to the top of the
notch. But Tyndall's party, after arriving at the shoulder, were led by
his guides along the crest of the ridge,
and consequently when they got to its
northern end they came to the top of
the notch, instead of the bottom—to the
dismay of all but the Carrels. Dr. Tyndall's words are : "The ridge was here
split by a deep cleft which separated it
from the final precipice, and the case
became more hopeless as we came more
near." The professor adds : "The
mountain is 14,800 feet high, and 14,600
feet had been acomplished." He greatly deceived himself : by the barometric
measurements of Signor Giordano the
notch is no less than 800 feet below the
summit. The guide Walter (Dr. Tyndall says) said it was impossible to proceed, and the Carrels, appealed to for
their opinion (this is their own account),
gave as an answer, "We are porters—
ask your guides." Bennen, thus left to
himself, "was finally forced to accept
defeat." Tyndall had nevertheless accomplished an advance of about four
hundred feet over one of the most difficult parts of the mountain.

The Val Tournanche is one of the
most charming valleys in the Italian

Alps: it is a paradise to an artist, and if the space at my command were greater, I would willingly linger over its groves of chestnuts, its bright trickling rills and its roaring torrents, its upland unsuspected valleys and its noble cliffs. The path rises steeply from Chatillon, but it is well shaded, and the heat of the summer sun is tempered by cool air and spray which comes off the ice-cold streams. One sees from the path, at several places on the right bank of the valley, groups of arches which have been built high up against the faces of the cliffs. Guide-books repeat—on whose authority I know not—that they are the remains of a Roman aqueduct. They have the Roman boldness of conception, but the work has not the usual Roman solidity. The arches have always seemed to me to be the remains of an *unfinished* work, and I learn from Jean-Antoine Carrel that there are other groups of arches, which are not seen from the path, all having the same appearance. It may be questioned whether those seen near the village of Antey are Roman. Some of them are semicircular, whilst others are distinctly

pointed. Here is one of the latter, which might pass for fourteenth-century work or later—a two-centred arch, with mean voussoirs and the masonry in rough courses. These arches are well worth the attention of an archæologist, but some difficulty will be found in approaching them closely.

We sauntered up the valley, and got to Breuil when all were asleep. A halo round the moon promised watery weather, and we were not disappointed, for on the next day (August 1) rain fell

heavily, and when the clouds lifted for a time we saw that new snow lay thickly over everything higher than nine thousand feet. J.-A. Carrel was ready and waiting (as I had determined to give the bold cragsman another chance); and he did not need to say that the Matterhorn would be impracticable for several days after all this new snow, even if the weather were to arrange itself at once. Our first day together was accordingly spent upon a neighboring summit, the Cimes Blanches—a degraded mountain well known for its fine panoramic view. It was little that we saw, for in every direction except to the south writhing masses of heavy clouds obscured everything; and to the south our view was intercepted by a peak higher than the Cimes Blanches, named the Grand Tournalin. But we got some innocent pleasure out of watching the gambolings of a number of goats, who became fast friends after we had given them some salt—in fact, too fast, and caused us no little annoyance when we were descending. "Carrel," I said, as a number of stones whizzed by which they had dislodged, "this must be put a stop to." "Diable!" he grunted, "it is very well to talk, but how will you do it?" I said that I would try; and sitting down poured a little brandy into the hollow of my hand, and allured the nearest goat with deceitful gestures. It was one who had gobbled up the paper in which the salt had been carried—an animal of enterprising character—and it advanced fearlessly and licked up the brandy. I shall not easily forget its surprise. It stopped short and coughed, and looked at me as much as to say, "Oh, you cheat!" and spat and ran away, stopping now and then to cough and spit again. We were not troubled any more by those goats.

More snow fell during the night, and our attempt on the Matterhorn was postponed indefinitely. Carrel and I wandered out again in the afternoon, and went, first of all, to a favorite spot with tourists near the end of the Görner glacier (or, properly speaking, the Boden glacier), to a little verdant flat studded with *Euphrasia officinalis*, the delight of swarms of bees, who gather there the honey which afterward appears at the *table d'hôte*.

On our right the glacier torrent thundered down the valley through a gorge with precipitous sides, not easily approached, for the turf at the top was slippery, and the rocks had everywhere been rounded by the glacier, which formerly extended far away. This gorge seems to have been made chiefly by the torrent, and to have been excavated

WATER-WORN ROCKS IN THE GORGE BELOW THE GÖRNER GLACIER.

subsequently to the retreat of the glacier. It seems so, because not merely upon its walls are there the marks of running water, but even upon the rounded rocks at the top of its walls, at a height of seventy or eighty feet above the present level of the torrent, there are some of those queer concavities which rapid streams alone are known to produce on rocks.

A little bridge, apparently frail, spans the torrent just above the entrance to this gorge, and from it one perceives being fashioned in the rocks below con-

cavities similar to those to which reference has just been made. The torrent is seen hurrying forward. Not everywhere. In some places the water strikes projecting angles, and, thrown back by them, remains almost stationary, eddying round and round: in others, obstructions fling it up in fountains, which play perpetually on the *under* surfaces of overhanging masses; and sometimes do so in such a way that the water not only works upon the under surfaces, but round the corner; that is to say, upon the surfaces which are *not* opposed to the general direction of the current. In all cases *concavities* are being produced. Projecting angles are rounded, it is true, and are more or less convex, but they are overlooked on account of the prevalence of concave forms.

Cause and effect help each other here. The inequalities of the torrent bed and walls cause its eddyings, and the eddies fashion the concavities. The more profound the latter become, the more disturbance is caused in the water. The destruction of the rocks proceeds at an ever-increasing rate, for the larger the amount of surface that is exposed, the greater are the opportunities for the assaults of heat and cold.

When water is in the form of glacier it has not the power of making concavities such as these in rocks, and of working upon surfaces which are not opposed to the direction of the current. Its nature is changed: it operates in a different way, and it leaves marks which are readily distinguished from those produced by torrent action.

The prevailing forms which result from glacier action are more or less *convex*. Ultimately, all angles and almost all curves are obliterated, and large areas of flat surfaces are produced. This perfection of abrasion is rarely found except in such localities as have sustained a grinding much more severe than that which has occurred in the Alps. Not merely can the operations of extinct glaciers be traced in detail by means of the bosses of rock popularly termed *roches moutonnées*, but their effects in the aggregate, on a range of mountains or an entire country, can be recognized sometimes at a distance of fifteen or twenty miles, from the incessant repetition of these convex forms.

We finished up the 3d of August with a walk over the Findelen glacier, and returned to Zermatt at a later hour than we intended, both very sleepy. This is noteworthy only on account of that which followed. We had to cross the Col de Valpelline on the next day, and an early start was desirable. Monsieur Seiler, excellent man! knowing this, called us himself, and when he came to my door I answered, "All right, Seiler, I will get up," and immediately turned over to the other side, saying to myself, "First of all, ten minutes' more sleep." But Seiler waited and listened, and, suspecting the case, knocked again : "Herr Whymper, have you got a light ?" Without thinking what the consequences might be, I answered, "No ;" and then the worthy man actually forced the lock off his own door to give me one. By similar and equally friendly and disinterested acts Monsieur

Seiler has acquired his enviable reputation.

At four A. M. we left his Monte Rosa hotel, and were soon pushing our way through the thickets of gray alder that skirt the path up the exquisite little valley which leads to the Z'muttgletscher.

Nothing can seem or be more inaccessible than the Matterhorn upon this side, and even in cold blood one holds

STRIATIONS PRODUCED BY GLACIER ACTION (AT GRINDELWALD).

his breath when looking at its stupendous cliffs. There are but few equal to them in size in the Alps, and there are none which can more truly be termed *precipices*. Greatest of them all is the immense north cliff, that which bends over toward the Z'muttgletscher. Stones which drop from the top of that amazing wall fall for about fifteen hundred feet before they touch anything, and those which roll down from above and bound over it fall to a much greater depth, and leap wellnigh one thousand feet beyond its base. This side of the mountain has always seemed sombre, sad, terrible: it is painfully suggestive of decay, ruin and death; and it is now, alas! more than terrible by its associations.

"There is no aspect of destruction about the Matterhorn cliffs," says Professor Ruskin. Granted—when they are seen from afar. But approach and sit down by the side of the Z'muttgletscher, and you will hear that their piecemeal destruction is proceeding ceaselessly, incessantly. You will *hear*, but probably you will not *see;* for even when the descending masses thunder as loudly as heavy guns, and the echoes roll back from the Ebihorn opposite, they will still be as pin-points against this grand old face, so vast is its scale.

If you would see the "aspects of destruction," you must come still closer and climb its cliffs and ridges, or mount to the plateau of the Matterhorngletscher, which is cut up and ploughed up by these missiles, and strewn on the surface with their smaller fragments: the larger masses, falling with tremendous velocity, plunge into the snow and are lost to sight.

The Matterhorngletscher, too, sends down *its* avalanches, as if in rivalry with the rocks behind. Round the whole of its northern side it does not terminate in the usual manner by gentle slopes, but comes to a sudden end at the top of the steep rocks which lie betwixt it and the Z'muttgletscher; and seldom does an hour pass without a huge slice breaking away and falling with dreadful uproar on to the slopes below, where it is re-compacted.

The desolate, outside pines of the Z'mutt forests, stripped of their bark and blanched by the weather, are a fit foreground to a scene that can hardly be surpassed in solemn grandeur. It is a subject worthy of the pencil of a great painter, and one which would tax the powers of the very greatest.

Higher up the glacier the mountain is less savage in appearance, but it is not less impracticable; and three hours later, when we arrived at the island of rock called the Stockje (which marks the end of the Z'muttgletscher proper, and which separates its higher feeder, the Stockgletscher, from its lower but greater one, the Tiefenmatten), Carrel himself, one of the least demonstrative of men, could not refrain from expressing wonder at the steepness of its faces, and at the audacity that had prompted us to camp upon the south-west ridge, the profile of which is seen very well from the Stockje. Carrel then saw the north and north-west sides of the mountain for the first time, and was more firmly persuaded than ever that an ascent was possible *only* from the direction of Breuil.

Three years afterward, I was traversing the same spot with the guide Franz Biener, when all at once a puff of wind brought to us a very bad smell, and on looking about we discovered a dead chamois half-way up the southern cliffs of the Stockje. We clambered up, and found that it had been killed by a most uncommon and extraordinary accident. It had slipped on the upper rocks, had rolled over and over down a slope of débris without being able to regain its feet, had fallen over a little patch of rocks that projected through the débris, and had caught the points of both horns on a tiny ledge not an inch broad. It had just been able to touch the débris where it led away down from the rocks, and had pawed and scratched until it could no longer touch. It had evidently been starved to death, and we found the poor beast almost swinging in the air, with its head thrown back and tongue protruding, looking to the sky as if imploring help.

We had no such excitement as this in 1863, and crossed this easy pass to the chalets of Prerayen in a very leisurely fashion. From the summit to Prerayen let us descend in one step. The way has been described before, and those who wish for information about it should consult the description of Mr. Jacomb, the discoverer of the pass. Nor need we stop at Prerayen, except to remark

"THE CHIMNEY."

(ON THE SOUTH-WEST RIDGE OF THE MATTERHORN.)

Page 64.

that the owner of the chalets (who is usually taken for a common herdsman) must not be judged by appearances. He is a man of substance, he has many flocks and herds; and although, when approached politely, he is courteous, he can (and probably will) act as the *master* of Prerayen if his position is *not* recognized, and with all the importance of a man who pays taxes to the extent of five hundred francs per annum to his government.

The hill tops were clouded when we rose from our hay on the 5th of August. We decided not to continue the tour of our mountain immediately, and returned over our track of the preceding day to the highest chalet on the left bank of the valley, with the intention of attacking the Dent d'Erin on the next morning. We were interested in this summit, more on account of the excellent view which it commanded of the south-west ridge and the terminal peak of the Matterhorn than from any other reason.

The Dent d'Erin had not been ascended at this time, and we had diverged from our route on the 4th, and had scrambled some distance up the base of Mont Brulé, to see how far its southwestern slopes were assailable. We were divided in opinion as to the best way of approaching the peak. Carrel, true to his habit of sticking to rocks in preference to ice, counseled ascending by the long buttress of the Tête de Bella Cia (which descends toward the west, and forms the southern boundary of the last glacier that falls into the Glacier de Zardesan), and thence traversing the heads of all the tributaries of the Zardesan to the western and rocky ridge of the Dent. I, on the other hand, proposed to follow the Glacier de Zardesan itself throughout its entire length, and from the plateau at its head (where my proposed route would cross Carrel's) to make directly toward the summit up the snow-covered glacier slope, instead of by the western ridge. The hunchback, who was accompanying us on these excursions, declared in favor of Carrel's route, and it was accordingly adopted.

5

The first part of the programme was successfully executed; and at half-past ten A. M. on the 6th of August we were sitting astride the western ridge, at a height of about twelve thousand five hundred feet, looking down upon the Tiefenmatten glacier. To all appearance, another hour would place us on the summit, but in another hour we found that we were not destined to succeed. The ridge (like all of the principal rocky ridges of the great peaks upon which I have stood) had been completely shattered by frost, and was nothing more than a heap of piled-up fragments. It was always narrow, and where it was narrowest it was also the most unstable and the most difficult. On neither side could we ascend it by keeping a little below its crest — on the side of the Tiefenmatten because it was too steep, and on both sides because the dislodgment of a single block would have disturbed the equilibrium of those which were above. Forced, therefore, to keep to the very crest of the ridge, and unable to deviate a single step either to the right or to the left, we were compelled to trust ourselves upon unsteady masses, which trembled under our tread, which sometimes settled down, grating in a hollow and ominous manner, and which seemed as if a very little shake would send the whole roaring down in one awful avalanche.

I followed my leader, who said not a word, and did not rebel until we came to a place where a block had to be surmounted which lay poised across the ridge. Carrel could not climb it without assistance, or advance beyond it until I joined him above; and as he stepped off my back on to it I felt it quiver and bear down upon me. I doubted the possibility of another man standing upon it without bringing it down. Then I rebelled. There was no honor to be gained by persevering, or dishonor in turning from a place which was dangerous on account of its excessive difficulty. So we returned to Prerayen, for there was too little time to allow us to reascend by the other route, which was subsequently shown to be the right way up the mountain.

Four days afterward a party of Englishmen (including my friends W. E. Hall, Crauford Grove and Reginald Macdonald) arrived in the Valpelline, and (unaware of our attempt) on the 12th, under the skillful guidance of Melchior Anderegg, made the first ascent of the Dent d'Erin by the route which I had proposed. This is the only mountain which I have essayed to ascend that has not, sooner or later, fallen to me. Our failure was mortifying, but I am satisfied that we did wisely in returning, and that if we had persevered by Carrel's route another Alpine accident would have been recorded. I have not heard that another ascent has been made of the Dent d'Erin.

On the 7th of August we crossed the Va Cornère pass, and had a good look at the mountain named the Grand Tournalin as we descended the Val de Chignana. This mountain was seen from so many points, and was so much higher than any peak in its immediate neighborhood, that it was bound to give a very fine view; and (as the weather continued unfavorable for the Matterhorn) I arranged with Carrel to ascend it the next day, and despatched him direct to the village of Val Tournanche to make the necessary preparations, whilst I, with Meynet, made a short cut to Breuil, at the back of Mont Panquero, by a little pass locally known as the Col de Fenêtre. I rejoined Carrel the same evening at Val Tournanche, and we started from that place at a little before five A. M. on the 8th to attack the Tournalin.

Meynet was left behind for that day, and most unwillingly did the hunchback part from us, and begged hard to be allowed to come. "Pay me nothing, only let me go with you. I shall want but a little bread and cheese, and of that I won't eat much. I would much rather go with you than carry things down the valley." Such were his arguments, and I was really sorry that the rapidity of our movements obliged us to desert the good little man.

Carrel led over the meadows on the south and east of the bluff upon which the village of Val Tournanche is built, and then by a zigzag path through a long and steep forest, making many short cuts, which showed he had a thorough knowledge of the ground. After we came again into daylight our route took us up one of those little, concealed lateral valleys which are so numerous on the slopes bounding the Val Tournanche.

This valley, the Combe de Ceneil, has a general easterly trend, and contains but one small cluster of houses (Ceneil). The Tournalin is situated at the head of the combe, and nearly due east of the village of Val Tournanche, but from that place no part of the mountain is visible. After Ceneil is passed it comes into view, rising above a cirque of cliffs (streaked by several fine waterfalls), at the end of the combe. To avoid these cliffs the path bends somewhat to the south, keeping throughout to the left bank of the valley; and at about thirty-five hundred feet above Val Tournanche, and fifteen hundred feet above Ceneil, and a mile or so to its east, arrives at the base of some moraines, which are remarkably large, considering the dimensions of the glaciers which formed them. The ranges upon the western side of the Val Tournanche are seen to great advantage from this spot, but here the path ends and the way steepens.

When we arrived at these moraines we had a choice of two routes—one continuing to the east over the moraines themselves, and the débris above them, and a large snow-bed still higher up, to a kind of col or depression to the south of the peak, from whence an easy ridge led toward the summit; the other, over a shrunken glacier on our north-east (now, perhaps, not in existence), which led to a well-marked col on the north of the peak, from whence a less easy ridge rose directly to the highest point. We followed the first named of these routes, and in a little more than half an hour stood upon the col, which commanded a most glorious view of the southern side of Monte Rosa, and of the ranges to its east and to the east of the Val d'Ayas.

Whilst we were resting at this point a large party of vagrant chamois arrived on the summit of the mountain from the northern side, some of whom, by their statuesque position, seemed to appreciate the grand panorama by which they were surrounded, while others amused themselves, like two-legged tourists, in rolling stones over the cliffs. The clatter of these falling fragments made us look up. The chamois were so numerous that we could not count them, clustered around the summit, totally unaware of our presence; and they scattered in a panic, as if a shell had burst amongst them, when saluted by the cries of my excited comrade, plunging wildly down in several directions, with unfaltering and unerring bounds, with such speed and with such grace that we were filled with admiration and respect for their mountaineering abilities.

The ridge that led from the col toward the summit was singularly easy, although well broken up by frost, and Carrel thought that it would not be difficult to arrange a path for mules out of the shattered blocks; but when we arrived on the summit we found ourselves separated from the very highest point by a cleft which had been concealed up to that time: its southern side was nearly perpendicular, but it was only fourteen or fifteen feet deep. Carrel lowered me down, and afterward descended on to the head of my axe, and subsequently on to my shoulders, with a cleverness which was almost as far removed from my awkwardness as his own efforts were from those of the chamois. A few easy steps then placed us on the highest point. It had not been ascended before, and we commemorated the event by building a huge cairn, which was seen for many a mile, and would have lasted for many a year had it not been thrown down by the orders of Canon Carrel, on account of its interrupting the sweep of a camera which he took to the lower summit in 1868 in order to photograph the

panorama. According to that well-known mountaineer, the summit of the Grand Tournalin is 6100 feet above the village of Val Tournanche, and 11,155 feet above the sea. Its ascent (including halts) occupied us only four hours.

CARREL LOWERED ME DOWN.

I recommend the ascent of the Tournalin to any person who has a day to spare in the Val Tournanche. It should be remembered, however (if its ascent is made for the sake of the view), that these southern Pennine Alps seldom remain unclouded after midday, and indeed frequently not later than ten or eleven A. M. Toward sunset the equilibrium of the atmosphere is restored, and the clouds very commonly disappear.

I advise the ascent of this mountain, not on account of its height or from its accessibility or inaccessibility, but simply for the wide and splendid view which may be seen from its summit. Its position is superb, and the list of the peaks which can be seen from it includes almost the whole of the principal mountains of the Cottian, Dauphiné, Graian, Pennine and Oberland groups. The view has, in the highest perfection, those elements of picturesqueness which are wanting in the purely panoramic views of higher summits. There are three principal sections, each with a central or dominating point, to which the eye is naturally drawn. All three alike are pictures in themselves, yet all are dissimilar. In the south, softened by the vapors of the Val d'Aoste, extends the long line of the Graians, with mountain after mountain twelve thousand five hundred feet and upward in height. It is not upon these, noble as some of them are, that the eye will rest, but upon the Viso, far off in the background. In the west and toward the north the range of Mont Blanc and some of the greatest of the Central Pennine Alps (including the Grand Combin and the Dent Blanche) form the background, but they are overpowered by the grandeur of the ridges which culminate in the Matterhorn. Nor in the east and north, where pleasant grassy slopes lead downward to the Val d'Ayas, nor upon the glaciers and snow-fields above them, nor upon the Oberland in the background, will the eye long linger, when immediately in front, several miles away, but seeming close at hand, thrown out by the pure azure sky, there are the glittering crests of Monte Rosa.

Those who would, but cannot, stand upon the highest Alps may console themselves with the knowledge that they do not usually yield the views that make the strongest and most permanent impressions. Marvelous some of the panoramas seen from the greatest peaks undoubtedly are, but they are necessarily without those isolated and central points which are so valuable pictorially. The eye roams over a multitude of objects (each perhaps grand individually), and, distracted by an embarrassment of riches, wanders from one to another, erasing by the contemplation of the next the effect that was produced by the last; and when those happy moments are over, which always fly with too great rapidity, the summit is left with an impression that is seldom durable because it is usually vague.

No views create such lasting impressions as those which are seen but for a moment when a veil of mist is rent in twain and a single spire or dome is disclosed. The peaks which are seen at these moments are not perhaps the greatest or the noblest, but the recollection of them outlives the memory of any panoramic view, because the picture, photographed by the eye, has time to dry, instead of being blurred while yet wet by contact with other impressions. The reverse is the case with the bird's-eye panoramic views from the great peaks, which sometimes embrace a hundred miles in nearly every direction. The eye is confounded by the crowd of details, and unable to distinguish the relative importance of the objects which are seen. It is almost as difficult to form a just estimate (with the eye) of the respective heights of a number of peaks from a very high summit as it is from the bottom of a valley. I think that the grandest and most satisfactory stand-points for viewing mountain scenery are those which are sufficiently elevated to give a feeling of depth as well as of height—which are lofty enough to exhibit wide and varied views, but not so high as to sink everything to the level of the spectator. The view from the Grand Tournalin is a favorable example of this class of panoramic views.

We descended from the summit by the northern route, and found it tolerably stiff clambering as far as the col, but thence, down the glacier, the way was straightforward, and we joined the route taken on the ascent at the foot of the ridge leading toward the east. In the evening we returned to Breuil.

There is an abrupt rise in the valley about two miles to the north of the village of Val Tournanche, and just above this step the torrent has eaten its way into its bed and formed an extraordinary chasm, which has long been known by the name Gouffre des Busserailles. We lingered about this spot to listen to the thunder of the concealed water, and to watch its tumultuous boiling as it issued from the gloomy cleft, but our efforts to peer into the mysteries of the place were baffled. In November, 1865, the intrepid Carrel induced two trusty comrades — the Maquignazes of Val

Tournanche—to lower him by a rope into the chasm and over the cataract. The feat required iron nerves and muscles and sinews of no ordinary kind, and its performance alone stamps Carrel as a man of dauntless courage. One of the Maquignazes subsequently descended in the same way, and these two men were so astonished at what they saw that they forthwith set to work with hammer and chisel to make a way into this romantic gulf. In a few days they constructed a rough but convenient plank gallery into the centre of the *gouffre*, along its walls, and on payment of a toll of half a franc any one can now enter the Gouffre des Busserailles.

I cannot, without a couple of sections and a plan, give an exact idea to the reader of this remarkable place. It corresponds in some of its features to the gorge figured upon page 62, but it exhibits in a much more notable manner the characteristic action and power of running water. The length of the chasm or *gouffre* is about three hundred and twenty feet, and from the top of its walls to the surface of the water is about one hundred and ten feet. At no part can the entire length or depth be seen at a glance, for, although the width at some places is fifteen feet or more, the view is limited by the sinuosities of the walls. These are everywhere polished to a smooth, vitreous - in - appearance surface. In some places the torrent has wormed into the rock, and has left natural bridges. The most extraordinary features of the Gouffre des Busserailles, however, are the caverns (or *marmites*, as they are termed) which the water has hollowed out of the heart of the rock. Carrel's plank path leads into one of the greatest — a grotto that is about twenty-eight feet across at its largest diameter, and fifteen or sixteen feet high, roofed above by the living rock, and with the torrent roaring fifty feet or thereabouts below, at the bottom of a fissure. This cavern is lighted by candles, and talking in it can only be managed by signs.

I visited the interior of the *gouffre* in 1869, and my wonder at its caverns was increased by observing the hardness of the hornblende out of which they have been hollowed. Carrel chiseled off a large piece, which is now lying before me. It has a highly polished, glassy surface, and might be mistaken, for a moment, for ice-polished rock. But the water has found out the atoms which were least hard, and it is dotted all over with minute depressions, much as the face of one is who has suffered from smallpox. The edges of these little hollows are *rounded*, and all the surfaces of the depressions are polished nearly or quite as highly as the general surface of the fragment. The water has drilled more deeply into some veins of steatite than in other places, and the presence of the steatite may possibly have had something to do with the formation of the *gouffre*.

I arrived at Breuil again after an absence of six days, well satisfied with my tour of the Matterhorn, which had been rendered very pleasant by the willingness of my guides and by the kindliness of the natives. But it must be admitted that the inhabitants of the Val Tournanche are behind the times. Their paths are as bad as, or worse than, they were in the time of De Saussure, and their inns are much inferior to those on the Swiss side. If it were otherwise there would be nothing to prevent the valley becoming one of the most popular and frequented of all the valleys in the Alps ; but as it is, tourists who enter it seem to think only about how soon they can get out of it, and hence it is much less known than it deserves to be on account of its natural attractions.

CHAPTER VII.

OUR SIXTH ATTEMPT TO ASCEND THE MATTERHORN.

CARREL had *carte blanche* in the matter of guides, and his choice fell upon his relative Cæsar, Luc Meynet and two others whose names I do not know. These men were now brought together, and our preparations were completed, as the weather was clearing up.

We rested on Sunday, August 9, eagerly watching the lessening of the mists around the great peak, and started just before dawn upon the 10th, on a still and cloudless morning, which seemed to promise a happy termination to our enterprise.

By going always, but gently, we arrived upon the Col du Lion before nine o'clock. Changes were apparent. Familiar ledges had vanished; the platform whereon my tent had stood looked very forlorn; its stones had been scattered by wind and frost, and had half disappeared; and the summit of the col itself, which in 1862 had always been respectably broad and covered by snow, was now sharper than the ridge of any church roof, and was hard ice. Already we had found that the bad weather of the past week had done its work. The rocks for several hundred feet below the col were varnished with ice. Loose, incoherent snow covered the older and harder beds below, and we nearly lost our leader through its treacherousness. He stepped on some snow which seemed firm, and raised his axe to deliver a swinging blow, but just as it was highest the crust of the slope upon which he stood broke away, and poured down in serpentine streams, leaving long bare strips, which glittered in the sun, for they were glassy ice. Carrel, with admirable readiness, flung himself back on to the rock off which he had stepped, and was at once secured. He simply remarked, "It is time we were tied up," and after we had been tied up he went to work again as if nothing had happened.

We had abundant illustrations during the next two hours of the value of a rope to climbers. We were tied up rather widely apart, and advanced generally in pairs. Carrel, who led, was followed closely by another man, who lent him a shoulder or placed an axe-head under his feet when there was need; and when this couple were well placed, the second pair advanced in similar fashion, the rope being drawn in by those above and paid out gradually by those below. The leading men advanced, or the third pair, and so on. This manner of progression was slow but sure. One man only moved at a time, and if he slipped (and we frequently did slip), he could slide scarcely a foot without being checked by the others. The certainty and safety of the method gave confidence to the one who was moving, and not only nerved him to put out his powers to the utmost, but sustained nerve in really difficult situations. For these rocks (which, it has been already said, were easy enough under ordinary circumstances) were now difficult in a high degree. The snow-water, which had trickled down for many days past in little streams, had taken, naturally, the very route by which we wished to ascend; and, re-frozen in the night, had glazed the slabs over which we had to pass—sometimes with a fine film of ice as thin as a sheet of paper, and sometimes so thickly that we could almost cut footsteps in it. The weather was superb, the men made light of the toil, and shouted to rouse the echoes from the Dent d'Hérens.

We went on gayly, passed the second tent-platform, the Chimney and the other well-remembered points, and reckoned confidently on sleeping that night upon the top of "the shoulder;" but before we had well arrived at the foot of the Great Tower, a sudden rush of cold air warned us to look out.

It was difficult to say where this air came from: it did not blow as a wind, but descended rather as the water in a shower-bath. All was tranquil again: the atmosphere *showed* no signs of disturbance: there was a dead calm, and not a speck of cloud to be seen anywhere. But we did not remain very long in this state. The cold air came again, and this time it was difficult to say where it did not come from. We jammed down our hats as it beat against the ridge and screamed amongst the crags. Before we had got to the foot of the Tower mists had been formed above and below. They appeared at first in small, isolated patches (in sev-

—TENT.

THE CRAGS OF THE MATTERHORN, DURING THE STORM, MIDNIGHT, AUGUST 10, 1863. Page 71.

eral places at the same time), which danced and jerked and were torn into shreds by the wind, but grew larger under the process. They were united together and rent again, showing us the blue sky for a moment, and blotting it out the next, and augmented incessantly until the whole heavens were filled with whirling, boiling clouds. Before we could take off our packs and get under any kind of shelter a hurricane of snow burst upon us from the east. It fell so thickly that in a few minutes the ridge was covered by it. "What shall we do?" I shouted to Carrel. "Monsieur," said he, "the wind is bad, the weather has changed, we are heavily laden. Here is a fine *gîte :* let us stop. If we go on we shall be half frozen. That is *my* opinion." No one differed from him ; so we fell to work to make a place for the tent, and in a couple of hours completed the platform which we had commenced in 1862. The clouds had blackened during that time, and we had hardly finished our task before a thunder-storm broke upon us with appalling fury. Forked lightning shot out at the turrets above and at the crags below. It was so close that we quailed at its darts. It seemed to scorch us; we were in the very focus of the storm. The thunder was simultaneous with the flashes, short and sharp, and more like the noise of a door violently slammed, multiplied a thousand-fold, than any noise to which I can compare it.

When I say that the thunder was *simultaneous* with the lightning, I speak as an inexact person. My meaning is, that the time which elapsed between seeing the flash and hearing the report was inappreciable to me. I wish to speak with all possible precision, and there are two points in regard to this storm upon which I can speak with some accuracy. The first is in regard to the distance of the lightning from our party. We *might* have been eleven hundred feet from it if a second of time had elapsed between seeing the flashes and hearing the reports ; and a second of time is not appreciated by inexact persons. It was certain that we were

sometimes less than that distance from the lightning, because I saw it pass in front of well-known points on the ridge, both above and below us, which were less (sometimes considerably less) than a thousand feet distant.

Secondly, in regard to the difficulty of distinguishing sounds which are merely echoes from true thunder or the noise which occurs simultaneously with lightning. Arago entered into this subject at some length in his Meteorological Essays, and seemed to doubt if it would ever be possible to determine whether echoes are *always* the cause of the rolling sounds commonly called thunder. I shall not attempt to show whether the rolling sounds should ever or never be regarded as true thunder, but only that during this storm upon the Matterhorn it was possible to distinguish the sound of the thunder itself from the sounds (rolling and otherwise) which were merely the echoes of the first, original sound.

At the place where we were camped a remarkable echo could be heard (one so remarkable that if it could be heard in this country it would draw crowds for its own sake) : I believe it came from the cliffs of the Dent d'Hérens. It was a favorite amusement with us to rouse this echo, which repeated any sharp cry in a very distinct manner several times, after the lapse of something like a dozen seconds. The thunderstorm lasted nearly two hours, and raged at times with great fury ; and the prolonged rollings from the surrounding mountains after one flash had not usually ceased before another set of echoes took up the discourse, and maintained the reverberations without a break. Occasionally there was a pause, interrupted presently by a single clap, the accompaniment of a single discharge, and after such times I could recognize the echoes from the Dent d'Hérens by their peculiar repetitions, and by the length of time which had passed since the reports had occurred of which they were the echoes.

If I had been unaware of the existence of this echo, I should have supposed that the resounds were original reports of explosions which had been unnoticed, since in intensity they were scarcely distinguishable from the true thunder, which during this storm seemed to me, upon every occasion, to consist of a single harsh, instantaneous sound.*

Or if, instead of being placed at a distance of less than a thousand feet from the points of explosion (and consequently hearing the report almost in the same moment as we saw the flash, and the rollings after a considerable interval of time), we had been placed so that the original report had fallen on our ears nearly at the same moment as the echoes, we should probably have considered that the successive reports and rollings of the echoes were reports of successive explosions occurring nearly at the same moment, and that they were not echoes at all.

This is the only time (out of many storms witnessed in the Alps) I have obtained evidence that the rollings of thunder are actually echoes, and that they are not, necessarily, the reports of a number of discharges over a long line, occurring at varying distances from the spectator, and consequently unable to arrive at his ear at the same moment, although they follow each other so swiftly as to produce a sound more or less continuous.†

* The same has seemed to me to be the case at all times when I have been close to the points of explosion. There has been always a distinct interval between the first explosion and the rolling sounds and secondary explosions which I have *believed* to be merely echoes; but it has never been possible (except in the above-mentioned case) to *identify* them as such. Others have observed the same. " The geologist, Professor Theobald, of Chur, who was in the Solferino storm, between the Tschiertscher and Urden Alp, in the electric clouds, says that the peals were short, like cannon-shots, but of a clearer, more cracking tone, and that the rolling of the thunder was only heard farther on."—Berlepsch's *Alps*, English ed., p. 133.

† Mr. J. Glaisher has frequently pointed out that all sounds in balloons at some distance from the earth are notable for their brevity. " It is one sound only : *there is no reverberation, no reflection ;* and this is characteristic of all sounds in the balloon—one clear sound, continuing during its own vibrations, then gone in a moment."—*Good Words*, 1863, p. 224. I learn from Mr. Glaisher that the thunder-claps which have been heard by him during his " travels in the air " have been no exception to the general rule, and the absence of rolling has fortified his belief that the rolling sounds which accompany thunder are echoes, and echoes *only*.

The wind during all this time seemed to blow tolerably consistently from the east. It smote the tent so vehemently (notwithstanding it was partly protected by rocks) that we had grave fears our refuge might be blown away bodily, with ourselves inside ; so, during some of the lulls, we issued out and built a wall to windward. At half-past three the wind changed to the north-west, and the clouds vanished. We immediately took the opportunity to send down one of the porters (under protection of some of the others a little beyond the Col du Lion), as the tent would accommodate only five persons. From this time to sunset the weather was variable. It was sometimes blowing and snowing hard, and sometimes a dead calm. The bad weather was evidently confined to the Mont Cervin, for when the clouds lifted we could see everything that could be seen from our gîte. Monte Viso, a hundred miles off, was clear, and the sun set gorgeously behind the range of Mont Blanc. We passed the night comfortably, even luxuriously, in our blanket-bags, but there was little chance of sleeping, between the noise of the wind, of the thunder and of the falling rocks. I forgave the thunder for the sake of the lightning. A more splendid spectacle than its illumination of the Matterhorn crags I do not expect to see.

We turned out at 3.30 A. M. on the 11th, and were dismayed to find that it still continued to snow. At 9 A. M. the snow ceased to fall, and the sun showed itself feebly, so we packed up our baggage and set out to try to get upon "the shoulder." We struggled upward until eleven o'clock, and then it commenced to snow again. We held a council : the opinions expressed at it were unanimous against advancing, and I decided to retreat ; for we had risen less than three hundred feet in the past two hours, and had not even arrived at the rope which Tyndall's party left behind attached to the rocks, in 1862. At the same rate of progression it would have taken us from four to five hours to get upon "the shoulder." Not one of us cared to attempt to do so under the existing circumstances; for, besides having to move our own weight, which was sufficiently troublesome at this part of the ridge, we had to transport much heavy baggage, tent, blankets, provisions, ladder and four hundred and fifty feet of rope, besides many other smaller matters. These, however, were not the most serious considerations. Supposing that we got upon "the shoulder," we might find ourselves detained there several days, unable either to go up or down.* I could not risk any such detention, being under obligations to appear in London at the end of the week.

We got to Breuil in the course of the afternoon: it was quite fine there, and the tenants of the inn received our statements with evident skepticism. They

MONSIEUR FAVRE.

were astonished to learn that we had been exposed to a snow-storm of twenty-six hours' duration. "Why," said Favre, the innkeeper, "*we* have had no snow: it has been fine all the time you have been absent, and there has been only that small cloud upon the mountain." Ah! that small cloud! None except those who have had experience of it can tell what a formidable obstacle it is.

Why is it that the Matterhorn is subject to these abominable variations of weather? The ready answer is, "Oh, the mountain is so isolated, it attracts

* Since then (on at least one occasion) several persons have found themselves in this predicament for five or six consecutive days.

the clouds." This is not a sufficient answer. Although the mountain *is* isolated, it is not so much more isolated than the neighboring peaks that it should gather clouds when none of the others do so. It will not at all account for the cloud to which I refer, which is not formed by an aggregation of smaller, stray clouds drawn together from a distance (as scum collects round a log in the water), but is created against the mountain itself, and springs into existence where no clouds were seen before. It is formed and hangs chiefly against the southern sides, and particularly against the south-eastern side. It frequently does not envelop the summit, and rarely extends down to the Glacier du Lion and to the Glacier du Mont Cervin below. It forms in the finest weather—on cloudless and windless days.

I conceive that we should look to differences of temperature rather than to the height or isolation of the mountain for an explanation. I am inclined to attribute the disturbances which occur in the atmosphere of the southern sides of the Matterhorn on fine days principally to the fact that the mountain is a *rock* mountain—that it receives a great amount of heat, and is not only warmer itself, but is surrounded by an atmosphere of a higher temperature, than such peaks as the Weisshorn and the Lyskamm, which are eminently *snow* mountains.

In certain states of the atmosphere its temperature may be tolerably uniform over wide areas and to great elevations. I have known the thermometer to show seventy degrees in the shade at the top of an Alpine peak more than thirteen thousand feet high, and but a very few degrees higher six or seven thousand feet lower. At other times there will be a difference of forty or fifty degrees (Fahrenheit) between two stations, the higher not more than six or seven thousand feet above the lower.

Provided that the temperature was uniform, or nearly so, on all sides of the Matterhorn, and to a considerable distance above its summit, no clouds would be likely to form upon it. But if the atmosphere immediately surrounding it is warmer than the contiguous strata, a local "courant ascendant" must necessarily be generated; and portions of the cooler superincumbent (or circumjacent) air will naturally be attracted toward the mountain, where they will speedily condense the moisture of the warm air in contact with it. I cannot explain the down-rushes of cold air which occur on it when all the rest of the neighborhood appears to be tranquil, in any other way. The clouds are produced by the contact of two strata of air (of widely different temperatures) charged with invisible moisture, as surely as certain colorless fluids produce a white, turbid liquid when mixed together. The order has been, wind of a low temperature, mist, rain, snow or hail.

This opinion is borne out to some extent by the behavior of the neighboring mountains. The Dom (14,935 feet) and the Dent Blanche (14,318) have both of them large cliffs of bare rock upon their southern sides, and against those cliffs clouds commonly form (during fine, still weather) at the same time as the cloud on the Matterhorn; whilst the Weisshorn (14,804) and the Lyskamm (14,889)—mountains of about the same altitude, and which are in corresponding situations to the former pair—usually remain perfectly clear.

I arrived at Chatillon at midnight on the 11th, defeated and disconsolate, but, like a gambler who loses each throw, only the more eager to have another try, to see if the luck would change; and returned to London ready to devise fresh combinations and to form new plans.

CROSSING THE CHANNEL.

PART V.

A NIGHT WITH CROZ. (*See page* 90.)

CHAPTER VIII.

FROM ST. MICHEL ON THE MONT CENIS ROAD,
BY THE COL DES AIGUILLES D'ARVE, COL
DE MARTIGNARE AND THE BRÈCHE DE LA
MEIJE, TO LA BÉRARDE.

WHEN we arrived upon the highest summit of Mont Pelvoux, in Dauphiné, in 1861, we saw, to our surprise and disappointment, that it was not the culminating point of the district, and that another mountain, distant about a couple of miles, and separated from us by an impassable gulf, claimed that distinction. I was troubled in spirit about this mountain, and my thoughts often reverted to the great wall-sided peak,

75

second in apparent inaccessibility only to the Matterhorn. It had, moreover, another claim to attention—it was the highest mountain in France.

The year 1862 passed away without a chance of getting to it, and my holiday was too brief in 1863 even to think about it; but in the following year it was possible, and I resolved to set my mind at rest by completing the task which had been left unfinished in 1861.

In the mean time, others had turned their attention to Dauphiné. First of

MICHEL-AUGUST CROZ (1865).

all (in 1862) came Mr. F. Tuckett—that mighty mountaineer, whose name is known throughout the length and breadth of the Alps — with the guides Michel Croz, Peter Perrn and Bartolommeo Peyrotte, and great success attended his arms. But Mr. Tuckett halted before the Pointe des Écrins, and, dismayed by its appearance, withdrew his forces to gather less dangerous laurels elsewhere.

His expedition, however, threw some light upon the Écrins. He pointed out the direction from which an attack was most likely to be successful, and Mr.

William Mathews and the Rev. T. G. Bonney (to whom he communicated the result of his labors) attempted to execute the ascent, with the brothers Michel and J. B. Croz, by following his indications, but they too were defeated.

The guide Michel Croz had thus been engaged in both of these expeditions in Dauphiné, and I naturally looked to him for assistance. Mr. Mathews (to whom I applied for information) gave him a high character, and concluded his reply to me by saying "he was only happy when upward of ten thousand feet high."

I know what my friend meant. Croz was happiest when he was employing his powers to the utmost. Places where you and I would "toil and sweat, and yet be freezing cold," were bagatelles to him, and it was only when he got above the range of ordinary mortals, and was required to employ his magnificent strength and to draw upon his unsurpassed knowledge of ice and snow, that he could be said to be really and truly happy.

Of all the guides with whom I traveled, Michel Croz was the man who was most after my own heart. He did not work like a blunt razor and take to his toil unkindly. He did not need urging or to be told a second time to do anything. You had but to say *what* was to be done and *how* it was to be done, and the work *was* done if it was possible. Such men are not common, and when they are known they are valued. Michel was not widely known, but those who did know him came again and again. The inscription placed upon his tomb truthfully records that he was "beloved by his comrades and esteemed by travelers."

At the time that I was planning my journey, my friends Messrs. A. W. Moore and Horace Walker were also drawing up their programme, and, as we found that our wishes were very similar, we agreed to unite our respective parties. My friends had happily secured Christian Almer of Grindelwald as their guide. The combination of Croz and Almer was a perfect one. Both men were in the prime of life, both were endued with strength and activity far beyond the average, and the courage and the knowledge of each were alike undoubted. The temper of Almer it was impossible to ruffle : he was ever obliging and enduring — a bold but a safe man. That which he lacked in fire, in dash, was supplied by Croz, who, in his turn, was kept in place by Almer. It is pleasant to remember how they worked together, and how each one confided to you that he liked the other *so* much because he worked *so* well ; but it is sad, very sad, to those who have known the men, to know that they can never work together again.

We met at St. Michel on the Mont Cenis road at mid-day on June 20, 1864, and proceeded in the afternoon over the Col de Valloires to the village of the same name. The summit of this pretty little pass is about thirty-five hundred feet above St. Michel, and from it we had a fair view of the Aiguilles d'Arve, a group of three peaks of singular form, which it was our especial object to investigate. They had been seen by ourselves and others from numerous distant points, and always looked very high and very inaccessible ; but we had been unable to obtain any information about them, except the few words in Joanne's *Itinéraire du Dauphiné.* Having made out from the summit of the Col de Valloires that they could be approached from the valley of Valloires, we hastened down to find a place where we could pass the night, as near as possible to the entrance of the little valley leading up to them.

By nightfall we arrived at the entrance to this little valley (Vallon des Aiguilles d'Arve), and found some buildings placed just where they were wanted. The proprietress received us with civility, and placed a large barn at our disposal, on the condition that no lights were struck or pipes smoked therein ; and when her terms were agreed to, she took us into her own chalet, made up a huge fire, heated a gallon of milk and treated us with genuine hospitality.

In the morning we found that the Val-

lon des Aiguilles d'Arve led away nearly due west from the valley of Valloires and that the village of Bonnenuit was placed (in the latter valley) almost exactly opposite to the junction of the two.

At 3.55 A. M. on the 21st we set out up the Vallon, passed for a time over pasture-land, and then over a stony waste, deeply channeled by water-courses. At 5.30 the two principal Aiguilles were well seen, and as by this time it was evident that the authors of the Sardinian official map had romanced as extensively in this neighborhood as elsewhere, it was necessary to hold a council.

Three questions were submitted to it : Firstly, Which is the highest of these Aiguilles ? Secondly, Which shall we go up ? Thirdly, How is it to be done ?

The French engineers, it was said, had determined that the two highest of them were respectively 11,513 and 11,529 feet in height ; but we were without information as to which two they had measured. Joanne indeed said (but without specifying whether he meant all three) that the Aiguilles had been several times ascended, and particularly mentioned that the one of 11,513 feet was "relatively easy."

We therefore said, "We will go up the peak of 11,529 feet." But that determination did not settle the second question. Joanne's "relatively easy" peak, according to his description, was evidently the most northern of the three. *Our* peak, then, was to be one of the other two, but which of them ? We were inclined to favor the central one, but it was hard to determine, they looked so equal in height. When, however, the council came to study the third question, "How is it to be done?" it was unanimously voted that upon the eastern and southern sides it was certainly relatively difficult, and that a move should be made round to the northern side.

The movement was duly executed, and after wading up some snow-slopes of considerable steepness (going occasionally beyond 40°), we found ourselves in a gap or nick between the central and northernmost Aiguille at 8.45 A. M. We then studied the northern face of our intended peak, and finally arrived at the conclusion that it was relatively impracticable. Croz shrugged his big shoulders, and said, "My faith! I think you will do well to leave it to others." Almer was more explicit, and volunteer-

THE AIGUILLES D'ARVE, FROM ABOVE THE CHALETS OF RIEU BLANC.

ed the information that a thousand francs would not tempt him to *try* it. We then turned to the northernmost peak, but found its southern faces even more hopeless than the northern faces of the central one. We enjoyed accordingly the unwonted luxury of a three hours' rest on the top of our pass, for pass we were determined it should be.

We might have done worse. We were ten thousand three hundred or ten thousand four hundred feet above the level of the sea, and commanded a most picturesque view of the mountains of the Tarentaise, while somewhat east of south we saw the monarch of the Dauphiné *massif*, whose closer acquaintance it was our intention to make. Three sunny hours passed away, and then we turned to the descent. We saw the distant pastures of a valley (which we supposed was the Vallon or Ravine de la Sausse), and a long snow-slope leading down to them. But from that slope we were cut off by precipitous rocks, and our first impression was that we should have to return in our track. Some running up and down, however, discovered two little gullies filled with threads of snow, and down the most northern of these we decided to go. It was a steep way, but a safe one, for the cleft was so narrow that we could press the shoulder against one side whilst the feet were against the other, and the last remnant of the winter's snow, well hardened, clung to the rift with great tenacity, and gave us a path when the rocks refused one. In half an hour we got to the top of the great snow-slope. Walker said, "Let us glissade;" the guides, "No, it is too steep." Our friend, however, started off at a standing glissade, and advanced for a time very skillfully; but after a while he lost his balance, and progressed downward and backward with great rapidity, in a way that seemed to us very much like tumbling heels over head. He let go his axe and left it behind, but it overtook him and batted him heartily. He and it traveled in this fashion for some hundreds of feet, and at last subsided into the rocks at the bottom. In a few moments we were reassured as to his safety by hearing him ironically request us not to keep him waiting down there.

We others followed the tracks shown by the dotted line upon the engraving (making zigzags to avoid the little groups of rocks which jutted through the snow, by which Walker had been upset), descended by a *sitting* glissade, and rejoined our friend at the bottom. We then turned sharply to the left, and tramped down the summit ridge of an old moraine of great size. Its mud was excessively hard, and where some large erratic blocks lay perched upon its crest we were obliged to cut steps (in the mud) with our ice-axes.

Guided by the sound of a distant "moo," we speedily found the highest chalets in the valley, named Rieu Blanc. They were tenanted by three old women (who seemed to belong to one of the missing links sought by naturalists) destitute of all ideas except in regard to cows, and who spoke a barbarous patois wellnigh unintelligible to the Savoyard Croz. They would not believe that we had passed between the Aiguilles: "It is impossible, the *cows* never go there." "Could we get to La Grave over yonder ridge?" "Oh yes! the *cows* often crossed!" Could they show us the way? No, but we could follow the *cow*-tracks.

We stayed a while near these chalets

to examine the western sides of the Aiguilles d'Arve, and, according to our united opinion, the central one was as inaccessible from this direction as from the east, north or south. On the following day we saw them again, from a height of about eleven thousand feet, in a south-easterly direction, and our opinion remained unchanged.

We saw (on June 20-22) the central Aiguille from all sides, and very nearly completely round the southernmost one. The northern one we also saw on all sides excepting from the north. (It is, however, precisely from this direction M. Joanne says that its ascent is relatively easy.) We do not, therefore, venture to express any opinion respecting its ascent, except as regards its actual summit. This is formed of two curious prongs or pinnacles of rock, and we do not understand in what way they (or either of them) can be ascended; nor shall we be surprised if this ascent is discovered to have been made in spirit rather than body—in fact, in the same manner as the celebrated ascent of Mont Blanc, "not entirely to the summit, but as far as the Montanvert!"

All three of the Aiguilles *may* be accessible, but they look as inaccessible as anything I have seen. They are the highest summits between the valleys of the Romanche and the Arc: they are placed slightly to the north of the watershed between those two valleys, and a line drawn through them runs pretty nearly north and south.

We descended by a rough path from Rieu Blanc to the chalets of La Sausse, which give the name to the Vallon or Ravine de la Sausse in which they are situated. This is one of the numerous branches of the valley that leads to St. Jean d'Arve, and subsequently to St. Jean de Maurienne.

Two passes, more or less known, lead from this valley to the village of La Grave (on the Lautaret road) in the valley of the Romanche—viz., the Col de l'Infernet and the Col de Martignare. The former pass was crossed just thirty years ago by J. D. Forbes, and was mentioned by him in his *Norway and* *its Glaciers.* The latter one lies to the north of the former, and is seldom traversed by tourists, but it was convenient for us, and we set out to cross it on the morning of the 22d, after having passed a comfortable but not luxurious night in the hay at La Sausse, where, however, the simplicity of the accommodation was more than counterbalanced by the civility and hospitality of the people in charge.*

We left the chalets at 4.15 A. M. under a shower of good wishes from our hostesses, proceeded at first toward the upper end of the ravine, then doubled back up a long buttress which projects in an unusual way, and went toward the Col de Martignare; but before arriving at its summit we again doubled and resumed the original course. At 6 A. M. we stood on the watershed, and followed it toward the east, keeping for some distance strictly to the ridge, and afterward diverging a little to the south to avoid a considerable secondary aiguille, which prevented a straight track being made to the summit at which we were aiming. At 9.15 we stood on its top, and saw at once the lay of the land.

We were very fortunate in the selection of our summit. Not to speak of other things, it gave a grand view of the ridge which culminates in the peak called La Meije (13,080 feet), which used to be mentioned by travelers under the name Aiguille du Midi de la Grave. It

* While stopping in the hospice on the Col de Lautaret in 1869, I was accosted by a middle-aged peasant, who asked if I would ride (for a consideration) in his cart toward Briançon. He was inquisitive as to my knowledge of his district, and at last asked, "Have you been at La Sausse?" "Yes." "Well, then, I tell you, *you saw there some of the first people in the world.*" "Yes," I said, "they were primitive, certainly." But he was serious, and went on: "Yes, real brave people;" and slapping his knee to give emphasis, "*but that they are first-rate for minding the cows!*"

After this he became communicative. "You thought, probably," said he, "when I offered to take you down, that I was some poor ——, not worth a *sou;* but I will tell you, that was my mountain—*my* mountain—that you saw at La Sausse: they were *my* cows, a hundred of them altogether." "Why, you are rich!" "Passably rich. I have another mountain on the Col du Galibier, and another at Villeneuve." He (although a common peasant in outward appearance) confessed to being worth four thousand pounds.

is the last, the only, great Alpine peak which has never known the foot of man, and one cannot speak in exaggerated terms of its jagged ridges, torrential glaciers and tremendous precipices. But were I to discourse upon these things without the aid of pictures, or to endeavor to convey in words a sense of the loveliness of curves, of the beauty of color or of the harmonies of sound, I should try to accomplish that which is impossible, and at the best should succeed in but giving an impression that the things spoken of may have been pleasant to hear or to behold, although they are perfectly incomprehensible to read about. Let me therefore avoid these things, not because I have no love for or thought of them, but because they cannot be translated into language; and presently, when topographical details must of necessity be returned to again, I will endeavor to relieve the poverty of the pen by a free use of the pencil.

Whilst we sat upon the Aiguille de la Sausse our attention was concentrated on a point that was immediately opposite—on a gap or cleft between the Meije and the mountain called the Rateau. It was, indeed, in order to have a good view of this place that we made the ascent of the Aiguille. It (that is, the gap itself) looked, as my companions remarked, obtrusively and offensively a pass. It had not been crossed, but it ought to have been; and this seemed to have been recognized by the natives, who called it, very appropriately, the Brèche de la Meije. It led to La Bérarde, a miserable village, without interest, without commerce, and almost without population. Why, then, did we wish to cross it? Because we were bound to the Pointe des Écrins, to which La Bérarde was the nearest inhabited place.

When we sat upon the Aiguille de la Sausse we were rather despondent about our prospects of crossing the Brèche, which seemed to present a combination of all that was formidable. There was evidently but one way by which it could be approached. We saw that at the top of the pass there was a steep wall of snow or ice (so steep that it was most likely ice), protected at its base by a big schrund or moat, which severed it from the snow-fields below. Then (tracking our course downward) we saw undulating snow-fields leading down to a great glacier. The snow-fields would be easy work, but the glacier was riven and broken in every direction, huge crevasses seemed to extend entirely across it in some places, and everywhere it had that strange twisted look which tells of the unequal motion of the ice. Where could we get on to it? At its base it came to a violent end, being cut short by a cliff, over which it poured periodical avalanches, as we saw by a great triangular bed of débris below. We could not venture there—the glacier must be taken in flank. But on which side? Not on the west—no one could climb those cliffs. It must, if anywhere, be by the rocks on the east, and *they* looked as if they were *roches moutonnées*.

So we hurried down to La Grave, to hear what Melchior Anderegg (who had just passed through the village with the family of our friend Walker) had to say on the matter. Who is Melchior Anderegg? Those who ask the question cannot have been in Alpine Switzerland, where the name of Melchior is as well known as the name of Napoleon. Melchior, too, is an emperor in his way—a very prince among guides. His empire is amongst the "eternal snows"—his sceptre is an ice-axe.

Melchior Anderegg—more familiarly and perhaps more generally known simply as Melchior—was born at Zaun, near Meiringen, on April 6, 1828. He was first brought into public notice in Hinchcliff's *Summer Months in the Alps*, and was known to very few persons at the time that little work was published. In 1855 he was "Boots" at the Grimsel hotel, and in those days when he went out on expeditions it was for the benefit of his master, the proprietor: Melchior himself only got the *trinkgelt*. In 1856 he migrated to the Schwarenbach inn on the Gemmi, where he employed his time in carving objects for sale. In 1858 he made numerous expeditions with Messrs. Hinchcliff and Stephen, and

proved to his employers that he possessed first-rate skill, indomitable courage and an admirable character. His position has never been doubtful since that year, and for a long time there has been no guide whose services have been more in request: he is usually engaged a year in advance.

MELCHIOR ANDEREGG IN 1864.

It would be almost an easier task to say what he has not done than to catalogue his achievements. Invariable success attends his arms: he leads his followers to victory, but not to death. I believe that no accident has ever befallen travelers in his charge. Like his friend Almer, he can be called a *safe* man. It is the highest praise that can be given to a first-rate guide.

Early in the afternoon we found ourselves in the little inn at La Grave, on the great Lautaret road, a rickety, tumble-down sort of place, with nothing stable about it, as Moore wittily remarked, except the smell. Melchior had gone,

6

and had left behind a note which said, "I think the passage of the Brèche is possible, but that it will be very difficult." His opinion coincided with ours, and we went to sleep, expecting to be afoot about eighteen or twenty hours on the morrow.

At 2.40 the next morning we left La Grave, in a few minutes crossed the Romanche, and at 4 A. M. got to the moraine of the eastern branch of the glacier that descends from the Brèche.* The rocks by which we intended to ascend were placed between the two branches of this glacier, and still looked smooth and unbroken. But by five o'clock we were upon them. We had been deluded by them. No carpenter could have planned a more convenient staircase. They were not *moutonné:* their smooth look from a distance was only owing to their singular firmness. In an hour we had risen above the most crevassed portion of the glacier, and began to look for a way on to it. Just at the right place there was a patch of old snow at the side, and, instead of gaining the ice by desperate acrobatic feats, we passed from the rocks on to it as easily as one walks across a gangway. At half-past six we were on the centre of the glacier, and the inhabitants of La Grave turned out *en masse* into the road and watched us

SCALE, THREE MILES TO AN INCH.

* Our route from La Grave to La Bérarde will be seen on the accompanying map.

with amazement as they witnessed the falsification of their confident predictions. Well might they stare, for our little caravan, looking to them like a train of flies on a wall, crept up and up, without hesitation and without a halt — lost to their sight one minute as it dived into a crevasse, then seen again clambering up the other side. The higher we rose the easier became the work, the angles lessened and our pace increased. The snow remained shadowed, and we walked as easily as on a high road; and when (at 7.45) the summit of the Brèche was seen, we rushed at it as furiously as if it had been a breach in the wall of a fortress, carried the moat by a dash, with a push behind and a pull before, stormed the steep slope above, and at 8.50 stood in the little gap, 11,054 feet above the level of the sea. The Brèche was won. Well might they stare—five hours and a quarter had sufficed for sixty-five hundred feet of ascent.† We screamed triumphantly as they turned in to breakfast.

Our day's work was as good as over (for we knew from Messrs. Mathews and Bonney that there was no difficulty upon the other side), and we abandoned ourselves to ease and luxury; wondering alternately, as we gazed upon the Rateau and the Écrins, how the one mountain could possibly hold itself together, and whether the other would hold out against us. The former looked so rotten that it seemed as if a puff of wind or a clap of thunder might dash the whole fabric to pieces, while the latter asserted itself the monarch of the group, and towered head and shoulders above all the rest of the peaks which form the great horseshoe of Dauphiné. At length a cruel rush of cold air made us shiver, and shift our quarters to a little grassy plot three thousand feet below—an oasis in a desert—where we lay nearly four hours admiring the splendid wall which protects the summit of the Meije from assault upon this side.‡ Then we tramp-

† Taking one kind of work with another, a thousand feet of height per hour is about as much as is usually accomplished on great Alpine ascents.

‡ This wall may be described as an exaggerated Gemmi, as seen from Leukerbad. From the highest

ed down the Vallon des Étançons, a howling wilderness, the abomination of desolation ; destitute alike of animal or vegetable life ; pathless, of course ; suggestive of chaos, but of little else ; covered almost throughout its entire length with débris, from the size of a walnut up to that of a house : in a word, it looked as if half a dozen moraines of first-rate dimensions had been carted and shot into it.   Our tempers were soured by constant pitfalls : it was impossible to take the eyes from the feet,

and if an unlucky individual so much as blew his nose without standing still to perform the operation, the result was either an instantaneous tumble or a barked shin or a half-twisted ankle. There was no end to it, and we became more savage at every step, unanimously agreeing that no power on earth would ever induce us to walk up or down this particular valley again.   It was not just to the valley, which was enclosed by noble mountains—unknown, it is true, but worthy of a great reputation, and

THE VALLON DES ÉTANÇONS (LOOKING TOWARD LA BÉRARDE).

which, if placed in other districts, would be sought after and cited as types of daring form and graceful outline.

CHAPTER IX.

THE ASCENT OF THE POINTE DES ÉCRINS.

BEFORE five o'clock on the afternoon of June 23 we were trotting down the

summit of La Meije right down to the Glacier des Étançons (a depth of about thirty-two hundred feet), the cliff is all but perpendicular, and appears to be completely unassailable.   The dimensions of these pages are insufficient to do justice to this magnificent wall, which is the most imposing of its kind that I have seen ; otherwise it would have been engraved.

steep path that leads into La Bérarde. We put up, of course, with the chasseur-guide Rodier (who, as usual, was smooth and smiling), and after congratulations were over we returned to the exterior to watch for the arrival of one Alexander Pic, who had been sent overnight with our baggage *viâ* Freney and Venos. But when the night fell and no Pic appeared, we saw that our plans must be modified, for he was necessary to our very existence : he carried our food, our tobacco, our all.   So, after some discussion, it was agreed that a portion of our programme should be abandoned, that the night of the 24th should be passed at the head of the Glacier de la Bonne Pierre, and that on the 25th a push should be made for the summit of the Écrins. We then went to straw.

Our porter Pic strolled in next morning with his usual jaunty air, and we seized upon our tooth-brushes, but upon looking for the cigars we found starvation staring us in the face. "Hullo! Monsieur Pic, where are our cigars?" "Gentlemen," he began, "I am deso-lated!" and then, quite pat, he told a long rigmarole about a fit on the road, of brigands, thieves, of their ransacking the knapsacks when he was insensible, and of finding them gone when he revived. "Ah, Monsieur Pic! we see what it is—you have smoked them yourself!" "Gentlemen, I never smoke—*never!*" Whereupon we inquired secretly if he was known to smoke, and found that he was. However, he said that he had never spoken truer words, and perhaps

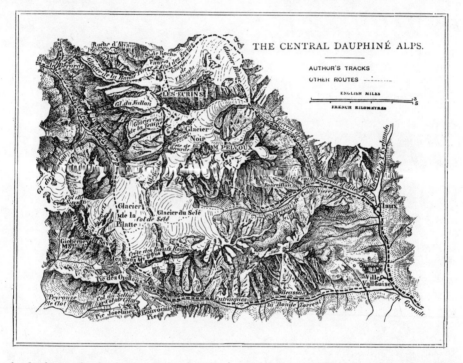

THE CENTRAL DAUPHINÉ ALPS.

AUTHOR'S TRACKS
OTHER ROUTES ------

ENGLISH MILES
FRENCH KILOMETRES

he had not, for he is reported to be the greatest liar in Dauphiné!

We were now able to start, and set out at 1.15 P. M. to bivouac upon the Glacier de la Bonne Pierre, accompanied by Rodier, who staggered under a load of blankets. Many slopes had to be mounted, and many torrents to be crossed, all of which have been described by Mr. Tuckett. We, however, avoided the difficulties he experienced with the latter by crossing them high up, where they were subdivided. But when we got on to the moraine on the right bank of the glacier (or, properly speaking, on to one of the moraines, for there are several), mists descended, to our great hindrance, and it was 5.30 before we arrived on the spot at which it was intended to camp.

Each one selected his nook, and we then joined round a grand fire made by our men. Fortnum & Mason's portable soup was sliced up and brewed, and was excellent; but it should be said that before it *was* excellent three times the quantity named in the directions had to be used. Art is required in drinking as in making this soup, and one point is this: always let your friends drink first;

not only because it is more polite, but because the soup has a tendency to burn the mouth if taken too hot, and one drink of the bottom is worth two of the top, as all the goodness settles.

While engaged in these operations the mist that enveloped the glacier and surrounding peaks was becoming thinner : little bits of blue sky appeared here and there, until suddenly, when we were looking toward the head of the glacier, far, far above us, at an almost inconceivable height, in a tiny patch of blue, appeared a wonderful rocky pinnacle, bathed in the beams of the fast-sinking sun. We were so electrified by the glory of the sight that it was some seconds before we realized what we saw, and understood that that astounding point, removed apparently miles from the earth, was one of the highest summits of Les Écrins, and that we hoped, before another sun had set, to stand upon an even loftier pinnacle. The mists rose and fell, presenting us with a series of dissolving views of ravishing grandeur, and finally died away, leaving the glacier and its mighty bounding precipices under an exquisite pale blue sky, free from a single speck of cloud.

The night passed over without anything worth mention, but we had occasion to observe in the morning an instance of the curious evaporation that is frequently noticeable in the High Alps. On the previous night we had hung up on a knob of rock our mackintosh bag containing five bottles of Rodier's bad wine. In the morning, although the stopper appeared to have been in all night, about four-fifths had evaporated. It was strange : my friends had not taken any, neither had I, and the guides each declared that they had not seen any one touch it. In fact, it was clear that there was no explanation of the phenomenon but in the dryness of the air. Still, it is remarkable that the dryness of the air (or the evaporation of wine) is always greatest when a stranger is in one's party : the dryness caused by the presence of even a single Chamounix porter is sometimes so great that not four-fifths but the entire quantity disappears. For

a time I found difficulty in combating this phenomenon, but at last discovered that if I used the wine-flask as a pillow during the night the evaporation was completely stopped.

At 4 A. M. we moved off across the glacier in single file toward the foot of a great gully which led from the upper slopes of the Glacier de la Bonne Pierre to the lowest point in the ridge that runs from the Écrins to the mountain called Roche Faurio—cheered by Rodier, who now returned with his wraps to La Bérarde.

By five minutes to six we were at the top of the gully (a first-rate couloir about one thousand feet high), and within sight of our work. Hard, thin and wedge-like as the Écrins had looked from afar, it had never looked so hard and so thin as it did when we emerged from the top of the couloir through the gap in the ridge : no tender shadows spoke of broad and rounded ridges, but sharp and shadowless its serrated edges stood out against the clear sky. It had been said that the route must be taken by one of the ridges of the final peak, but both were alike repellent, hacked and notched in numberless places. They reminded me of my failure on the Dent d'Hérens in 1863, and of a place on a similar ridge from which advance or retreat was alike difficult. But, presuming one or other of these ridges or arêtes to be practicable, there remained the task of getting to them, for completely round the base of the final peak swept an enormous bergschrund, almost separating it from the slopes which lay beneath. It was evident thus early that the ascent would not be accomplished without exertion, and that it would demand all our faculties and all our time. In more than one respect we were favored. The mists were gone, the day was bright and perfectly calm, there had been a long stretch of fine weather beforehand, and the snow was in excellent order ; and, most important of all, the last new snow which had fallen on the final peak, unable to support itself, had broken away and rolled in a mighty avalanche over schrund, névé, séracs, over hills and valleys in the glacier (leveling one and filling the other), completely down to the col, where

it lay in huge jammed masses, powerless to harm us; and had made a broad track,

of the map at page 84, leading from Roche Faurio toward the W.N.W. We arrived upon the plateau of the Glacier de l'Encula, behind this ridge, from the direction of D, and then made a nearly straight track to the left hand of the bergschrund at A.

almost a road, over which, for part of the way at least, we might advance with rapidity.

We took in all this in a few minutes, and seeing there was no time to be lost, despatched a hasty meal, left knapsacks, provisions and all encumbrances by the col, started again at half-past six, and made direct for the left side of the schrund, for it was there alone that a passage was practicable. We crossed it at 8.10. Our route can now be followed upon the annexed outline. The arrow

marked D points out the direction of the Glacier de la Bonne Pierre. The ridge in front, that extends right across, is the ridge that is partially shown on the top

Thus far there was no trouble, but the nature of the work changed immediately. If we regard the upper seven hundred feet alone of the final peak of the Écrins, it may be described as a three-sided pyramid. One face is toward the Glacier Noir, and forms one of the sheerest precipices in the Alps. Another is toward the Glacier du Vallon, and is less steep and less uniform in angle than the first. The third is toward the Glacier de l'Encula, and it was by this one we approached the summit. Imagine a triangular plane seven hundred or eight hundred feet high, set at an angle exceeding 50°; let it be smooth, glassy; let the uppermost edges be cut into spikes and teeth, and let them be bent, some one way, some another. Let the glassy face be covered with minute fragments of rock, scarcely attached, but varnished with ice: imagine this, and then you will have a very faint idea of the face of the Écrins on which we stood. It was not possible to avoid detaching stones, which, as they fell, caused words unmentionable to rise. The greatest friends would have reviled each other in such a situation. We gained the eastern arête, and endeavored for half an hour to work upward toward the summit, but it was useless (each yard of progress cost an incredible time); and having no desire to form the acquaintance of the Glacier Noir in a precipitate manner, we beat a retreat and returned to the schrund. We again held a council, and it was unanimously decided that we should be beaten if we could not cut along the upper edge of the schrund, and, when nearly beneath the summit, work up to it. So Croz took off his coat and went to work, on ice— not that black ice so often mentioned and so seldom seen, but on ice as hard as ice could be. Weary work for the guides. Croz cut for more than half an hour, and we did not seem to have advanced at all. Some one behind, seeing how great the labor was and how slow the progress, suggested that after all we might do better on the arête. Croz's blood was up, and, indignant at this slight on his powers, he ceased working, turned in his steps, and rushed toward me with a haste that made me shudder: "By all means let us go there! —the sooner the better." No slight was intended, and he resumed his work, after a time being relieved by Almer. Half-past ten came: an hour had passed— they were still cutting. Dreary work for us, for there was no capering about to be done here; hand as well as foot holes were necessary; the fingers and toes got very cold; the ice, as it boomed in bounding down the bergschrund, was very suggestive; conversation was very restricted, separated as we were by our tether of twenty feet apiece. Another hour passed. We were now almost immediately below the summit, and we stopped to look up. We were nearly as far off it (vertically) as we had been more than three hours before. The day seemed going against us. The only rocks near at hand were scattered, no bigger than tea-cups, and most of these, we found afterward, were glazed with ice. Time forbade cutting right up to

the summit, even had it been possible, which it was not. We decided to go up to the ridge again by means of the rocks, but had we not had a certain confidence in each other, it unquestionably would not have been done; for this, it must be understood, was a situation where not only *might* a slip have been fatal to every one, but it would have been so beyond doubt: nothing, moreover, was easier than to make one. It was a place where all had to work in unison, where there must be no slackening of the rope and no unnecessary tension. For another hour we were in this trying situation, and at 12.30 we gained the arête again, but at a much higher point (B), close to the summit. Our men were, I am afraid, wellnigh worn out: cutting up a couloir one thousand feet high was not the right sort of preparation for work of this kind. Be it so or not, we were all glad to rest for a short time, for we had not sat down a minute since leaving the col, six hours before. Almer, however, was restless, knowing that mid-day was past, and that much remained to be accomplished, and untied himself and commenced working toward the summit. Connecting the teeth of rock were beds of snow, and Almer, but a few feet from me, was crossing the top of one of these, when suddenly, without a moment's warning, it broke away under him and plunged down on to the glacier. As he staggered for a second, one foot in the act of stepping and the other on the falling mass, I thought him lost, but he happily fell on to the right side and stopped himself. Had he taken the step with his right instead of his left foot, he would, in all probability, have fallen several hundred feet without touching anything, and would not have been arrested before reaching the glacier, a vertical distance of at least three thousand feet.

Small, ridiculously small, as the distance was to the summit, we were occupied nearly another hour before it was gained. Almer was a few feet in front, and he, with characteristic modesty, hesitated to step on the highest point, and drew back to allow us to pass. A cry was raised for Croz, who had done the chief part of the work, but he declined the honor, and we marched on to the top simultaneously—that is to say, clustered round it, a yard or two below, for it was much too small to get upon.

According to my custom, I bagged a piece from off the highest rock (chlorite slate), and I found afterward that it had a striking similarity to the final peak of the Écrins. I have noticed the same

FRAGMENT FROM THE SUMMIT OF THE POINTE DES ÉCRINS.

thing on other occasions, and it is worthy of remark that not only do fragments of such rock as limestone often present the characteristic forms of the cliffs from which they have been broken, but that morsels of mica slate will represent, in a wonderful manner, the identical shape of the peaks of which they have formed part. Why should it not be so if the mountain's mass is more or less homogeneous? The same causes which produce the small forms fashion the large ones: the same influences are at work— the same frost and rain give shape to the mass as well as to its parts.

Did space permit me, I could give but a sorry idea of the view, but it will be readily imagined that a panorama extending over as much ground as the whole of England is one worth taking some trouble to see, and one which is not often to be seen even in the Alps. No clouds obscured it, and a list of the

summits that we saw would include nearly all the highest peaks of the chain. I saw the Pelvoux now—as I had seen the Écrins from it three years before— across the basin of the Glacier Noir. It is a splendid mountain, although in height it is equaled, if not surpassed, by its neighbor, the Aléfroide.

We could stay on the summit but a short time, and at a quarter to two prepared for the descent. Now, as we looked down, and thought of what we had passed over in coming up, we one and all hesitated about returning the same way. Moore said, No. Walker said the same, and I too—the guides were both of the same mind: this, be it remarked, although we had considered that there was no chance whatever of getting up any other way. But those "last rocks" were not to be forgotten. Had they but protruded to a moderate extent, or had they been merely glazed, we should doubtless still have tried; but they were not reasonable rocks—they would neither allow us to hold nor would do it themselves. So we turned to the western arête, trusting to luck that we should find a way down to the schrund, and some means of getting over it afterward. Our faces were a tolerable index to our thoughts, and apparently the thoughts of the party were not happy ones. Had any one then said to me, "You are a great fool for coming here," I should have answered with humility, "It is too true." And had my monitor gone on to say, "Swear you will never ascend another mountain if you get down safely," I am inclined to think I should have taken the oath. In fact, the game here was not worth the risk. The guides felt it as well as ourselves, and as Almer led off he remarked, with more piety than logic, "The good God has brought us up, and he will take us down in safety;" which showed pretty well what he was thinking about.

The ridge down which we now endeavored to make our way was not inferior in difficulty to the other. Both were serrated to an extent that made it impossible to keep strictly to them, and obliged us to descend occasionally for

DESCENDING THE WESTERN ARÉTE OF THE POINTE DES ÉCRINS.

Page 89.

some distance on the northern face and then mount again. Both were so rotten that the most experienced of our party, as well as the least, continually upset blocks large and small. Both arêtes were so narrow, so thin, that it was often a matter for speculation on which side an unstable block would fall.

At one point it seemed that we should be obliged to return to the summit and try the other way down. We were on the very edge of the arête: on one side was the enormous precipice facing the Pelvoux, which is not far from perpendicular—on the other a slope exceeding 50°. A deep notch brought us to an abrupt halt. Almer, who was leading, advanced cautiously to the edge on his hands and knees and peered over: his care was by no means unnecessary, for the rocks had broken away from under us unexpectedly several times. In this position he looked down for some moments, and then without a word turned his head and looked at us. His face *may* have expressed apprehension or alarm, but it certainly did not show hope or joy. We learned that there was no means of getting down, and that we must, if we wanted to pass it, jump across on to an unstable block on the other side. It was decided that it should be done, and Almer, with a larger extent of rope than usual, jumped: the rock swayed as he came down upon it, but he clutched a large mass with both arms and brought himself to anchor. That which was both difficult and dangerous for the first man was easy enough for the others, and we got across with less trouble than I expected, stimulated by Croz's perfectly just observation, that if we couldn't get across there we were not likely to get down the other way.

We had now arrived at C, and could no longer continue on the arête, so we commenced descending the face again. Before long we were close to the schrund, but unable to see what it was like at this part, as the upper edge bent over. Two hours had already passed since leaving the summit, and it began to be highly probable that we should have to spend a night on the Glacier Blanc. Almer,

who yet led, cut ~~steps~~ right down to the edge, but still he could not see below : therefore, warning us to hold tight, he made his whole body rigid, and (standing in the large step which he had cut for the purpose) had the upper part of his person lowered out until he saw what he wanted. He shouted that our work was finished, made me come close to the edge and untie myself, advanced the others until he had rope enough, and then with a loud *jodel* jumped down on to soft snow. Partly by skill and partly by luck he had hit the crevasse at its easiest point, and we had only to make a downward jump of eight or ten feet.

It was now 4.45 P. M. : we had been more than eight hours and a half accomplishing the ascent of the final peak, which, according to an observation by Mr. Bonney in 1862, is only 525 feet high.* During this period we had not stopped for more than half an hour, and our nerves and muscles had been kept at the highest degree of tension the whole time. It may be imagined that we accepted the ordinary conditions of glacier traveling as an agreeable relief, and that that which at another time might have seemed formidable we treated as the veriest bagatelle. Late in the day as it was, and soft as was the snow, we put on such pace that we reached the Col des Écrins in less than forty minutes. We lost no time in arranging our baggage, for we had still to traverse a long glacier, and to get clear of two ice-falls before it was dark ; so at 5.35 we resumed the march, adjourning eating and drinking, and put on a spurt which took us clear of the Glacier Blanc by 7.45 P. M. We got clear of the moraine of the Glacier Noir at 8.45, just as the last remnant of daylight vanished. Croz and myself were a trifle in advance of the others, and fortunately so for us ; for as they were about to commence the descent of the snout of the glacier, the whole of the moraine that rested on its

* See vol. i., p. 73, of *Alpine Journal.* We considered the height assigned to the final peak by Mr. Bonney was too small, and thought it should have been two hundred feet more.

face peeled off and came down with a tremendous roar.

We had now the pleasure of walking over a plain that is known by the name of the Pré de Madame Carle, covered with pebbles of all sizes and intersected by numerous small streams or torrents. Every hole looked like a stone, every stone like a hole, and we tumbled about from side to side until our limbs and our tempers became thoroughly jaded. My companions, being both short-sighted, found the traveling especially disagreeable; so there was little wonder that when we came upon a huge mass of rock as big as a house, which had fallen from the flanks of Pelvoux, a regular cube that offered no shelter whatever, Moore cried out in ecstasy, "Oh, how delightful! the very thing I have been longing for! Let us have a perfectly extemporaneous bivouac." This, it should be said, was when the night threatened thunder and lightning, rain and all other delights.

The pleasures of a perfectly extemporaneous bivouac under these circumstances not being novelties to Croz and myself, we thought we would. try for the miseries of a roof, but Walker and Almer, with their usual good-nature, declared it was the very thing that they too were longing for; so the trio resolved to stop. We generously left them all the provisions (a dozen cubic inches or thereabouts of bacon fat and half a candle), and pushed on for the chalets of Aléfroide, or at least we thought we did, but could not be certain. In the course of half an hour we got uncommonly close to the main torrent, and Croz all at once disappeared. I stepped cautiously forward to peer down into the place where I thought he was, and quietly tumbled head over heels into a big rhododendron bush. Extricating myself with some trouble, I fell backward over some rocks, and got wedged in a cleft so close to the torrent that it splashed all over me.

The colloquy which then ensued amid the thundering of the stream was as follows: "Hullo, Croz! "Eh, monsieur?" "Where are you?" "Here, sieur?" "Where are you?" "Here,

monsieur." "Where *is* here?" "I don't know: where are you?" "Here, Croz;" and so on.

The fact was, from the intense darkness and the noise of the torrent, we had no idea of each other's situation: in the course of ten minutes, however, we joined together again, agreed we had quite enough of that kind of thing, and adjourned to a most eligible rock at 10.15.

How well I remember the night at that rock, and the jolly way in which Croz came out! We were both very wet about the legs, and both uncommonly hungry, but the time passed pleasantly enough round our fire of juniper, and until long past midnight we sat up recounting, over our pipes, wonderful stories of the most incredible description, in which, I must admit, my companion beat me hollow. Then throwing ourselves on our beds of rhododendron, we slept an untroubled sleep, and rose on a bright Sunday morning as fresh as might be, intending to enjoy a day's rest and luxury with our friends at La Ville de Val Louise.

I have failed to give the impression I wish if it has not been made evident that the ascent of the Pointe des Écrins was not an ordinary piece of work. There is an increasing disposition nowa-days, amongst those who write on the Alps, to underrate the difficulties and dangers which are met with, and this disposition is, I think, not less mischievous than the old-fashioned style of making everything terrible. Difficult as we found the peak, I believe we took it at the best, perhaps the only possible, time of the year. The great slope on which we spent so much time was, from being denuded by the avalanche of which I have spoken, deprived of its greatest danger. Had it had the snow still resting upon it, and had we persevered with the expedition, we should almost without doubt have ended with calamity instead of success. The ice of that slope is always below, its angle is severe, and the rocks do not project sufficiently to afford the support that snow requires to be stable when at a great angle. So far am I from desiring to tempt any one to repeat the expedition, that I put it on record as my belief, however sad and however miserable a man may have been, if he is found on the summit of the Pointe des Écrins after a fall of new snow, he is likely to experience misery far deeper than anything with which he has hitherto been acquainted.

PART VI.

CHAPTER X.

FROM VAL LOUISE TO LA BÉRARDE BY THE COL DE PILATTE.

FROM Ailefroide to Claux, but for the path, travel would be scarcely more easy than over the Pré de Madame Carle. The valley is strewn with immense masses of gneiss, from the size of a large house downward, and it is only occasionally that rock *in situ* is seen, so covered up is it by the débris, which seems to have been derived almost entirely from the neighboring cliffs.

It was Sunday, a day most calm and bright. Golden sunlight had dispersed the clouds and was glorifying the heights, and we forgot hunger through the brilliancy of the morning and beauty of the mountains.

We meant the 26th to be a day of rest, but it was little that we found in the cabaret of Claude Giraud, and we fled before the babel of sound which rose in intensity as men descended to a depth which is unattainable by the beasts of the field, and found at the chalets of Entraigues the peace that had been denied to us at Val Louise.

Again we were received with the most cordial hospitality. Everything that was eatable or drinkable was brought out and pressed upon us; very little curiosity was exhibited; all information that could be afforded was given; and when we retired to our clean straw we again congratulated each other that we had escaped from the foul den which is where a good inn should be, and had cast in our lot with those who dwell in chalets. Very luxurious that straw seemed after two nights upon quartz pebbles and glacier mud, and I felt quite aggrieved (expecting it was the summons for departure) when, about midnight, the heavy wooden door creaked on its hinges, and a man hem'd and ha'd to attract attention; but when it whispered, "Monsieur Edvard," I perceived my mistake: it was our Pelvoux companion, Monsieur Reynaud, the excellent *agent-voyer* of La Bessée.

Monsieur Reynaud had been invited to accompany us on the excursion that is described in this chapter, but had arrived at Val Louise after we had left, and had energetically pursued us during the night. Our idea was, that a pass might be made over the high ridge called (on the French map) Crête de Bœufs Rouges, near to the peak named Les Bans, which might be the shortest route in time (as it certainly would be in distance) from Val Louise across the central Dauphiné Alps. We had seen the northern (or Pilatte) side from the Brèche de la Meije, and it seemed to be practicable at one place near the above-mentioned mountain. More than that could not be told at a distance of eleven miles. We intended to try to hit a point on the ridge immediately above the part where it seemed to be easiest.

We left Entraigues at 3.30 on the morning of June 27, and proceeded, over very gently-inclined ground, toward the foot of the Pic de Bonvoisin (following, in fact, the route of the Col de Sellar, which leads from the Val Louise into the Val Godemar),* and at 5 A. M., finding that there was no chance of obtaining a view from the bottom of the valley of the ridge over which our route was to be taken, sent Almer up the lower slopes of the Bonvoisin to reconnoitre. He telegraphed that we might proceed, and at 5.45 we quitted the snow-beds at the bottom of the valley for the slopes which rose toward the north.

The course was north-north-west, and was prodigiously steep. *In less than two miles' difference of latitude we rose one mile of absolute height.* But the route was so far from being an exceptionally difficult one that at 10.45 we stood on the summit of the pass, having made an ascent of more than five thousand feet in five hours, inclusive of halts.

Upon the French map a glacier is laid down on the south of the Crête des Bœufs Rouges, extending along the entire length of the ridge, at its foot, from east to west. In 1864 this glacier did not exist as *one* glacier, but in the place where it should have been there were several small ones, all of which were, I believe, separated from each other.†

We commenced the ascent from the Val d'Entraigues to the west of the most western of these small glaciers, and quitted the valley by the first great gap in its cliffs after that glacier was passed. We did not take to the ice until it afforded an easier route than the rocks: then (at 8.30) Croz went to the front, and led with admirable skill through a maze of crevasses up to the foot of a great snow-couloir that rose from the head of the glacier to the summit of the ridge over which we had to pass.

We had settled beforehand in London, without knowing anything whatever about the place, that such a couloir as this should be in this angle; but when we got into the Val d'Entraigues, and found that it was not possible to see into the corner, our faith in its existence became less and less, until the telegraphing of Almer, who was sent up the opposite slopes to search for it, assured us that we were true prophets.

Snow-couloirs are nothing more or less than gullies partly filled by snow. They are most useful institutions, and may be considered as natural highways placed, by a kind Providence, in convenient situations for getting over places which would otherwise be inaccessible. They are a joy to the mountaineer, and, from afar, assure him of a path when all besides is uncertain; but they are grief to novices, who, when upon steep snow, are usually seized with two notions—first, that the snow will slip, and, secondly, that those who are upon it must slip too.

Nothing, perhaps, could look much more unpromising to those who do not know the virtues of couloirs than such a place as the engraving represents,‡ and if persons inexperienced in mountain-craft had occasion to cross a ridge or to climb rocks in which there were such couloirs, they would instinctively avoid them. But practiced mountaineers would naturally look to them for a path, and would follow them almost as a matter of course, unless they turned out to be filled with ice or too much swept by

---

* The height of Col de Sellar (or de Celar) is 10,073 feet (Forbes). I was told by peasants at Entraigues that sheep and goats can be easily taken across it.

† It is perhaps just possible, although improbable, that these little glaciers were united together at the time that the survey was made. Since then the glaciers of Dauphiné (as throughout the Alps generally) have shrunk very considerably. A notable diminution took place in their size in 1869, which was attributed by the natives to the very heavy rains of that year.

‡ This drawing was made to illustrate the remarks which follow. It does not represent any particular couloir, but it would serve, tolerably well, as a portrait of the one which we ascended when crossing the Col de Pilatte.

falling stones, or the rock at the sides proved to be of such an exceptional character as to afford an easier path than the snow.

Couloirs look prodigiously steep when seen from the front, and, so viewed, it is impossible to be certain of their inclination within many degrees. Snow, however, does actually lie at steeper angles in couloirs than in any other situation : forty-five to fifty degrees is not an uncommon inclination. Even at such angles, two men with proper axes can mount on snow at the rate of seven hundred to eight hundred feet per hour. The same amount can only be accomplished in the same time on steep rocks when they are of the very easiest character, and four or five hours may be readily spent upon an equal height of difficult rocks. Snow-couloirs are therefore to be commended because they economize time.

Of course, in all gullies one is liable to be encountered by falling stones. Most of those which fall from the rocks of a couloir sooner or later spin down the snow which fills the trough, and as their course and pace are more clearly apparent when falling over snow than when jumping from ledge to ledge, persons with lively imaginations are readily impressed by them. The grooves which are usually seen wandering down the length of snow-couloirs are deepened (and perhaps occasionally originated) by falling

ly only gutters, caused by water trickling off the rocks. Whether this is so or not, one should always consider the

stones, and they are sometimes pointed out by cautious men as reasons why couloirs should not be followed. I think they are very frequent-

possibility of being struck by falling stones, and, in order to lessen the risk as far as possible, should mount upon the sides of the snow and not up its centre. Stones that come off the rocks then fly over one's head or bound down the middle of the trough at safe distance.

At 9.30 A. M. we commenced the ascent of the couloir leading from the nameless glacier to a point in the ridge, just to the east of Mont Bans. So far, the route had been nothing more than a steep grind in an angle where little could be seen, but now views opened out in several directions, and the way began to be interesting. It was more so, perhaps, to us than to our companion, M. Reynaud, who had no rest in the last night. He was, moreover, heavily laden. Science was to be regarded—his pockets were stuffed with books; heights and angles were to be observed—his knapsack was filled with instruments ; hunger was to be guarded against—his shoulders were ornamented with a huge nimbus of bread, and a leg of mutton swung behind from his knapsack, looking like an overgrown tail. Like a good-hearted fellow, he had brought this food, thinking we might be in need of it. As it happened, we were well provided for, and, having our own packs to carry, could not relieve him of his superfluous burdens, which, naturally, he did not like to throw away. As the angles steepened the strain on his strength became more and more apparent. At last he began to groan. At first a most gentle and mellow groan, but as we rose so did his groans, till at last the cliffs were groaning in echo and we were moved to laughter.

Croz cut the way with unflagging energy throughout the whole of the ascent, and at 10.45 we stood on the summit of our pass, intending to refresh ourselves with a good halt; but just at that moment a mist, which had been playing about the ridge, swooped down and blotted out the whole of the view on the northern side. Croz was the only one who caught a glimpse of the descent, and it was deemed advisable to push on immediately while its recollection was fresh in his memory. We are consequently unable to tell anything about the summit of the pass, except that it lies immediately to the east of Mont Bans, and is elevated about eleven thousand three hundred feet above the level of the sea. It is the highest pass in Dauphiné. We called it the Col de Pilatte.

We commenced to descend toward the Glacier de Pilatte by a slope of smooth ice, the face of which, according to the measurement of Mr. Moore, had an inclination of 54°! Croz still led, and the others followed at intervals of about fifteen feet, all being tied together, and Almer occupying the responsible position of last man : the two guides were therefore about seventy feet apart. They were quite invisible to each other from the mist, and looked spectral even to us. But the strong man could be heard by all hewing out the steps below, while every now and then the voice of the steady man pierced the cloud : "Slip not, dear sirs : place well your feet : stir not until you are certain."

For three-quarters of an hour we progressed in this fashion. The axe of Croz all at once stopped. "What is the matter, Croz?" "Bergschrund, gentlemen." "Can we get over?" "Upon my word, I don't know : I think we must jump." The clouds rolled away right and left as he spoke. The effect was dramatic. It was a *coup de théâtre*, preparatory to the "great sensation leap" which was about to be executed by the entire company.

Some unseen cause, some cliff or obstruction in the rocks underneath, had caused our wall of ice to split into two portions, and the huge fissure which had thus been formed extended on each hand as far as could be seen. We, on the slope above, were separated from the slope below by a mighty crevasse. No running up and down to look for an easier place to cross could be done on an ice-slope of 54° : the chasm had to be passed then and there.

A downward jump of fifteen or sixteen feet, and a forward leap of seven or eight feet, had to be made at the same time. That is not much, you will say. It was not much : it was not the quantity, but it was the quality of the jump which gave to it its particular flavor. You had to hit a narrow ridge of ice. If that was passed, it seemed as if you might roll down for ever and ever. If it was not attained, you dropped into the crevasse below, which al-

"WE SAW A TOE—IT SEEMED TO BELONG TO MOORE—WE SAW REYNAUD A FLYING BODY."

Page 95.

though partly choked by icicles and snow that had fallen from above, was still gaping in many places, ready to receive an erratic body.

Croz untied Walker in order to get rope enough, and, warning us to hold fast, sprang over the chasm. He alighted cleverly on his feet, untied himself and sent up the rope to Walker, who followed his example. It was then my turn, and I advanced to the edge of the ice. The second which followed was what is called a supreme moment. That is to say, I felt supremely ridiculous. The world seemed to revolve at a frightful pace and my stomach to fly away. The next moment I found myself sprawling in the snow, and then, of course, vowed that it was nothing, and prepared to encourage my friend Reynaud.

He came to the edge and made declarations. I do not believe that he was a whit more reluctant to pass the place than we others, but he was infinitely more demonstrative: in a word, he was French. He wrung his hands: "Oh what a *diable* of a place !" "It is nothing, Reynaud," I said, "it is nothing." "Jump !" cried the others, "jump !" But he turned round, as far as one can do such a thing in an ice-step, and covered his face with his hands, ejaculating, "Upon my word, it is not possible. No, no, no ! it is not possible."

How he came over I do not know. We saw a toe—it seemed to belong to Moore ; we saw Reynaud, a flying body, coming down as if taking a header into water, with arms and legs all abroad, his leg of mutton flying in the air, his bâton escaped from his grasp ; and then we heard a thud as if a bundle of carpets had been pitched out of a window. When set upon his feet he was a sorry spectacle : his head was a great snowball, brandy was trickling out of one side of the knapsack, Chartreuse out of the other. We bemoaned its loss, but we roared with laughter.

I cannot close this chapter without paying a tribute to the ability with which Croz led us through a dense mist down the remainder of the Glacier de Pilatte.

As an exhibition of strength and skill it has probably never been surpassed in the Alps or elsewhere. On this almost unknown and very steep glacier he was perfectly at home, even in the mists. Never able to see fifty feet ahead, he still went on with the utmost certainty and without having to retrace a single step, and displayed from first to last consummate knowledge of the materials with which he was dealing. Now he cut steps down one side of a *sérac*, went with a dash at the other side, and hauled us up after him ; then cut away along a ridge until a point was gained from which we could jump on to another ridge ; then, doubling back, found a snow-bridge, across which he crawled on hands and knees, towed us across by the legs, ridiculing our apprehensions, mimicking our awkwardness, declining all help, bidding us only to follow him.

About 1 P. M. we emerged from the mist, and found ourselves just arrived upon the level portion of the glacier, having, as Reynaud properly remarked, come down as quickly as if there had not been any mist at all. Then we attacked the leg of mutton which my friend had so thoughtfully brought with him, and afterward raced down, with renewed energy, to La Bérarde.

Reynaud and I walked together to St. Christophe, where we parted. Since then we have talked over the doings of this momentous day, and I know that he would not, for a good deal, have missed the passage of the Col de Pilatte, although we failed to make it an easier or a shorter route than the Col du Selé. I rejoined Moore and Walker the same evening at Venos, and on the next day went with them over the Lautaret road to the hospice on its summit, where we slept.

So our little campaign in Dauphiné came to an end. It was remarkable for the absence of failures, and for the ease and precision with which all our plans were carried out. This was due very much to the spirit of my companions, but it was also owing to the fine weather which we were fortunate enough to enjoy, and to our making a very early start every morning. By beginning our work at or before the break of day on the longest days in the year, we were not only able to avoid hurrying when deliberation was desirable, but could afford to spend several hours in delightful ease whenever the fancy seized us.

I cannot too strongly recommend tourists in search of amusement to avoid the inns of Dauphiné. Sleep in the chalets. Get what food you can from the inns, but by no means attempt to pass a night in them. *Sleep* in them you cannot. M. Joanne says that the inventor of the insecticide powder was a native of Dauphiné. I can well believe it. He must have often felt the necessity of such an invention in his infancy and childhood.

CHAPTER XI.

PASSAGE OF THE COL DE TRIOLET, AND ASCENTS OF MONT DOLENT, AIGUILLE DE TRÉLATÊTE AND AIGUILLE D'ARGENTIÈRE.

TEN years ago very few people knew from personal knowledge how extremely inaccurately the chain of Mont Blanc was delineated. During the previous half century thousands had made the tour of the chain, and in that time at least a thousand individuals had stood upon its highest summit; but out of all this number there was not one capable, willing or able to map the mountain which, until recently, was regarded as the highest in Europe.

Many persons knew that great blunders had been perpetrated, and it was notorious that even Mont Blanc itself was represented in a ludicrously incorrect manner on all sides excepting the north; but there was not, perhaps, a single individual who knew, at the time to which I refer, that errors of no less than one thousand feet had been committed in the determination of heights at each end of the chain, that some glaciers were represented of double their real dimensions, and that ridges and mountains were laid down which actually had no existence.

One portion alone of the entire chain had been surveyed, at the time of which

I speak, with anything like accuracy. It was not done (as one would have expected) by a government, but by a private individual—by the British De Saussure, the late J. D. Forbes. In the year 1842 he "made a special survey of the Mer de Glace of Chamounix and its tributaries, which in some of the following years he extended by further observations, so as to include the Glacier des Bossons." The map produced from this survey was worthy of its author, and subsequent explorers of the region he investigated have been able to detect only trivial inaccuracies in his work.

The district surveyed by Forbes remained a solitary bright spot in a region where all besides was darkness until the year 1861. Praiseworthy attempts were made by different hands to throw light upon the gloom, but these efforts were ineffectual, and showed how labor may be thrown away by a number of observers working independently without the direction of a single head.

In 1861, Sheet xxii, of Dufour's Map of Switzerland appeared. It included the section of the chain of Mont Blanc that belonged to Switzerland, and this portion of the sheet was executed with the admirable fidelity and thoroughness which characterizes the whole of Dufour's unique map. The remainder of the chain (amounting to about four-fifths of the whole) was laid down after the work of previous topographers, and its wretchedness was made more apparent by contrast with the finished work of the Swiss surveyors.

Strong hands were needed to complete the survey, and it was not long before the right men appeared.

In 1863, Mr. Adams-Reilly, who had been traveling in the Alps during several years, resolved to attempt a survey of the unsurveyed portions of the chain of Mont Blanc. He provided himself with a good theodolite, and, starting from a base-line measured by Forbes in the valley of Chamounix, determined the positions of no less than two hundred points. The accuracy of his work may be judged from the fact that, after having turned many corners and carried his observations over a distance of fifty miles, his Col Ferret "fell within two hundred yards of the position assigned to it by General Dufour !"

In the winter of 1863 and the spring of 1864, Mr. Reilly constructed an entirely original map from his newly-acquired data. The spaces between his trigonometrically-determined points he filled in after photographs and a series of panoramic sketches which he made from his different stations. The map so produced was an immense advance upon those already in existence, and it was the first which exhibited the great peaks in their proper positions.

This extraordinary piece of work revealed Mr. Reilly to me as a man of wonderful determination and perseverance. With very small hope that my proposal would be accepted, I invited him to take part in renewed attacks on the Matterhorn. He entered heartily into my plans, and met me with a counter-proposition—namely, that I should accompany him on some expeditions which he had projected in the chain of Mont Blanc. The unwritten contract took this form : I will help you to carry out your desires, and you shall assist me to carry out mine. I eagerly closed with an arrangement in which all the advantages were upon my side.

Before I pass on to these expeditions it will be convenient to devote a few paragraphs to the topography of the chain of Mont Blanc.

At the present time the chain is divided betwixt France, Switzerland and Italy. France has the lion's share, Switzerland the most fertile portion, and Italy the steepest side. It has acquired a reputation which is not extraordinary, but which is not wholly merited. It has neither the beauty of the Oberland nor the sublimity of Dauphiné. But it attracts the vulgar by the possession of the highest summit in the Alps. If that is removed, the elevation of the chain is in nowise remarkable. In fact, excluding Mont Blanc itself, the mountains of which the chain is made up are *less* important than those of the Oberland and the central Pennine groups.

The ascent of Mont Blanc has been made from several directions, and perhaps there is no single point of the compass from which the mountain cannot be ascended. But there is not the least probability that any one will discover easier ways to the summit than those already known.

I believe it is correct to say that the Aiguille du Midi and the Aiguille de Miage were the only two summits in the chain of Mont Blanc which had been ascended at the beginning of 1864.* The latter of these two is a perfectly insignificant point, and the former is only a portion of one of the ridges just now mentioned, and can hardly be regarded as a mountain separate and distinct from Mont Blanc. The really great peaks of the chain were considered inaccessible, and, I think, with the exception of the Aiguille Verte, had never been assailed.

The finest as well as the highest peak in the chain (after Mont Blanc itself) is the Grandes Jorasses. The next, without a doubt, is the Aiguille Verte. The Aiguille de Bionnassay, which in actual height follows the Verte, should be considered as a part of Mont Blanc ; and in the same way the summit called Les Droites is only a part of the ridge which culminates in the Verte. The Aiguille de Trélatête is the next on the list that is entitled to be considered a separate mountain, and is by far the most important peak (as well as the highest) at the south-west end of the chain. Then comes the Aiguille d'Argentière, which occupies the same rank at the north-east end as the last-mentioned mountain does in the south-west. The rest of the aiguilles are comparatively insignificant; and although some of them (such as the Mont Dolent) look well from low elevations, and seem to possess a certain importance, they sink into their proper places directly one arrives at a considerable altitude.

The summit of the Aiguille Verte would have been one of the best stations out of all these mountains for the purposes of my friend. Its great height and its iso-

* Besides Mont Blanc itself.

lated and commanding position make it a most admirable point for viewing the intricacies of the chain, but he exercised a wise discretion in passing it by, and in selecting as our first excursion the passage of the Col de Triolet.

We slept under some big rocks on the Couvercle on the night of July 7, with the thermometer at 26.5° Fahr., and at 4.30 on the 8th made a straight track to the north of the Jardin, and thence went in zigzags, to break the ascent, over the upper slopes of the Glacier de Talèfre toward the foot of the Aiguille de Triolet. Croz was still my guide; Reilly was accompanied by one of the Michel Payots of Chamounix; and Henri Charlet, of the same place, was our porter.

The way was over an undulating plain of glacier of moderate inclination until the corner leading to the col, from whence a steep secondary glacier led down into the basin of the Talèfre. We experienced no difficulty in making the ascent of this secondary glacier with such ice-men as Croz and Payot, and at 7.50 A. M. arrived on the top of the so-called pass, at a height, according to Mieulet, of 12,162 feet, and 4530 above our camp on the Couvercle.

The descent was commenced by very steep, firm rocks, and then by a branch of the Glacier de Triolet. Schrunds* were abundant: there were no less than five extending completely across the glacier, all of which had to be jumped. Not one was equal in dimensions to the extraordinary chasm on the Col de Pilatte, but in the aggregate they far surpassed it. "Our lives," so Reilly expressed it, "were made a burden to us with schrunds."

Several spurs run out toward the south-east from the ridge at the head of the Glacier de Triolet, and divide it into a number of bays. We descended the most northern of these, and when we emerged from it on to the open glacier, just at the junction of our bay with the next one, we came across a most beautiful ice-arch festooned with icicles, the decaying remnant of an old sérac,

* Great crevasses. A bergschrund is a schrund, but something more.

which stood isolated full thirty feet above the surface of the glacier! It was an accident, and I have not seen its like elsewhere. When I passed the spot in 1865 no vestige of it remained.

We flattered ourselves that we should arrive at the chalets of Pré du Bar very early in the day, but, owing to much time being lost on the slopes of Mont Rouge, it was nearly 4 P. M. before we got to them. There were no bridges across the torrent nearer than Gruetta, and rather than descend so far we preferred to round the base of Mont Rouge and to cross the snout of the Glacier du Mont Dolent.

We occupied the 9th with the ascent of the Mont Dolent. This was a miniature ascent. It contained a little of everything. First we went up to the Col Ferret (No. 1), and had a little grind over shaly banks; then there was a little walk over grass; then a little tramp over a moraine (which, strange to say, gave a pleasant path); then a little zigzagging over the snow-covered glacier of Mont Dolent. Then there was a little bergschrund; then a little wall of snow, which we mounted by the side of a little buttress; and when we struck the ridge descending south-east from the summit, we found a little arête of snow leading to the highest point. The summit itself was little—very small indeed: it was the loveliest little cone of snow that was ever piled up on mountain-top; so soft, so pure, it seemed a crime to defile it. It was a miniature Jungfrau, a toy summit: you could cover it with the hand.

But there was nothing little about the *view* from the Mont Dolent. [Situated at the junction of three mountain-ridges, it rises in a positive steeple far above anything in its immediate neighborhood, and certain gaps in the surrounding ridges, which seem contrived for that especial purpose, extend the view in almost every direction. The precipices which descend to the Glacier d'Argentière I can only compare to those of the Jungfrau, and the ridges on both sides of that glacier, especially the steep rocks of Les Droites and Les Courtes, surmounted by the sharp snow-peak of the Aiguille Verte, have almost the effect of the Grandes Jorasses. Then, framed as it were between the massive tower of the Aiguille de Triolet and the more distant Jorasses, lies, without exception, the most delicately beautiful picture I have ever seen—the whole *massif* of Mont Blanc, raising its great head of snow far above the tangled series of flying buttresses which uphold the Monts Maudits, supported on the left by Mont Peuteret and by the mass of ragged aiguilles which overhangs the Brenva. This aspect of Mont Blanc is not new, but from this point its *pose* is unrivaled, and it has all the superiority of a picture grouped by the hand of a master. . . . The view is as extensive as, and far more lovely than, that from Mont Blanc itself.] *

We went down to Cormayeur, and on the afternoon of July 10 started from that place to camp on Mont Suc, for the ascent of the Aiguille de Trélatête, hopeful that the mists which were hanging about would clear away. They did not, so we deposited ourselves and a vast load of straw on the moraine of the Miage Glacier, just above the Lac de Combal, in a charming little hole which some solitary shepherd had excavated beneath a great slab of rock. We spent the night there and the whole of the next day, unwilling to run away, and equally so to get into difficulties by venturing into the mist. It was a dull time, and I grew restless. Reilly read to me a lecture on the excellence of patience, and composed himself in an easy attitude to pore over the pages of a yellow-covered book. "Patience," I said to him viciously, "comes very easy to fellows who have shilling novels, but I have not got one. I have picked all the mud out of the nails of my boots, and have skinned my face: what shall I do?" "Go and study the moraine of the Miage," said he. I went, and came back after an hour. "What news?" cried Reilly, raising himself on his elbow. "Very little: it's a big moraine, bigger than I thought, with ridge outside ridge, like a fortified camp;

* The bracketed paragraphs in this chapter are extracted from the notes of Mr. Reilly.

and there are walls upon it which have been built and loopholed, as if for defence." "Try again," he said as he threw himself on his back.

But I went to Croz, who was asleep, and tickled his nose with a straw until he awoke; and then, as that amusement was played out, watched Reilly, who was getting numbed, and shifted uneasily from side to side, and

threw himself on his stomach, and rested his head on his elbows, and lighted his pipe and puffed at it savagely. When I looked again, how was Reilly?

An indistinguishable heap—arms, legs, head, stones and straw, all mixed together, his hat flung on one side, his novel tossed far away! Then I went to him and read him a

lecture on the excellence of patience.

Bah! it was a dull time. Our mountain, like a beautiful coquette, sometimes unveiled herself for a moment and looked charming above, al-

though very mysterious below. It was not until eventide she allowed us to approach her: then, as darkness came on, the curtains were withdrawn, the light drapery was lifted, and we stole up on tiptoe through the grand portal framed by Mont Suc. But night advanced rapidly, and we found ourselves left out in the cold, without a hole to creep into or shelter from overhanging rock. We might have fared badly except for our good plaids. But when they were sewn together down their long edges, and one end tossed over our rope (which was passed round some rocks), and the other secured by stones, there was sufficient

protection; and we slept on this exposed ridge, ninety-seven hundred feet above the level of the sea, more soundly perhaps than if we had been lying on feather beds.

We left our bivouac at 4.45 A. M., and at 9.40 arrived upon the highest of the three summits of the Trélatête by passing over the lowest one. It was well above everything at this end of the chain, and the view from it was extraordinarily magnificent. The whole of the western face of Mont Blanc was

OUR CAMP ON MONT SUC.

spread out before us : we were the first by whom it had been ever seen. I cede the description of this view to my comrade, to whom it rightfully belongs.

[For four years I had felt great interest in the geography of the chain : the year before I had mapped, more or less successfully, all but this spot, and this spot had always eluded my grasp. The praises, undeserved as they were, which my map had received, were as gall and wormwood to me when I thought of that great slope which I had been obliged to leave a blank, speckled over with unmeaning dots of rock, gathered from

previous maps, for I had consulted them all without meeting an intelligible representation of it. From the surface of the Miage glacier I had gained nothing, for I could only see the feet of magnificent ice-streams, but no more ; but now, from the top of the dead wall of rock which had so long closed my view, I saw those fine glaciers from top to bottom, pouring down their streams, nearly as large as the Bossons, from Mont Blanc, from the Bosse and from the Dôme.

The head of Mont Blanc is supported on this side by two buttresses, between which vast glaciers descend. Of these the most southern takes its rise at the foot of the precipices which fall steeply down from the Calotte,* and its stream, as it joins that of the Miage, is cut in two by an enormous *rognon* of rock. Next, to the left, comes the largest of the buttresses of which I have spoken, almost forming an aiguille in itself. The next glacier (Glacier du Dôme) descends from a large basin which receives the snows of the summit-ridge between the Bosse and the Dôme, and it is divided from the third and last glacier by another buttress, which joins the summit-ridge at a point between the Dôme and the Aiguille de Bionnassay.]

The great buttresses betwixt these magnificent ice-streams have supplied a large portion of the enormous masses of débris which are disposed in ridges round about, and are strewn over, the termination of the Glacier de Miage in the Val Véni. These moraines † used to be classed amongst the wonders of the world. They are very large for a glacier of the size of the Miage.

The dimensions of moraines are not ruled by those of glaciers. Many small glaciers have large moraines, and many large ones have small moraines. The size of the moraines of any glacier depends mainly upon the area of rock-surface that is exposed to atmospheric influences within the basin drained by the glacier, upon the nature of such rock, whether it is friable or resistant, and upon the dip of strata. Moraines most likely will be small if little rock-surface is exposed; but when large ones are seen, then, in all probability, large areas of rock, uncovered by snow or ice, will be found in immediate contiguity to the glacier. The Miage glacier has large ones, because it receives detritus from many great cliffs and ridges. But if this glacier, instead of lying, as it does, at the bottom of a trough, were to

fill that trough, if it were to completely envelop the Aiguille de Trélatête and the other mountains which border it, and were to descend from Mont Blanc unbroken by rock or ridge, it would be as destitute of morainic matter as the great Mer de Glace of Greenland. For if a country or district is *completely* covered up by glacier, the moraines may be of the very smallest dimensions.

The contributions that are supplied to moraines by glaciers themselves, from the abrasion of the rocks over which their ice passes, are minute compared with the accumulations which are furnished from other sources. These great rubbish-heaps are formed—one may say almost entirely—from débris which falls or is washed down the flanks of mountains, or from cliffs bordering glaciers; and are composed, to a very limited extent only, of matter that is ground, rasped or filed off by the friction of the ice.

If the contrary view were to be adopted, if it could be maintained that "glaciers, *by their motion, break off masses of rock from the sides and bottoms of their valley-courses*, and crowd along everything that is movable, so as to form large accumulations of débris in front and along their sides," ‡ the conclusion could not be resisted, the greater the glacier the greater should be the moraine.

This doctrine does not find much favor with those who have personal knowledge of what glaciers do at the present time. From De Saussure ? downward it has been pointed out, time after time, that moraines are chiefly formed from débris coming from rocks or soil *above* the ice, not from the bed over which it passes. But amongst the writings of modern speculators upon glaciers and glacier-action in bygone times it is not uncommon to find the

---

* The Calotte is the name given to the dome of snow at the summit of Mont Blanc.

† I do not know the origin of the term *moraine.* De Saussure says (vol. i. p. 380, ? 536), "The peasants of Chamounix call these heaps of débris *the moraine* of the glacier." It may be inferred from this that the term was a local one, peculiar to Chamounix.

‡ *Atlas of Physical Geography*, by Augustus Peterman and the Rev. T. Milner. The italics are not in the original.

? "The stones that are found upon the upper extremities of glaciers are of the same nature as the mountains which rise above; but, as the ice carries them down into the valleys, they arrive between rocks of a totally different nature from their own."—De Saussure, ? 536

notions entertained that moraines represent the amount of *excavation* (such is the term employed) performed by glaciers, or at least are comprised of matter which has been excavated by glaciers; that vast moraines have necessarily been produced by vast glaciers; and that a great extension of glaciers—a glacial period—necessarily causes the production of vast moraines. It is needless to cite more than one or two examples to show that such generalizations cannot be sustained. Innumerable illustrations might be quoted.

In the chain of Mont Blanc one may compare the moraines of the Miage with those of the Glacier d'Argentière. The latter glacier drains a basin equal to or exceeding that of the former, but its moraines are small compared with those of the former. More notable still is the disparity of the moraines of the Görner glacier (that which receives so many branches from the neighborhood of Monte Rosa) and of the Z'Muttgletscher. The area drained by the former greatly exceeds the basin of the Z'Mutt, yet the moraines of the Z'Mutt are incomparably larger than those of the Görner. No one is likely to say that the Z'Mutt and Miage glaciers have existed for a far greater length of time than the other pair: an explanation must be sought amongst the causes to which reference has been made.

More striking still is it to see the great interior Mer de Glace of Greenland almost without moraines. This vast ice-plateau, although smaller than it was in former times, is still so extensive that the whole of the glaciers of the Alps might be merged into it without its bulk being perceptibly increased. If the size of moraines bore any sort of relation to the size of glaciers, the moraines of Greenland should be far greater than those of the Alps.

This interior ice-reservoir of Greenland, enormous as it is, must be considered as but the remnant of a mass which was incalculably greater, and which is unparalleled at the present time outside the Antarctic Circle. With the exception of localities where the rocks are easy of disintegration, and the traces of glacier-action have been to a great extent destroyed, the whole country bears the marks of the grinding and polishing of ice; and, judging by the flatness of the curves of the *roches moutonnées*, and by the perfection of the polish which still remains upon the rocks after they have sustained (through many centuries) extreme variations of temperature, the period during which such effects were produced must have widely exceeded in duration the "glacial period" of Europe. If moraines were built from matter excavated by glaciers, the moraines of Greenland should be the greatest in the world!

The absence of moraines upon and at the termination of this great Mer de Glace is due to the want of rocks rising above the ice.* On two occasions in 1867 I saw, at a glance, at least six hundred square miles of it from the summits of small mountains on its outskirts. Not a single peak or ridge was to be seen rising above, nor a single rock reposing upon, the ice. The country was completely covered up by glacier: all was ice as far as the eye could see.†

There is evidence, then, that considerable areas of exposed rock-surface are essential to the production of large moraines, and that glacial periods do not necessarily produce vast moraines—that moraines are not built up of matter which is excavated by glaciers, but simply illustrate the powers of glaciers for transportation and arrangement.

We descended in our track to the Lac de Combal, and from thence went over the Col de la Seigne to Les Motets, where we slept: on July 13 crossed the Col du Mont Tondu to Contamines (in a sharp thunderstorm), and the Col de Voza to

---

* I refer to those portions of it which I have seen in the neighborhood of Disco Bay. There are moraines in this district, but they were formed when the great Mer de Glace stretched nearer to the sea—when it sent arms down through the valleys in the belt of land which now intervenes between sea and glacier.

† The interior of Greenland appears to be absolutely covered by glacier between 68° 30′ and 70° N. lat. Others speak of peaks peeping through the ice to the north and south of this district, but I suspect that these peaks are upon the outskirts of the great Mer de Glace

Chamounix. Two days only remained for excursions in this neighborhood, and we resolved to employ them in another attempt to ascend the Aiguille d'Argentière, upon which mountain we had been cruelly defeated just eight days before.

It happened in this way: Reilly had a notion that the ascent of the aiguille could be accomplished by following the ridge leading to its summit from the Col du Chardonnet. At half-past six on the morning of the 6th we found ourselves accordingly on the top of that pass, which is about eleven thousand or eleven thousand one hundred feet above the level of the sea. The party consisted of our friend Moore and his guide Almer, Reilly and his guide François Couttet, myself and Michel Croz. So far, the weather had been calm and the way easy, but immediately we arrived on the summit of the pass we got into a furious wind. Five minutes earlier we were warm—now we were frozen. Fine snow, whirled up into the air, penetrated every crack in our harness, and assailed our skins as painfully as if it had been red hot instead of freezing cold. The teeth chattered involuntarily; talking was laborious; the breath froze instantaneously; eating was disagreeable; sitting was impossible.

We looked toward our mountain: its aspect was not encouraging. The ridge that led upward had a spiked arête, palisaded with miniature aiguilles, banked up at their bases by heavy snow-beds, which led down at considerable angles, on one side toward the Glacier de Saleinoz, on the other toward the Glacier du Chardonnet. Under any circumstances it would have been a stiff piece of work to clamber up that way. Prudence and comfort counseled, "Give it up." Discretion overruled valor. Moore and Almer crossed the Col du Chardonnet to go to Orsières, and we others returned toward Chamounix.

But when we got some distance down, the evil spirit which prompts men to ascend mountains tempted us to stop and to look back at the Aiguille d'Argentière. The sky was cloudless; no wind could be felt, nor sign of it perceived; it was

only eight o'clock in the morning; and there, right before us, we saw another branch of the glacier leading high up into the mountain—far above the Col du Chardonnet—and a little couloir rising from its head almost to the top of the peak. This was clearly the right route to take. We turned back and went at it.

The glacier was steep, and the snow-gully rising out of it was steeper. Seven hundred steps were cut. Then the couloir became *too* steep. We took to the rocks on its left, and at last gained the ridge, at a point about fifteen hundred feet above the col. We faced about to the right and went along the ridge, keeping on some snow a little below its crest, on the Saleinoz side. Then we got the wind again, but no one thought of turning, for we were within two hundred and fifty feet of the summit.

The axes of Croz and Couttet went to work once more, for the slope was about as steep as snow could be. Its surface was covered with a loose, granular crust, dry and utterly incoherent, which slipped away in streaks directly it was meddled with. The men had to cut through this into the old beds underneath, and to pause incessantly to rake away the powdery stuff, which poured down in hissing streams over the hard substratum. Ugh! how cold it was! How the wind blew! Couttet's hat was torn from its fastenings and went on a tour in Switzerland. The flour-like snow, swept off the ridge above, was tossed spirally upward, eddying in *tourmentes*, then, dropped in lulls or caught by other gusts, was flung far and wide to feed the Saleinoz.

"My feet are getting suspiciously numbed," cried Reilly: "how about frost-bites?" "Kick hard, sir," shouted the men: "it's the only way." *Their* fingers were kept alive by their work, but it was cold for their feet, and they kicked and hewed simultaneously. I followed their example, but was too violent, and made a hole clean through my footing. A clatter followed as if crockery had been thrown down a well.

I went down a step or two, and discovered in a second that all were standing over a cavern (not a crevasse, speaking properly) that was bridged over by a thin vault of ice, from which great icicles hung in grooves. Almost in the same minute Reilly pushed one of his hands right through the roof. The whole party might have tumbled through at any moment. "Go ahead, Croz: we are over a chasm!" "We know it," he answered, "and we can't find a firm place."

In the blandest manner my comrade inquired if to persevere would not be to do that which is called "tempting Providence." My reply being in the affirmative, he further observed, "Suppose we go down?" "Very willingly." "Ask the guides." They had not the least objection; so we went down, and slept that night at the Montanvert.

Off the ridge we were out of the wind. In fact, a hundred feet down *to windward*, on the slope fronting the Glacier du Chardonnet, we were broiling hot: there was not a suspicion of a breeze. Upon that side there was nothing to tell that a hurricane was raging a hundred feet higher; the cloudless sky looked tranquillity itself; whilst to leeward the only sign of a disturbed atmosphere was the friskiness of the snow upon the crests of the ridges.

We set out on the 14th, with Croz, Payot and Charlet, to finish off the work which had been cut short so abruptly, and slept, as before, at the Chalets de Lognan. On the 15th, about midday, we arrived upon the summit of the aiguille, and found that we had actually been within one hundred feet of it when we turned back upon the first attempt.

It was a triumph to Reilly. In this neighborhood he had performed the feat (in 1863) of joining together "two mountains, each about thirteen thousand feet high, standing on the map about a mile and a half apart." Long before we made the ascent he had procured evidence which could not be impugned that the Pointe des Plines, a fictitious summit which had figured on other

maps as a distinct mountain, could be no other than the Aiguille d'Argentière, and he had accordingly obliterated it from the preliminary draft of his map. We saw that it was right to do so. The Pointe des Plines did not exist. We had ocular demonstration of the accuracy of his previous observations.

I do not know which to admire most, the fidelity of Mr. Reilly's map or the indefatigable industry by which the materials were accumulated from which it was constructed. To men who are sound in limb it may be amusing to arrive on a summit (as we did upon the top of Mont Dolent), sitting astride a ridge too narrow to stand upon, or to do battle with a ferocious wind (as we did on the top of the Aiguille de Trélatête), or to feel half frozen in midsummer (as we did on the Aiguille d'Argentière). But there is extremely little amusement in making sketches and notes under such conditions. Yet upon all these expeditions, under the most adverse circumstances and in the most trying situations, Mr. Reilly's brain and fingers were always at work. Throughout all he was ever alike—the same genial, equable-tempered companion, whether victorious or whether defeated; always ready to sacrifice his own desires to suit our comfort and convenience. By a most happy union of audacity and prudence, combined with untiring perseverance, he eventually completed his self-imposed task—a work which would have been intolerable except as a labor of love, and which, for a single individual, may wellnigh be termed herculean.

We separated upon the level part of the Glacier d'Argentière, Reilly going with Payot and Charlet *via* the chalets of Lognan and de la Pendant, whilst I, with Croz, followed the right bank of the glacier to the village of Argentière. At 7 P. M. we entered the humble inn, and ten minutes afterward heard the echoes of the cannon which were fired upon the arrival of our comrades at Chamounix.

PART VII.

CHAPTER XII.
MOMING PASS—ZERMATT.

ON July 10, Croz and I went to Sierre, in the Valais, *viâ* the Col de Balme, the Col de la Forclaz and Martigny. The Swiss side of the Forclaz is not creditable to Switzerland. The path from Martigny to the summit has undergone successive improvements in these latter years, but mendicants permanently disfigure it.

We passed many tired pedestrians toiling up this oven, persecuted by trains of parasitic children. These children swarm there like maggots in a rotten cheese. They carry baskets of fruit with which to plague the weary tourist. They flit around him like flies; they thrust the fruit in his face; they pester him with their pertinacity. Beware of them!— taste, touch not their fruit. In the eyes of these children each peach, each grape, is worth a prince's ransom. It is of no use to be angry: it is like flapping wasps — they only buzz the more. Whatever you do or whatever you say, the end will be the same. "Give me something" is the alpha and omega of all their addresses. They learn the phrase, it is· said, before they are taught the alphabet. It is in all their mouths. From the tiny toddler up to the maiden of sixteen, there is nothing heard but one universal chorus of "Give me something: will you have the goodness to give me something?"

From Sierre we went up the Val d'Anniviers to Zinal, to join our former companions, Moore and Almer. Moore was ambitious to discover a shorter way from Zinal to Zermatt than the two passes which were known.[*] He had shown to me, upon Dufour's map, that a direct line connecting the two places passed exactly over the depression between the Zinal-Rothhorn and the Schallhorn. He was confident that a passage could be effected over this depression, and was sanguine that it would (in consequence of its directness) prove to be a quicker route than the circuitous ones over the Triftjoch and the Col Durand.

He was awaiting us, and we immediately proceeded up the valley and across the foot of the Zinal glacier to the Arpitetta Alp, where a chalet was supposed to exist in which we might pass the night. We found it at length,[†] but it was not

[*] The Col de Zinal or Triftjoch, between the Trifthorn and the Ober Gabelhorn, and the Col Durand, between the last-mentioned mountain and the Dent Blanche.

[†] High above the Glacier de Moming at the foot of the Crête de Milton.

equal to our expectations. It was not one of those fine timbered chalets with huge overhanging eaves, covered with pious sentences carved in unintelligible characters. It was a hovel, growing, as it were, out of the hillside, roofed with rough slabs of slaty stone, without door or window, surrounded by quagmires of ordure and dirt of every description.

A foul native invited us to enter. The interior was dark, but when our eyes became accustomed to the gloom we saw that our palace was in plan about fifteen by twenty feet: on one side it was scarcely five feet high, but on the other was nearly seven. On this side there was a raised platform about six feet wide, littered with dirty straw and still dirtier sheepskins. This was the bed-room. The remainder of the width of the apartment was the parlor. The rest was the factory. Cheese was the article which was being fabricated, and the foul native was engaged in its manufacture. He was garnished behind with a regular cowherd's one-legged stool, which gave him a queer, uncanny look when it was elevated in the air as he bent over into his tub, for the making of his cheese required him to blow into a tub for ten minutes at a time. He then squatted on his stool to gain breath, and took a few whiffs at a short pipe, after which he blew away more vigorously than before. We were told that this procedure was necessary: it appeared to us to be nasty. It accounts, perhaps, for the flavor possessed by certain Swiss cheeses.

Big black and leaden-colored clouds rolled up from Zinal, and met in combat on the Moming glacier with others which descended from the Rothhorn. Down came the rain in torrents and crash went the thunder. The herd-boys hurried under shelter, for the frightened cattle needed no driving, and tore spontaneously down the Alp as if running a steeple-chase. Men, cows, pigs, sheep and goats forgot their mutual animosities, and rushed to the only refuge on the mountain. The spell was broken which had bound the elements for some weeks past, and the *cirque* from the Weisshorn to Lo Besso was the theatre in which they spent their fury.

A sullen morning succeeded an angry night. We were undecided in our council whether to advance or to return down the valley. Good seemed likely to overpower bad; so, at 5.40, we left the chalet *en route* for our pass [amidst the most encouraging assurances from all the people on the Alp that we need not distress ourselves about the weather, as it was not possible to get to the point at which we were aiming].*

Our course led us at first over ordinary mountain-slopes, and then over a flat expanse of glacier. Before this was quitted it was needful to determine the exact line which was to be taken. We were divided betwixt two opinions. I advocated that a course should be steered due south, and that the upper plateau of the Moming glacier should be attained by making a great détour to our right. This was negatived without a division. Almer declared in favor of making for some rocks to the south-west of the Schallhorn, and attaining the upper plateau of the glacier by mounting them. Croz advised a middle course, up some very steep and broken glacier. Croz's route seemed likely to turn out to be impracticable, because much step-cutting would be required upon it. Almer's rocks did not look good: they were, possibly, unassailable. I thought both routes were bad, and declined to vote for either of them. Moore hesitated, Almer gave way, and Croz's route was adopted.

He did not go very far, however, before he found that he had undertaken too much, and after [glancing occasionally round at us, to see what we thought about it, suggested that it might, after all, be wiser to take to the rocks of the Schallhorn]. That is to say, he suggested the abandonment of his own and the adoption of Almer's route. No one opposed the change of plan, and in the absence of instructions to the contrary he proceeded to cut steps across an ice-slope toward the rocks.

When we quitted the slopes of the Arpitetta Alp we took a south-easterly course over the Moming glacier. We halted to settle the plan of attack shortly after we got upon the ice. The rocks of the Schallhorn, whose ascent Almer recommended, were then to our southeast. Croz's proposed route was to the south-west of the rocks, and led up the southern side of a very steep and broken glacier.* The part he intended to traverse was, in a sense, undoubtedly practicable. He gave it up because it would have involved too much step-cutting. But the part of this glacier which intervened between his route and Almer's rocks was, in the most complete sense of the word, impracticable. It passed over a continuation of the rocks, and was broken in half by them. The upper portion was separated from the lower portion by a long slope of ice that had been built up from the débris of the glacier which had fallen from above. The foot of this slope was surrounded by immense quantities of the larger avalanche blocks. These we cautiously skirted, and when Croz halted they had been left far below, and we were half-way up the side of the great slope which led to the base of the ice-wall above.

Across this ice-slope Croz now proceeded to cut. It was executing a flank movement in the face of an enemy by whom we might be attacked at any moment. The peril was obvious. It was a monstrous folly. It was foolhardiness. A retreat should have been sounded.†

"I am not ashamed to confess," wrote Moore in his Journal, "that during the whole time we were crossing this slope my heart was in my mouth, and I never felt relieved from such a load of care as when, after, I suppose, a passage of about twenty minutes, we got on to the rocks and were in safety. . . . I have never heard a positive oath come from Almer's mouth, but the language in which he kept up a running commentary, more to himself than to me, as we went along, was stronger than I should have given him credit for using. His prominent feeling seemed to be one of *indignation*

that we should be in such a position, and self-reproach at being a party to the proceeding; while the emphatic way in which, at intervals, he exclaimed, ' Quick ! be quick !' sufficiently betokened his alarm."

It was not necessary to admonish Croz to be quick. He was as fully alive to the risk as any of the others. He told me afterward that this place was not only the most dangerous he had ever crossed, but that no consideration whatever would tempt him to cross it again. Manfully did he exert himself to escape from the impending destruction. His head, bent down to his work, never turned to the right or to the left. One, two, three, went his axe, and then he stepped on to the spot where he had been cutting. How painfully insecure should we have considered those steps at any other time ! But now we thought of nothing but the rocks in front, and of the hideous *séracs*, lurching over above us, apparently in the act of falling.

We got to the rocks in safety, and if they had been doubly as difficult as they were, we should still have been well content. We sat down and refreshed the inner man, keeping our eyes on the towering pinnacles of ice under which we had passed, but which now were almost beneath us. Without a preliminary warning sound one of the largest —as high as the Monument at London Bridge—fell upon the slope below. The stately mass heeled over as if upon a hinge (holding together until it bent thirty degrees forward), then it crushed out its base, and, rent into a thousand fragments, plunged vertically down upon the slope that we had crossed ! Every atom of our track that was in its course was obliterated : all the new snow was swept away, and a broad sheet of smooth, glassy ice showed the resistless force with which it had fallen.

It was inexcusable to follow such a perilous path, but it is easy to understand why it was taken. To have retreated from the place where Croz suggested a change of plan, to have descended below the reach of danger, and to have mounted again by the route

* Through what is technically called an " ice-fall."
† The responsibility did not rest with Croz. His part was to advise, but not to direct.

which Almer suggested, would have been equivalent to abandoning the excursion, for no one would have passed another night in the chalet on the Arpitetta Alp. "Many," says Thucydides, "though seeing well the perils ahead, are forced along by fear of dishonor, as the world calls it, so that, vanquished by a

position, that an error of judgment had been committed.

After a laborious trudge over many species of snow, and through many varieties of vapor—from the quality of a Scotch mist to that of a London fog—we at length stood on the depression between the Rothhorn and the Schallhorn.* A steep wall of snow was upon the Zinal side of the summit, but what the descent was like on the other side we could not tell, for a billow of snow tossed over its crest by the western winds, suspended over Zermatt with motion arrested, resembling an ocean wave frozen in the act of breaking, cut off the view.†

Croz, held hard in by the others, who kept down the Zinal side, opened his shoulders, flogged down the foam, and cut away the cornice to its junction with the summit; then boldly leaped down, and called on us to follow him.

It was well for us now that we had such a man as leader. An inferior or less daring guide would have hesitated to enter upon the descent in a dense

ICE-AVALANCHE ON THE MOMING PASS.

mere word, they fall into irremediable calamities." Such was nearly the case here. No one could say a word in justification of the course which was adopted; all were alive to the danger that was being encountered; yet a grave risk was deliberately, although unwillingly, incurred, in preference to admitting, by withdrawal from an untenable

mist, and Croz himself would have done right to pause had he been less mag-

* The summit of the pass has been marked on Dufour's map 3793 mètres, or 12,444 feet.

† These snow-cornices are common on the crests of high mountain-ridges, and it is always prudent (just before arriving upon the summit of a mountain or ridge) to *sound* with the alpenstock; that is to say, drive it in, to discover whether there is one or not. Men have often narrowly escaped losing their lives from neglecting this precaution.

THE SUMMIT OF THE MOMING PASS IN 1864.

Page 108.

nificent in *physique*. He acted rather than said, "Where snow lies fast, there man can go; where ice exists, a way may be cut; it is a question of power: I have the power—all you have to do is to follow me." Truly, he did not spare himself, and could he have performed the feats upon the boards of a theatre that he did upon this occasion, he would have brought down the house with thunders of applause. Here is what Moore wrote in *his* Journal:

[The descent bore a strong resemblance to the Col de Pilatte, but was very much steeper and altogether more difficult, which is saying a good deal. Croz was in his element, and selected his way with marvelous sagacity, while Almer had an equally honorable, and perhaps more responsible, post in the rear, which he kept with his usual steadiness. . . . One particular passage has impressed itself on my mind as one of the most nervous I have ever made. We had to pass along a crest of ice, a mere knife-edge—on our left a broad crevasse, whose bottom was lost in blue haze, and on our right, at an angle of seventy degrees or more, a slope falling to a similar gulf below. Croz, as he went along the edge, chipped small notches in the ice, in which we placed our feet, with the toes well turned out, doing all we knew to preserve our balance. While stepping from one of these precarious footholds to another, I staggered for a moment. I had not really lost my footing, but the agonized tone in which Almer, who was behind me, on seeing me waver, exclaimed, "Slip not, sir!" gave us an even livelier impression than we already had of the insecurity of the position. . . . One huge chasm, whose upper edge was far above the lower one, could neither be leaped nor turned, and threatened to prove an insuperable barrier. But Croz showed himself equal to the emergency. Held up by the rest of the party, he cut a series of holes for the hands and feet, down and along the almost perpendicular wall of ice forming the upper side of the schrund. Down this slippery staircase we crept, with our faces to the wall, until a point was reached where the width of the chasm was not too great for us to drop across. Before we had done we got quite accustomed to taking flying leaps over the schrunds. . . . To make a long story short: after a most desperate and exciting struggle, and as bad a piece of ice-work as it is possible to imagine, we emerged on to the upper plateau of the Hohlicht glacier.]

The glimpses which had been caught of the lower part of the Hohlicht glacier were discouraging, so it was now determined to cross over the ridge between it and the Rothhorn glacier. This was not done without great trouble. Again we rose to a height exceeding twelve thousand feet. Eventually we took to the track of the despised Triftjoch, and descended by the well-known but rough path which leads to that pass, arriving at the Monte Rosa hotel at Zermatt at 7.20 P. M. We occupied nearly twelve hours of actual walking in coming from the chalet on the Arpitetta Alp (which was two and a half hours above Zinal), and we consequently found that the Moming pass was not the shortest route from Zinal to Zermatt, although it was the most direct.

Two dozen guides — good, bad and indifferent, French, Swiss and Italian — can commonly be seen sitting on the wall in front of the Monte Rosa hotel, waiting on their employers and looking for employers, watching new arrivals, and speculating on the number of francs which may be extracted from their pockets. The *messieurs* — sometimes strangely and wonderfully dressed —stand about in groups, or lean back in chairs, or lounge on the benches which are placed by the door. They wear extraordinary boots, and still more remarkable head-dresses. Their peeled, blistered and swollen faces are worth studying. Some, by the exercise of watchfulness and unremitting care, have been fortunate enough to acquire a fine raw sienna complexion. But most of them have not been so happy. They have been scorched on rocks and roasted on glaciers. Their cheeks—first puffed, then cracked—have exuded a turpentine-like matter, which has coursed down their faces, and has dried in patches like the resin on the trunks of pines. They have removed it, and at the same time have pulled off large flakes of their skin. They have gone from bad to worse—their case has become hopeless — knives and scissors have been called into play : tenderly and daintily they have endeavored to reduce their cheeks to one uniform hue. It is not to be done. But they have gone on, fascinated, and at last have brought their unhappy countenances to a state of helpless and complete ruin. Their lips are cracked, their cheeks are swollen, their eyes are bloodshot, their noses are peeled and indescribable.

Such are the pleasures of the mountaineer ! Scornfully and derisively the last-comer compares the sight with his own flaccid face and dainty hands, unconscious that he too, perhaps, will be numbered with those whom he now ridicules.

There is a frankness of manner about these strangely-appareled and queer-faced men which does not remind one of drawing-room or city life ; and it is good to see—in this club-room of Zermatt—those cold bodies, our too-frigid countrymen, melt together when they are brought into contact; and it is pleasant to witness the hearty welcome given to the new-comers by the host and his excellent wife.*

I left this agreeable society to seek letters at the post. They yielded disastrous intelligence. My holiday was brought to an abrupt termination, and I awaited the arrival of Reilly (who was convoying the stores for the attack on the Matterhorn) only to inform him that our arrangements were upset; then traveled home, day and night, as fast as express-trains would carry me.

* This opportunity has been taken to introduce to the reader some of the most expert amateur mountaineers of the time, and a few of the guides who have been or will be mentioned in the course of this narrative.

Peter Perrn is on the extreme right. Then come young Peter Taugwalder (upon the bench) and J. J. Maquignaz (leaning against the door-post). Franz Andermatten occupies the steps, and Ulrich Lauener towers in the background.

CHAPTER XIII.

THE ASCENT OF THE GRAND CORNIER.

OUR career in 1864 had been one of unbroken success, but the great ascent upon which I had set my heart was not attempted, and until it was accomplished I was unsatisfied. Other things, too, influenced me to visit the Alps once more. I wished to travel elsewhere, in places where the responsibility of direction would rest with myself alone. It was well to know how far my judgment in the choice of routes could be relied upon.

The journey of 1865 was chiefly undertaken, then, to find out to what extent I was capable of selecting paths over mountainous country. The programme which was drawn up for this journey was rather ambitious, since it included almost all of the great peaks which had not then been ascended, but it was neither lightly undertaken nor hastily executed. All pains were taken to secure success. Information was sought from those who could give it, and the defeats of others were studied, that their errors might be avoided. The results which followed came not so much, perhaps, from luck, as from forethought and careful calculation.

For success does not, as a rule, come by chance, and when one fails there is a reason for it. But when any notable or so-called brilliant thing is done, we are too apt to look upon the success alone, without considering how it was accomplished, whilst when men fail we inquire why they have not succeeded. So failures are oftentimes more instructive than successes, and the disappointments of some become profitable to others.

Up to a certain point the programme was completely and happily carried out. Nothing but success attended our efforts so long as the excursions were executed as they had been planned. Most of them were made upon the very days which had been fixed for them months beforehand ; and all were accomplished, comparatively speaking, so easily that their descriptions must be, in the absence of difficulty and danger, less interesting to the general reader than they would have been if our course had been marked by blunders and want of judgment. Before proceeding to speak of these excursions, it will not be entirely useless to explain the reasons which influenced the selection of the routes which were adopted upon them.

In the course of the past five seasons my early practices were revolutionized. My antipathy to snow was overcome, and my predilection for rocks was modified. Like all those who are not mountaineers born, I was, at the first, extremely nervous upon steep snow. The snow seemed bound to slip, and all those who were upon it to go along with it. Snow of a certain quality is undoubtedly liable to slip when it is at a certain inclination. The exact states which are dangerous or safe it is not possible to describe in writing. That is only learnt by experience, and confidence upon snow is not really felt until one has gained experience. Confidence gradually came to me, and as it came so did my partiality for rocks diminish. For it was evident, to use a common expression, that it paid better to travel upon snow than upon rocks. This applies to snow-beds pure and simple, or to snow which is lying over glacier; and in the selection of routes it has latterly always been my practice to look for the places where snow-slopes or snow-covered glaciers reach highest into mountains.

It is comparatively seldom, however, that an ascent of a great mountain can be executed exclusively upon snow and glacier. Ridges peep through which have to be surmounted. In my earlier scramblings I usually took to, or was taken upon, the summits (or arêtes) of the ridges, and a good many mountaineers habitually take to them on principle, as the natural and proper way. According to my experience, it is seldom well to do so when any other course is open. As I have already said, and presently shall repeat more particularly, the crests of all the main ridges of the great peaks of the Alps are shattered and cleft by frost; and it not unfrequently happens that a notch in a ridge, which appears perfectly insignificant from a

distance, is found to be an insuperable barrier to farther progress, and a great détour or a long descent has to be made to avoid the obstacle. When committed to an arête, one is tied, almost always, to a particular course, from which it is difficult to deviate. Much loss of time must result if any serious obstruction occurs, and total defeat is not at all improbable.

But it seldom happens that a great Alpine peak is seen that is cut off abruptly, in all directions, from the snows and glaciers which surround it. In its gullies snow will cling, although its faces may be too steep for the formation of permanent snow-beds. The merits of these snow-gullies (or couloirs) have been already pointed out, and it is hardly necessary to observe, after that which was just now said about snow, that ascents of snow-gullies (with proper precautions) are very much to be preferred to ascents of rocky arêtes.

By following the glaciers, the snow-slopes above, and the couloirs rising out of them, it is usually possible to get very close to the summits of the great peaks in the Alps. The final climb will, perhaps, necessarily be by an arête. The less of it the better.

It occasionally occurs that considerable mountain-slopes or faces are destitute of snow-gullies. In that case it will, very likely, be best to adhere to the faces (or to the gullies or minor ridges upon them), rather than take to the great ridges. Upon a face one can move to the right or to the left with more facility than upon the crest of a ridge, and when a difficulty is arrived at, it is, consequently, less troublesome to circumvent.

In selecting the routes which were taken in 1865, I looked, first, for places where glaciers and snow extended highest up into the mountains which were to be ascended or the ridges which were to be crossed; next, for gullies filled with snow leading still higher; and finally, from the heads of the gullies we completed the ascents, whenever it was practicable, by faces instead of by arêtes. The ascent of the Grand Cornier (13,022), of the Dent Blanche (14,318), Grandes Jorasses (13,700), Aiguille Verte (13,540), Ruinette (12,727), and the Matterhorn (14,780), were all accomplished in this way, besides the other excursions which will be referred to by and by. The route selected before the start was made was in every case strictly followed out.

We inspected all of these mountains from neighboring heights before entering upon their ascents. I explained to the guides the routes I proposed to be taken, and (when the courses were at all complicated) sketched them out on paper to prevent misunderstanding. In some few cases they suggested variations, and in every case the route was well discussed. The *execution* of the work was done by the guides, and I seldom interfered with or attempted to assist in it.

The 13th of June, 1865, I spent in the valley of Lauterbrunnen with the Rev. W. H. Hawker and the guides Christian and Ulrich Lauener, and on the 14th crossed the Petersgrat with Christian Almer and Johann Tännler to Turtman (Tourtemagne) in the Valais. Tännler

was then paid off, as Michel Croz and Franz Biener were awaiting me.

It was not possible to find two leading guides who worked together more harmoniously than Croz and Almer. Biener's part was subordinate to theirs, and he was added as a convenience rather than as a necessity. Croz spoke French alone, Almer little else than German. Biener spoke both languages, and was useful on that account; but he seldom went to the front, excepting during the early part of the day, when the work was easy, and he acted throughout more as a porter than as a guide.

The importance of having a reserve of power on mountain expeditions cannot be too strongly insisted upon. We always had some in hand, and were never pressed or overworked so long as we were together. Come what might, we were ready for it. But by a series of chances, which I shall never cease to regret, I was first obliged to part with Croz,* and then to dismiss the others; and so, deviating from the course that I had deliberately adopted, which was successful in practice because it was

* I engaged Croz for 1865 before I parted from him in 1864, but upon writing to him in the month of April to fix the dates of his engagement, I found that he had supposed he was free (in consequence of not having heard from me earlier), and had engaged himself to a Mr. B—— from the 27th of June. I endeavored to hold him to his promise, but he considered himself unable to withdraw from his later obligation. His letters were honorable to him. The following extract from the last one he wrote to me is given as an interesting souvenir of a brave and upright man:

sound in principle, became fortuitously a member of an expedition that ended with the catastrophe which brought my scrambles amongst the Alps to a close.

On June 15 we went from Turtman to Z'meiden, and thence over the Forcletta pass to Zinal. We diverged from the summit of the pass up some neighboring heights to inspect the Grand Cornier, and I decided to have nothing to do with its northern side. The mountain was more than seven miles away, but it was quite safe to pronounce it inaccessible from our direction.

On the 16th we left Zinal at 2.05 A.M., having been for a moment greatly surprised by an entry in the hotel-book,* and ascending by the Zinal glacier, and giving the base of our mountain a wide berth in order that it might the better be examined, passed gradually right round to its south before a way up it was seen. At 8.30 we arrived upon the plateau of the glacier that descends toward the east, between the Grand Cornier and the Dent Blanche, and from this place a route was readily traced. We steered to the north over the glacier, toward the ridge that descends to the east, gained it by mounting snow-slopes, and followed

it to the summit, which was arrived at before half-past twelve. From first to last the route was almost entirely over snow.

The ridges leading to the north and to the south from the summit of the Grand Cornier exhibited in a most striking manner the extraordinary effects that may be produced by violent alternations of heat and cold. The southern one was hacked and split into the wildest forms, and the northern one was not less cleft and impracticable, and offered

PART OF THE SOUTHERN RIDGE OF THE GRAND CORNIER.

the droll piece of rock-carving which is represented upon page 114. Some small blocks actually tottered and fell before our eyes, and starting others in their downward course, grew into a perfect avalanche, which descended with a solemn roar on the glaciers beneath.

It is natural that the great ridges should present the wildest forms — not on account of their dimensions, but by reason of their positions. They are exposed to the fiercest heat of the sun, and are seldom in shadow as long as it is above the horizon. They are entirely unprotected,

* It was an entry describing an ascent of the Grand Cornier (which we supposed had never been ascended) from the very direction which we had just pronounced to be hopeless! It was especially startling, because Franz Biener was spoken of in it as having been concerned in the ascent. On examining Biener, it was found that he had made the excursion, and had supposed at the time he was upon its summit that it was the Grand Cornier. He saw afterward that they had only ascended one of the several points upon the ridge running northward from the Grand Cornier—I believe, the Pigne de l'Allée (11,168 feet)!

8

and are attacked by the strongest blasts and by the most intense cold. The most durable rocks are not proof against such assaults. These grand, apparently solid, eternal mountains, seeming so firm, so immutable, are yet ever changing and crumbling into dust. These shattered ridges are evidence of their sufferings. Let me repeat that every principal ridge of every great peak in the Alps amongst those I have seen has been shattered in this way, and that every summit amongst the rock-summits upon which I have stood has

PART OF THE NORTHERN RIDGE OF THE GRAND CORNIER.

been nothing but a piled-up heap of fragments.

The minor ridges do not usually present such extraordinary forms as the principal ones. They are less exposed, and they are less broken up, and it is reasonable to assume that their annual degradation is less than that of the summit-ridges.

The wear and tear does not cease even in winter, for these great ridges are never completely covered up by snow, and the sun has still power.* The de-

struction is incessant, and increases as time goes on; for the greater the surfaces which are exposed to the practically inexhaustible powers of sun and frost, the greater ruin will be effected.

The rock-falls which are continually occurring upon all rock-mountains are, of course, caused by these powers. No one doubts it, but one never believes it so thoroughly as when the quarries are seen from which their materials have been hewn, and when the germs, so to speak, of these avalanches have been seen actually starting from above.

These falls of rock take place from two causes: first, from the heat of the sun detaching small stones or rocks which have been arrested on ledges or slopes and bound together by snow or ice. I have seen such released many times when the sun has risen high: they fall gently at first, gather strength, grow in volume, and at last rush down with a cloud trailing behind, like the dust after an express-train. Secondly, from the freezing of the water which trickles during the day into the clefts, fissures and crannies. This agency is naturally most active in the night, and then, or during very cold weather, the greatest falls take place.†

When one has continually seen and heard these falls, it is easily understood why the glaciers are laden with moraines. The wonder is, not that they are sometimes so great, but that they are not always greater. Irrespective of lithological considerations, one knows that this débris cannot have been excavated by the glaciers. The moraines are *borne*

---

* I wrote in the *Athenæum*, August 29, 1863, to the same effect: "This action of the frost does not cease in winter, inasmuch as it is impossible for the Matterhorn to be entirely covered by snow. Less precipitous mountains may be entirely covered up during winter, and if they do not then actually gain height, the wear and tear is, at least, suspended. . . . We arrive, therefore, at the conclusion that although such snow-peaks as Mont Blanc *may* in the course of ages grow higher, the Matterhorn must decrease in height." These remarks have received confirmation.

The men who were left by M. Dollfus-Ausset in his

observatory upon the summit of the Col Théodule during the winter of 1865, remarked that the snow was partially melted upon the rocks in their vicinity upon the 19th, 20th, 21st, 22d, 23d, 26th and 27th of December of that year, and on the 22d of December they entered in their journal: "Nous avons vu au Matterhorn que la neige se fondait sur roches et qu'il s'en écoulait de l'eau." — *Matériaux pour l'étude des Glaciers*, vol. viii. part i. p. 246, 1868; and vol. viii. part ii. p. 77, 1869.

† In each of the seven nights I passed upon the south-west ridge of the Matterhorn in 1861-'63 (at heights varying from 11,844 to 12,992 feet above the level of the sea), the rocks fell incessantly in showers and avalanches.

by glaciers, but they are *born* from the ridges. They are generated by the sun and delivered by the frost. "Fire," it is well said in Plutarch's life of Camillus, "is the most active thing in nature, and all generation is motion, or at least with motion : all other parts of matter without warmth lie sluggish and dead, and crave the influence of heat as their life, and when that comes upon them they immediately acquire some active or passive qualities." *

If the Alps were granted a perfectly invariable temperature, if they were no longer subjected alternately to freezing blasts and to scorching heat, they might more correctly be termed "eternal." They might continue to decay, but their abasement would be much less rapid.

When rocks are covered by a sheet of glacier they do enjoy an almost invariable temperature. The extremes of summer and winter are unknown to rocks which are so covered up: a range of a very few degrees is the most that is possible underneath the ice.† There is *then* little or no disintegration from unequal expansion and contraction. Frost *then* does not penetrate into the heart of the rock and cleave off vast masses. The rocks *then* sustain grinding instead of cleaving. Atoms *then* come away instead of masses. Fissures and overhanging surfaces are bridged, for the ice cannot get at them ; and after many centuries of grinding have been sustained, we still find numberless angular surfaces (in the *lee-sides*) which were fashioned before the ice began to work.

The points of difference which are so evident between the operations of heat, cold and water, and the action of gla-

ciers upon rocks, are as follow. The former take advantage of cracks, fissures, joints and soft places—the latter does not. The former can work *underneath* overhanging masses—the latter cannot. The effects produced by the former continually increase, because they continually expose fresh surfaces by forming new cracks, fissures and holes. The effects which the latter produces constantly diminish, because the area of the surfaces operated upon becomes less and less as they become smoother and flatter.

What can one conclude, then, but that sun, frost and water have had infinitely more to do than glaciers with the fashioning of mountain-forms and valley-slopes ? Who can refuse to believe that powers which are at work everywhere, which have been at work always, which are so incomparably active, capable and enduring, must have produced greater effects than a solitary power which is always local in its influence, which has worked *comparatively* but for a short time, which is always slow and feeble in its operations, and which constantly diminishes in intensity ? Yet there are some who refuse to believe that sun, frost and water have played an important part in modeling the Alps, and hold it as an article of their faith that the Alpine region "owes its present conformation mainly to the action of its ancient glaciers"! ‡

My reverie was interrupted by Croz observing that it was time to be off. Less than two hours sufficed to take us to the glacier plateau below (where we had left our baggage) : three-quarters of an hour more placed us upon the depression between the Grand Cornier and the Dent Blanche (Col du Grand Cornier), and at 6 P. M. we arrived at Albricolla. Croz and Biener hankered after milk, and descended to a village lower down the valley, but Almer and I stayed where we were, and passed a chilly night on some planks in a half-burnt chalet.

---

* Tonson's ed. of 1758. Bacon may have had this passage in mind when he wrote, "It must not be thought that heat generates motion, or motion heat (though in some respects this be true), but that the very essence of heat, or the substantial self of heat, is motion, and nothing else."—*Novum Organum,* book ii., Devey's translation.

† Doubtless, *at the sides* of glacier-beds the range of temperature is greater. But there is evidence that the winter cold does not penetrate to the innermost recesses of glacier-beds in the fact that streams continue to flow underneath the ice all the year round, winter as well as summer, in the Alps and (I was informed in Greenland) in Greenland. Even in midsummer the bottom temperature is close to 32° Fahr.

‡ Professor Tyndall "On the Conformation of the Alps," *Phil. Mag.,* Sept., 1862.

PART VIII.

CHAPTER XIV.
THE ASCENT OF THE DENT BLANCHE.

CROZ and Biener did not return until past 5 A.M. on June 17, and we then set out at once for Zermatt, intending to cross the Col d'Hérens. But we did not proceed far before the attractions of the Dent Blanche were felt to be irresistible, a n d we turned aside up the steep lateral glacier which descends along its south-western face.

LESLIE STEPHEN.

The Dent Blanche is a mountain little known except to the climbing fraternity. It was, and is, reputed to be one of the most difficult mountains in the Alps. Many attempts were made to scale it before its ascent was accomplished. Even Leslie Stephen himself, fleetest of foot of the whole Alpine brotherhood, once upon a time returned discomfited from it.

It was not climbed until 1862, but in that year Mr. T. S. Kennedy, with Mr. Wigram and the guides Jean B. Croz and Kronig, managed to conquer it.

They had a hard fight, though, before they gained the victory: a furious wind and driving snow, added to the natural difficulties, nearly turned the scale against them.

Mr. Kennedy described his expedition in a very interesting paper in the *Alpine Journal*. His account bore the impress of truth, but unbelievers said that it was impossible to have told (in weather such as was then experienced) whether the summit had actually been attained, and sometimes roundly asserted that the mountain, as the saying is, yet remained virgin.

I did not share these doubts, although they influenced me to make the ascent. I thought it might be possible to find an easier route than that taken by Mr. Kennedy, and that if we succeeded in discovering one we should be able at once to refute his traducers and to vaunt our superior wisdom. Actuated by these elevated motives, I halted my little army at the foot of the glacier, and inquired, "Which is best for us to do?— to ascend the Dent Blanche, or to cross to Zermatt?" They answered, with befitting solemnity, "We think Dent Blanche is best."

From the chalets of Abricolla the south-

THE BERGSCHRUND ON THE DENT BLANCHE IN 1865.

west face of the Dent Blanche is regarded almost exactly in profile. From thence it is seen that the angle of the face scarcely exceeds thirty degrees, and after observing this I concluded that the face would, in all probability, give an easier path to the summit than the crest of the very jagged ridge which was followed by Mr. Kennedy.

We zigzagged up the glacier along the foot of the face, and looked for a way on to it. We looked for some time in vain, for a mighty bergschrund effectually prevented approach, and, like a fortress' moat, protected the wall from assault. We went up and up, until, I suppose, we were not more than a thousand feet below the point marked 3912 mètres: then a bridge was discovered, and we dropped down on hands and knees to cross it.

A bergschrund, it has been said, is a schrund and something more than a schrund. A schrund is simply a big crevasse: a bergschrund is frequently, but not always, a big crevasse. The term is applied to the last of the crevasses one finds, in ascending, before quitting the glacier and taking to the rocks which bound it. It is the mountains' schrund. Sometimes it is *very* large, but early in the season (that is to say, in the month of June or before) bergschrunds are usually snowed up or well bridged over, and do not give much trouble. Later in the year, say in August, they are frequently very great hindrances, and occasionally are completely impassable.

We crossed the bergschrund of the Dent Blanche, I suppose, at a height of about twelve thousand feet above the level of the sea. Our work may be said to have commenced at that point. The face, although not steep in its general inclination, was so cut up by little ridges and cliffs, and so seamed with incipient couloirs, that it had all the difficulty of a much more precipitous slope. The difficulties were never great, but they were numerous, and made a very respectable total when put together. We passed the bergschrund soon after nine in the morning, and during the next eleven

hours halted only five and forty minutes. The whole of the remainder of the time was occupied in ascending and descending the twenty-four hundred feet which compose this south-western face; and inasmuch as one thousand feet per hour (taking the mean of ascent and descent) is an ordinary rate of progression, it is tolerably certain that the Dent Blanche is a mountain of exceptional difficulty.

The hindrances opposed to us by the mountain itself were, however, as nothing compared with the atmospheric obstructions. It is true there was plenty of—"Are you fast, Almer?" "Yes." "Go ahead, Biener." Biener, made secure, cried, "Come on, sir," and *monsieur* endeavored. "No, no," said Almer, "not there—*here!*" pointing with his bâton to the right place to clutch. Then 'twas Croz's turn, and we all drew in the rope as the great man followed. "Forward" once more—and so on.

Five hundred feet of this kind of work had been accomplished when we were saluted (not entirely unexpectedly) by the first gust of a hurricane which was raging above. The day was a lovely one for dwellers in the valleys, but we had long ago noted some light, gossamer clouds that were hovering round our summit, being drawn out in a suspicious manner into long, silky threads. Croz, indeed, prophesied before we had crossed the schrund that we should be beaten by the wind, and had advised that we should return. But I had retorted, "No, my good Croz, you said just now, 'Dent Blanche is best:' we must go up the Dent Blanche."

I have a very lively and disagreeable recollection of this wind. Upon the outskirts of the disturbed region it was only felt occasionally. It then seemed to make rushes at one particular man, and when it had discomfited him, it whisked itself away to some far-off spot, only to return presently in greater force than before.

My old enemy, the Matterhorn, seen across the basin of the Z'Muttgletscher, looked totally unassailable. "Do you think," the men asked, "that you or any one else will ever get up *that* mountain ?" And when, undismayed by their ridicule, I stoutly answered, "Yes, but not upon that side," they burst into derisive chuckles. I must confess that my hopes sank, for nothing can look, or be, more completely inaccessible than the Matterhorn on its northern and north-west sides.

"Forward" once again. We overtopped the Dent d'Hérens. "Not a thousand feet more : in three hours we shall be on the summit." "You mean *ten*," echoed Croz, so slow had been the progress. But I was not far wrong in the estimate. At 3.15 we struck the great ridge followed by Mr. Kennedy, close to the top of the mountain. The wind and cold were terrible there. Progress was oftentimes impossible, and we waited, crouching under the lee of rocks, listening to "the shrieking of the mindless wind," while the blasts swept across, tearing off the upper snow and blowing it away in streamers over the Schönbühl glacier—"nothing seen except an indescribable writhing in the air, like the wind made visible."

Our goal was concealed by the mist, though it was only a few yards away, and Croz's prophecy that we should stay all night upon the summit seemed likely to come true. The men rose with the occasion, although even their fingers had nearly lost sensation. There were no murmurings nor suggestions of return, and they pressed on for the little white cone which they knew must be near at hand. Stopped again—a big mass perched loosely on the ridge barred the way : we could not crawl over and scarcely dared creep round it. The wine went round for the last time. The liquor was half frozen—still we would more of it. It was all gone : the bottle was left behind, and we pushed on, for there was a lull.

The end came almost before it was expected. The clouds opened, and I saw that we were all but upon the highest point, and that between us and it, about twenty yards off, there was a little artificial pile of stones. Kennedy was a true man—it was a cairn which he

had erected. "What is that, Croz ?" "*Homme de pierres*," he bawled. It was needless to proceed farther : I jerked the rope from Biener, and motioned that we would go back. He did the same to Almer, and we turned immediately. *They* did not see the stones (they were cutting footsteps), and misinterpreted the reason of the retreat. Voices were inaudible and explanations impossible.

We commenced the descent of the face. It was hideous work. The men looked like impersonations of Winter, with their hair all frosted and their beards matted with ice. My hands were numbed—dead. I begged the others to stop. "We cannot afford to stop : we must continue to move," was their reply. They were right : to stop was to be entirely frozen. So we went down, gripping rocks varnished with ice, which pulled the skin from the fingers. Gloves were useless : they became iced too, and the bâtons slid through them as slippery as eels. The iron of the axes stuck to the fingers —it felt red hot ; but it was useless to shrink : the rocks and the axes had to be firmly grasped—no faltering would do here.

We turned back at 4.12 P. M., and at 8.15 crossed the bergschrund again, not having halted for a minute upon the entire descent. During the last two hours it was windless, but time was of such vital importance that we pressed on incessantly, and did not stop until we were fairly upon the glacier. Then we took stock of what remained of the tips of our fingers. There was not much skin left : they were perfectly raw, and for weeks afterward I was reminded of the ascent of the Dent Blanche by the twinges which I felt when I pulled on my boots. The others escaped with some slight frost-bites, and altogether we had reason to congratulate ourselves that we got off so lightly. The men complimented me upon the descent, and I could do the same honestly by them. If they had worked less vigorously or harmoniously, we should have been benighted upon the face, where there was not a single spot upon which it was possible to sit ; and if that had happened,

I do not think that one would have survived to tell the tale.

We made the descent of the glacier in a mist, and of the moraine at its base and of the slopes below in total darkness, and regained the chalets of Abricolla at 11.45 P. M. We had been absent eighteen and a half hours, and out of that time had been going not less than seventeen. That night we slept the sleep of those who are thoroughly tired.*

Two days afterward, when walking into Zermatt, whom should we meet but Mr. Kennedy! "Hullo!" we said, "we

T. S. KENNEDY.

have just seen your cairn on the top of the Dent Blanche." "No, you haven't," he answered very positively. "What do you mean?" "Why, that you cannot have seen my cairn, because I didn't make one!" "Well, but we saw *a* cairn." "No doubt: it was made by a man who went up the mountain last year with Lauener and Zurfluh." "O-o-h!" we said, rather disgusted at hearing news when we expected to communicate some —"O-o-h! Good-morning, Kennedy." Before this happened we managed to lose our way upon the Col d'Hérens, but an account of that must be reserved for the next chapter.

* The ascent of the Dent Blanche is the hardest that I have made. There was nothing upon it so difficult as the last five hundred feet of the Pointe des Ecrins, but on the other hand, there was hardly a step upon it which was positively easy. The whole of the face required actual climbing. There was probably very little difference in difficulty between the route we took in 1865 and that followed by Mr. Kennedy in 1862.

CHAPTER XV.

LOST ON THE COL D'HÉRENS.—MY SEVENTH ATTEMPT TO ASCEND THE MATTERHORN.

WE should have started for Zermatt about 7 A. M. on the 18th, had not Biener asked to be allowed to go to mass at Evolène, a village about two and a half hours from Abricolla. He received permission, on the condition that he returned not later than mid-day, but he did not come back until 2.30 P. M., and we thereby got into a pretty little mess.

The pass which we were about to traverse to Zermatt—the Col d'Hérens—is one of the few glacier-passes in this district which have been known almost from time immemorial. It is frequently crossed in the summer season, and is a very easy route, notwithstanding that the summit of the pass is 11,417 feet above the level of the sea.

From Abricolla to the summit the way lies chiefly over the flat Glacier de Ferpècle. The walk is of the most straightforward kind. The glacier rises in gentle undulations, its crevasses are small and easily avoided, and all you have to do, after once getting upon the ice, is to proceed due south in the most direct manner possible. If you do so, in two hours you should be upon the summit of the pass.

We tied ourselves in line, of course, when we entered upon the glacier, and placed Biener to lead, as he had frequently crossed the pass, supposing that his local knowledge might save us some time upon the other side. We had proceeded, I suppose, about halfway up, when a little thin cloud dropped down upon us from above, but it was so light, so gauzy, that we did not for a moment suppose that it would become embarrassing, and hence I neglected to note at the proper moment the course which we should steer—that is to say, to observe our precise situation in regard to the summit of the pass.

For some little time Biener progressed steadily, making a tolerably straight track, but at length he wavered, and deviated sometimes to the right and sometimes to the left. Croz rushed forward directly he saw this, and, taking the poor young man by his shoulders, gave him a good shaking, told him that he was an imbecile, to untie himself at once, and go to the rear. Biener looked half frightened, and obeyed without a murmur. Croz led off briskly, and made a good straight track for a few minutes, but then, it seemed to me, began to move steadily round to the left. I looked back, but the mist was now too thick to see our traces, and so we continued to follow our leader. At last the others (who were behind, and in a better position to judge) thought the same as I did, and we pulled up Croz to deliver our opinion. He took our criticism in good part, but when Biener opened his mouth, that was too much for him to stand, and he told the young man again, "You are imbecile: I bet you twenty francs to one that *my* track is better than *yours* — twenty francs! Now then, imbecile!"

Almer went to the front. He commenced by returning in the track for a hundred yards or so, and then started off at a tangent from Croz's curve. We kept this course for half an hour, and then were certain that we were not on the right route, because the snow became decidedly steep. We bore away more and more to the right to avoid this steep bank, but at last I rebelled, as we had for some time been going almost south-west, which was altogether the wrong direction. After a long discussion we returned some distance in our track, and then steered a little east of south, but we continually met steep snow-slopes, and to avoid them went right or left as the case might require.

We were greatly puzzled, and could not in the least tell whether we were too near the Dent Blanche or too close to the Tête Blanche. The mists had thickened, and were now as dense as a moderate London fog. There were no rocks or echoes to direct us, and the guidance of the compass brought us invariably against these steep snow-banks. The men were fairly beaten: they had all had a try, or more than one, and at last gave it up as a bad job, and asked what was to be done. It was 7.30 P. M., and

only an hour of daylight was left. We were beginning to feel used up, for we had wandered about at tiptop speed for the last three hours and a half; so I said, "This is my advice: let us turn in our track, and go back as hard as ever we can, not quitting the track for an instant." They were well content, but just as we were starting off the clouds lifted a little, and we thought we saw the col. It was then to our right, and we went at it with a dash, but before we had gone a hundred paces down came the mist again. We kept on nevertheless for twenty minutes, and then, as darkness was perceptibly coming on,. and the snow was yet rising in front, we turned back, and by running down the entire distance managed to get clear of the Ferpecle glacier just as it became pitch-dark. We arrived at our cheerless chalet in due course, and went to bed supperless, for our food was gone — all very sulky, not to say savage, agreeing in nothing except in bullying Biener.

At 7 A. M. on the 19th we set out, for the third time, for the Col d'Hérens. It was a fine day, and we gradually recovered our tempers as we saw the follies which had been committed on the previous evening. Biener's wavering track was not so bad, but Croz had swerved from the right route from the first, and had traced a complete semicircle, so that when we stopped him we were facing Abricolla, whence we had started. Almer had commenced with great discretion, but he kept on too long, and crossed the proper route. When I stopped them (because we were going south-west) we were a long way up the Tête Blanche! Our last attempt was in the right direction: we were actually upon the summit of the pass, and in another ten yards we should have commenced to go down hill! It is needless to point out that if the compass had been looked to at the proper moment—that is, immediately the mist came down—we should have avoided all our troubles. It was of little use afterward, except to tell us when we were going *wrong*.

We arrived at Zermatt in six and a half hours' walking from Abricolla, and

CAMP.

THE MATTERHORN FROM THE RIFFELBERG.

Page 121.

Seiler's hospitable reception set us all right again. On the 20th we crossed the Théodule pass, and diverged from its summit up the Théodulhorn (11,391) to examine a route which I suggested for the ascent of the Matterhorn; but before continuing an account of our proceedings, I must stop for a minute to explain why this new route was proposed, in place of that up the south-western ridge.

The Matterhorn may be divided into three sections—the first facing the Z'Mutt-gletscher, which looks, and is, completely unassailable; the second facing the east, which seems inaccessibility itself; the third facing Breuil, which does not look entirely hopeless. It was from this last direction that all my previous attempts were made. It was by the south-western ridge, it will be remembered, that not only I, but Mr. Hawkins, Professor Tyndall and the chasseurs of Val Tournanche, essayed to climb the mountain. Why, then, abandon a route which had been shown to be feasible up to a certain point?

I gave it up for four reasons: 1. On account of my growing disinclination for arêtes, and preference for snow and rock faces. 2. Because I was persuaded that meteorological disturbances (by which we had been baffled several times) might be expected to occur again and again. 3. Because I found that the east face was a gross imposition: it looked not far from perpendicular, while its angle was, in fact, scarcely more than 40°. 4. Because I observed for myself that the strata of the mountain dipped to the west-south-west. It is not necessary to say anything more than has been already said upon the first two of these four points, but upon the latter two a few words are indispensable. Let us consider, first, why most persons receive such an exaggerated impression of the steepness of the eastern face.

When one looks at the Matterhorn from Zermatt, the mountain is regarded (nearly) from the north-east. The face that fronts the east is consequently neither seen in profile nor in full front, but almost halfway between the two: it looks, therefore, more steep than it really is. The majority of those who visit Zermatt go up to the Riffelberg or to the Görnergrat, and from these places the mountain naturally looks still more precipitous, because its eastern face (which is almost all that is seen of it) is viewed more directly in front. From the Riffel hotel the slope seems to be set at an angle of seventy degrees. If the tourist continues to go southward, and crosses the Théodule pass, he gets, at one point, immediately in front of the eastern face, which then seems to be absolutely perpendicular. Comparatively few persons correct the erroneous impressions they receive in these quarters by studying the face in profile, and most go away with a very incorrect and exaggerated idea of the precipitousness of this side of the mountain, because they have considered the question from one point of view alone.

Several years passed away before I shook myself clear of my early and false impressions regarding the steepness of this side of the Matterhorn. First of all, I noticed that there were places on this eastern face where snow remained permanently all the year round. I do not speak of snow in gullies, but of the considerable slopes which are seen in the accompanying engraving about half-way up the face. Such beds as these could not continue to remain throughout the summer unless the snow had been able to accumulate in the winter in large masses; and snow cannot accumulate and remain in large masses, in a situation such as this, at angles much exceeding forty-five degrees.* Hence I was bound to conclude that the eastern face was many degrees removed from perpendicularity; and to be sure on this point, I went to the slopes between the Z'Mutt-gletscher and the Matterhorngletscher, above the chalets of Staffel, whence the face could be seen in profile. Its appearance from this direction would be amazing to one who had seen it only from the east. It looks so totally different from the apparently sheer and perfectly unclimbable cliff one sees from

---

* I prefer to be on the safe side. My impression is, that snow cannot accumulate in large masses *at* forty-five degrees.

the Riffelberg that it is hard to believe the two slopes are one and the same thing. Its angle scarcely exceeds forty degrees.

A great step was made when this was learned. This knowledge alone would not, however, have caused me to try an ascent by the eastern face instead of by the south-west ridge. Forty degrees may not seem a formidable inclination to the reader, nor is it for only a small cliff. But it is very unusual to find so steep a gradient maintained continuously as the general angle of a great mountain-slope, and very few instances can be quoted from the High Alps of such an angle being preserved over a rise of three thousand feet.

l do not think that the steepness or the height of this cliff would have deterred climbers from attempting to ascend it, if it had not, in addition, looked so repulsively smooth. Men despaired of finding anything to grasp. Now, some of the difficulties of the south-west ridge came from the smoothness of the rocks, although that ridge, even from a distance, seemed to be well broken up. How much greater, then, might not have been the difficulty of climbing a face which looked smooth and unbroken close at hand?

A more serious hindrance to mounting the south-west ridge is found in the dip of its rocks to the west-south-west. The great mass of the Matterhorn, it is now well ascertained, is composed of regularly stratified rocks, which rise toward the east. It has been mentioned in the text, more than once, that the rocks on some portions of the ridge leading from the Col du Lion to the summit dip outward, and that fractured edges overhang. This is shown very clearly in the annexed diagram, Fig. I. It will be readily understood that such an arrangement is not favorable for climbers, and that the degree of facility

Fig. 1.

with which rocks can be ascended that are so disposed must depend very much upon the frequency or paucity of fissures and joints. The rocks of the south-west ridge are sufficiently provided with cracks, but if it were otherwise, their texture and arrangement would render them unassailable.*

It is not possible to go a single time upon the rocks of the south-west ridge, from the Col du Lion to the foot of the Great Tower, without observing the prevalence of their outward dip, and that their fractured edges have a tendency to overhang; nor can one fail to notice that it is upon this account the débris which is rent off by frost does not remain *in situ*, but pours down in showers over the surrounding cliffs. Each day's work, so to speak, is cleared away —the ridge is swept clean: there is scarcely anything seen but firm rock.†

The fact that the mountain is composed of a series of stratified beds was pointed out long ago. De Saussure remarked it, and recorded explicitly in his *Travels* (§ 2243) that they "rose to the north-east at an angle of about forty-five degrees." Forbes noticed it also, but gave it as his opinion that the beds were "less inclined, or nearly horizontal." He added, "De Saussure is no doubt correct." The truth, I think, lies between the two.

I was acquainted with both of the above-quoted passages, but did not turn the knowledge to any practical account until I re-observed the same fact for myself. It was not until after my repulse in 1863 that I referred the peculiar difficulties of the south-west ridge to the dip of the strata, but when once persuaded that structure and not texture was the real impediment, it was reasonable to infer that the opposite side—that is to

---

* Weathered granite is an admirable rock to climb, its gritty texture giving excellent hold to the nails in one's boots. But upon such metamorphic schists as compose the mass of the great peak of the Matterhorn the texture of the rock itself is of no value.

† I refer here only to that portion of the ridge which is between the Col du Lion and the Great Tower. The remarks would not apply to the rocks higher up; higher still the rocks are firm again; yet higher (upon the "Shoulder") they are much disintegrated; and then, upon the final peak, they are again firm.

say, the eastern face—might be comparatively easy; in brief, that an arrangement should
be found like
Fig. 2, instead
of like Fig. 1.
This trivial
deduction was
the key to the
ascent of the
Matterhorn.

Fig. 2.

The point
was, Did the strata continue with a similar dip throughout the mountain? If
they did, then this great eastern face,
instead of being hopelessly impracticable, should be quite the reverse. In
fact, it should be a great natural staircase, with steps inclining inward; and
if it were so, its smooth aspect might be
of no account, for the smallest steps, inclined in this fashion, would afford good
footing.

They did so, so far as one could judge
from a distance. When snow fell in the
summer-time, it brought out long terraced
lines upon the mountain, rudely parallel
to each other; and the eastern face on
those occasions was often whitened almost completely over; while the other
sides, with the exception of the powder-
ed terraces, remained black, for the snow
could not rest upon them.

The very outline of the mountain, too,
confirmed the conjecture that its structure would assist an ascent on the eastern face, although it opposed one on all
other sides. Look at any photograph
of the peak from the north-east, and
you will see that upon the right-hand
side (that facing the Z'Muttgletscher)
there is an incessant repetition of overhanging cliffs and of slopes, all trending
downward; in short, that the character of
the whole of that side is similar to Fig. 1,
p. 122; and that upon the left hand (or
south-east) ridge the forms, so far as they
go, are suggestive of the structure shown
by Fig. 2, above. There is no doubt
that the contours of the mountain, seen
from this direction, have been largely influenced by the direction of its beds.

It was not therefore from a freak that
I invited Mr. Reilly to join in an attack

upon the eastern face, but from a grad-
ually-acquired conviction that it would
prove to give the easiest path to the
summit; and if we had not been obliged
to part the mountain would doubtless
have been ascended in 1864.

My guides readily admitted that they
had been greatly deceived as to the
steepness of the eastern face, when they
were halted to look at it in profile as we
came down the Z'Muttgletscher on our
way to Zermatt, but they were far from
being satisfied that it would turn out to
be easy to climb, and Almer and Biener
expressed themselves decidedly averse
to making an attempt upon it. I gave
way temporarily before their evident reluctance, and we made the ascent of the
Théodulhorn to examine an alternative
route, which I expected would commend
itself to them in preference to the other,
as a great part of it led over snow.

There is an immense gully in the Matterhorn which leads up from the Glacier
du Mont Cervin to a point high up on
the south-eastern ridge. I proposed to
ascend this to its head, and to cross over
the south-east ridge on to the eastern
face. This would have brought us on
a level with the bottom of the great snow-
slope shown upon the centre of the eastern face in the engraving. This snow-
slope was to be crossed diagonally, with
the view of arriving at the snow upon
the north-east ridge, which is shown
upon the same engraving about half an
inch from the summit. The remainder
of the ascent was to be made by the
broken rocks, mixed with snow, upon
the north side of the mountain. Croz
caught the idea immediately, and thought
the plan feasible: details were settled,
and we descended to Breuil. Luc Meynet the hunchback was summoned, and
expressed himself delighted to resume
his old vocation of tent-bearer; and
Favre's kitchen was soon in commotion
preparing three days' rations, for I intended to take that amount of time over
the affair—to sleep on the first night
upon the rocks at the top of the gully, to
make a push for the summit, and to return to the tent on the second day; and
upon the third to come back to Breuil.

We started at 5.45 A. M. on June 21, and followed the route of the Breuiljoch for three hours. We were then in full view of our gully, and turned off at right angles for it. The closer we approached the more favorable did it look. There was a good deal of snow in it, which was evidently at a small angle, and it seemed as if one-third of the ascent, at least, would be a very simple matter. Some suspicious marks in the snow at its base suggested that it was not free from falling stones, and as a measure of precaution we turned off on one side, worked up under cover of the cliffs, and waited to see if anything should descend. Nothing fell, so we proceeded up its right or northern side, sometimes cutting steps up the snow, and sometimes mounting by the rocks. Shortly before 10 A. M. we arrived at a convenient place for a halt, and stopped to rest upon some rocks close to the snow which commanded an excellent view of the gully.

While the men were unpacking the food I went to a little promontory to examine our proposed route more narrowly, and to admire our noble couloir, which led straight up into the heart of the mountain for fully one thousand feet. It then bent toward the north, and ran up to the crest of the south-eastern ridge. My curiosity was piqued to know what was round this corner, and whilst I was gazing up at it, and following with the eye the exquisitely drawn curves which wandered down the snow in the gully, all converging to a large rut in its centre, I saw a few little stones skidding down. I consoled myself with thinking that they would not interfere with us if we adhered to the side. But then a larger one came down, a solitary fellow, rushing at the rate of sixty miles an hour— and another—and another. I was unwilling to raise the fears of the men unnecessarily, and said nothing to them. They did not hear the stones. Almer was seated on a rock, carving large slices from a leg of mutton, the others were chatting, and the first intimation they had of danger was from a crash, a sudden roar, which reverberated awfully

amongst the cliffs ; and looking up they saw rocks, boulders and stones, big and little, dart round the corner eight hundred feet or so above us, fly with fearful fury against the opposite cliffs, rebound from them against the walls on our side, and descend ; some ricochetting from side to side in a frantic manner, some bounding down in leaps of a hundred feet or more over the snow, and more trailing down in a jumbled, confused mass, mixed with snow and ice, deepening the grooves which a moment before had excited my admiration.

The men looked wildly around for protection, and, dropping the food, dashed under cover in all directions. The precious mutton was pitched on one side, the wine-bag was let fall, and its contents gushed out from the unclosed neck, while all four cowered under defending rocks, endeavoring to make themselves as small as possible. Let it not be supposed that their fright was unreasonable or that I was free from it. I took good care to make myself safe, and went and cringed in a cleft until the storm had passed. But their scramble to get under shelter was indescribably ludicrous. Such a panic I have never witnessed, before or since, upon a mountain-side.

This ricochet practice was a novelty to me. It arose, of course, from the couloir being bent, and from the falling rocks having acquired great pace before they passed the angle. In straight gullies it will probably never be experienced. The rule is, as I have already remarked, that falling stones keep down the centres of gullies, and you are out of harm's way if you follow the sides.

There would have been singularly little amusement and very great risk in mounting this gully, and we turned our backs upon it with perfect unanimity. The question then arose, "What is to be done ?" I suggested climbing the rocks above us, but this was voted impossible. I thought the men were right, but would not give in without being assured of the fact, and clambered up to settle the question. In a few minutes I was brought to a halt. My forces were scattered : the little hunchback alone was closely following me, with a broad grin upon his face and the tent upon his shoulder; Croz, more behind, was still keeping an eye upon his monsieur; Almer, a hundred feet below, sat on a rock with his face buried in his hands; Biener was nowhere, out of sight. "Come down, come down," shouted Croz, "it is useless;" and I turned at length, convinced that it was even as he said. Thus my little plan was knocked on the head, and we were thrown back upon the original scheme.

We at once made a straight track for Mr. Morshead's Breuiljoch (which was the most direct route to take in order to get to the Hörnli, where we intended to sleep, preparatory to attacking the eastern face), and arrived upon its summit at 12.30 P. M. We were then unexpectedly checked. The pass, as one, had vanished! and we found ourselves cut off from the Furggengletscher by a small but precipitous wall of rock: the glacier had shrunk so much that descent was impracticable. During the last hour clouds had been coming up from the south: they now surrounded us, and it began to blow hard. The men clustered together, and advocated leaving the mountain alone. Almer asked, with more point than politeness, "Why don't

MY TENT-BEARER—THE HUNCHBACK.

you try to go up a mountain which *can* be ascended?" "It is impossible," chimed in Biener. "Sir," said Croz, "if we cross to the other side we shall lose three days, and very likely shall not succeed. You want to make ascents in the chain of Mont Blanc, and I believe they can be made. But I shall not be able to make them with you if I spend these days here, for I must be at Chamounix on the 27th." There was force in what he said, and his words made me hesitate. I relied upon his strong arms for some work which it was expected would be unusually difficult. Snow began to fall: that settled the matter, and

I gave the word to retreat. We went back to Breuil, and on to Val Tournanche, where we slept; and the next day proceeded to Chatillon, and thence up the valley of Aosto to Cormayeur.

I cannot but regret that the counsels of the guides prevailed. If Croz had not uttered his well-intentioned words he might still have been living. He parted from us at Chamounix at the appointed time, but by a strange chance we met again at Zermatt three weeks later; and two days afterward he perished before my eyes on the very mountain from which we turned away, at his advice on the 21st of June.

PART IX.

CHAPTER XVI.

VALLEY OF AOSTA, AND ASCENT OF THE GRANDES JORASSES.

THE valley of Aosta is famous for its bouquetins and infamous for its cretins. The bouquetin, steinbock, or ibex, was formerly widely distributed throughout the Alps. It is now confined almost entirely, or absolutely, to a small district in the south of the valley of Aosta, and fears have been repeatedly expressed in late years that it will speedily become extinct.

But the most sanguine person does not imagine that cretinism will be eradicated for many generations. It is widely spread throughout the Alps, it is by no means peculiar to the valley of Aosta, but nowhere does it thrust itself more frequently upon the attention of the traveler, and in no valley where "every prospect pleases" is one so often and so painfully reminded that "only man is vile."

It seems premature to fear that the bouquetins will soon become extinct. It is not easy to take a census of them, for, although they have local habitations, it is extremely difficult to find them at home. But there is good reason to believe that there are at least six hundred still roaming over the mountains in the neighborhood of the valleys of Grisanche, Rhèmes, Savaranche and Cogne.

It would be a pity if it were otherwise. They appeal to the sympathies of all as the remnants of a diminishing race, and no mountaineer or athletic person could witness without sorrow the extinction of an animal possessing such noble qualities; which a few months after birth can jump over a man's head at a bound, without taking a run; which passes its whole life in a constant fight for existence; which has such a keen appreciation of the beauties of Nature, and such disregard of pain, that it will "stand for hours like a statue in the midst of the bitterest storm, until the tips of its ears are frozen"! and which, when its last hour arrives, "climbs to the highest mountain-peaks, hangs on a rock with its horns, twists itself round and round upon them until they are worn off, and then falls down and expires"!!* Even Tschudi himself calls this story wonderful. He may well do so. I disclaim belief in it —the bouquetin is too fine a beast to indulge in such antics.

Forty-five keepers, selected from the most able chasseurs of the district, guard

* Tschudi's *Sketches of Nature in the Alps.*

126

its haunts. Their task is not a light one, although they are naturally acquainted with those who are most likely to attempt poaching. If they were withdrawn, it would not be long before the ibex would be an extinct wild animal, so far as the Alps are concerned. The passion for killing something, and the present value of the beast itself, would soon lead to its extermination. For as meat alone the

THE BOUQUETIN.

bouquetin is valuable, the gross weight of one that is full grown amounting to from one hundred and sixty to two hundred pounds, while its skin and horns are worth ten pounds and upward, according to condition and dimensions.

In spite of the keepers, and of the severe penalties which may be inflicted for killing a bouquetin, poaching occurs constantly. Knowing that this was the case, I inquired at Aosta, upon my last visit, if any skins or horns were for sale, and in ten minutes was taken into a garret where the remains of a splendid beast were concealed — a magnificent male, presumed to be more than twenty years old, as its massive horns had twenty-two more or less strongly-marked knobby rings. The extreme length of the skin, from the tip of the nose to the end of the tail, was one mètre sixty-nine centimètres (about five feet seven inches), and from the ground to the top of its back had been, apparently, about seventy-seven centimètres. It is rare to meet with a bouquetin of these dimensions, and the owner of this skin might have been visited with several years' imprisonment if it had been known that it was in his possession.

The chase of the bouquetin is properly considered a sport fit for a king, and His Majesty Victor Emmanuel, for whom it is reserved, is too good a sportsman to slaughter indiscriminately an animal which is an ornament to his domains. Last year (1869) seventeen fell to his gun at one hundred yards and upward. In 1868, His Majesty presented a fine specimen to the Italian Alpine Club. The members banqueted, I believe, upon its flesh, and they have had the skin stuffed and set up in their rooms at Aosta. It is said by connoisseurs to be badly stuffed—that it is not broad enough in the chest and is too large behind. Still, it looks well-proportioned, although it seems made for hard work rather than for feats of agility. From this specimen the accompanying engraving has been made.

It is a full-grown male about twelve years old, and if it stood upright would measure three feet three and a half inches from the ground to the base of its horns. Its extreme length is four feet seven inches. Its horns have eleven well-marked rings, besides one or two faintly-marked ones, and are (measured round their curvature) fifty-four and a half centimètres in length. The horns of the first-mentioned specimen (measured in the same way) had a length of only fifty-three and a half centimètres, although they were ornamented with nearly double the number of rings, and were presumably of double the age, of the other.*

The keepers and the chasseurs of this district not only say that the rings upon the horns of the ibex tell its age (each one reckoning as a year), but that the half-developed ones, which sometimes are very feebly marked indeed, show that the animal has suffered from hunger during the winter. Naturalists are skeptical upon this point, but inasmuch as they offer no better reason against the reputed fact than the natives do in its favor (one saying that it is not so, and the other saying that it is so), we may perhaps be permitted to consider it an open question. I can only say that if the faintly-marked rings do denote years of famine, the times for the bouquetin are very hard indeed; since in most of the horns which I have seen the lesser rings have been very numerous, and sometimes more plentiful than the prominent ones.

The chef of the keepers (who judges by the above-mentioned indications) tells me that the ibex not unfrequently arrives at the age of thirty years, and sometimes to forty or forty-five. He says, too, that it is not fond of traversing steep snow, and in descending a couloir that is filled with it will zig-zag down, by springing from one side to the other in leaps of fifty feet at a time! Jean Tairraz, the worthy landlord of the Hôtel du Mont Blanc at Aosta (who has had opportunities of observing the animal closely), assures me that at the age of four or five months it can easily

clear a height of nine or ten feet at a bound!

Long live the bouquetin! and long may its chase preserve the health of the mountaineering king, Victor Emmanuel! Long life to the bouquetin! but down with the cretin!

The peculiar form of idiocy which is called cretinism is so highly developed in the valley of Aosta, and the natives are so familiarized with it, that they are almost indignant when the surprised traveler remarks its frequency. One is continually reminded that it is not peculiar to the valley, and that there are cretins elsewhere. It is too true that this terrible scourge is widespread throughout the Alps and over the world, and that there are places where the proportion of cretins to population is, or has been, even greater than in the valley of Aosta; but I have never seen or heard of a valley so fertile and so charming —of one which, apart from cretinism, leaves so agreeable an impression upon the wayfarer—where equal numbers are reduced to a condition which any respectable ape might despise.

The whole subject of cretinism is surrounded with difficulty. The number of those who are afflicted by it is unknown, its cure is doubtful, and its origin is mysterious. It has puzzled the most acute observers, and every general statement in regard to it must be fenced by qualifications.

It is tolerably certain, however, that the centre of its distribution in the valley of Aosta is about the centre of the valley. The city of Aosta itself may be regarded as its head-quarters. It is there, and in the neighboring towns of Gignod, Villeneuve, St. Vincent and Verrex, and in the villages and upon the high-road between those places, that these distorted, mindless beings, more like brutes than men, commonly excite one's disgust by their hideous, loathsome and uncouth appearance, by their obscene gestures and by their senseless gabbling. The accompanying portrait of one is by no means overdrawn: some are too frightful for representation.

How can we account for this partic-

---

* Mr. King, in his *Italian Valleys of the Alps*, says, "In the pair [of horns] I possess, which are *two feet* long, there are eight of these yearly rings." It would seem, therefore (if the rings are annual ones), that the maximum length of horn is attained at a comparatively early age.

ular intensity toward the middle of the valley? Why is it that cretins become more and more numerous after Ivrea is passed, attain their highest ratio and lowest degradation at or about the chief town of the valley, and then diminish in numbers as its upper termination is approached? This maximum of intensity must certainly point to a cause, or to a combination of causes, operating about Aosta, which are less powerful at the two extremities of the valley; and if the reason for it could be determined, the springs of cretinism would be exposed.

The disease would be even more puz-

A CRETIN OF AOSTA.

zling than it is if it were confined to this single locality, and the inquirer were to find not merely that it was almost unknown upon the plains to the east and in the districts to the west, but that the valleys radiating north and south from the main valley were practically unaffected by it. For it is a remarkable circumstance, which has attracted the notice of all who have paid attention to cretinism, that the natives of the tributary valleys are almost free from the malady — that people of the same race, speaking the same language, breathing the same air, eating the same food, and

living the same life, enjoy almost entire immunity from it, while at the distance of a very few miles thousands of others are completely in its power.

A parallel case is found, however, on the other side of the Pennine Alps. The Rhone valley is almost equally disfigured by cretinism, and in it, too, the extremities of the valley are slightly affected compared with the intermediate districts —particularly those between Brieg and St. Maurice.* This second example strengthens the conviction that the great development of cretinism in the middle of the valley of Aosta is not the result of accidental circumstances.

It was formerly supposed that cretinism arose from the habitual drinking of snow- and glacier-water. De Saussure opposed to this conjecture the facts that the disease was entirely unknown precisely in those places where the inhabitants were most dependent upon these kinds of water, and that it was most common where such was not the case — that the high valleys were untainted, while the low ones were infected. The notion seems to have proceeded from cretins being confounded with persons who were merely goitred, or at least from the supposition that goitre was an incipient stage of cretinism.

Goitre, it is now well ascertained, is induced by the use of chemically impure water, and especially hard water; and the investigations of various observers have discovered that goitre has an intimate connection with certain geological formations. In harmony with these facts it is found that infants are seldom born with goitres, but that they develop as the child grows up, that they will sometimes appear and disappear from mere change of locality, and that it is possible to produce them intentionally.

It is not so certain that the causes which produce goitre should be regarded

* It was stated a few years ago that one in twenty-five of the natives of the Canton Valais (which is chiefly occupied by the valley of the Upper Rhone) were cretins. This would give about thirty-five hundred to the canton. At the same time the valley of Aosta contained about two thousand cretins.

9

as causes of the production or maintenance of cretinism. It is true that cretins are very generally goitrous, but it is also true that there are tens of thousands of goitrous persons who are entirely free from all traces of cretinism. Not only so, but that there are districts in the Alps and outside of them (even in our own country) where goitre is not rare, but where the cretin is unknown. Still, regarding the evil state of body which leads to goitre as being, possibly, in alliance with cretinism, it will not be irrelevant to give the former disease a little more attention before continuing the consideration of the main subject.

In this country the possession of a goitre is considered a misfortune rather than otherwise, and individuals who are afflicted with these appendages attempt to conceal their shame. In the Alps it is quite the reverse. In France, Italy and Switzerland it is a positive advantage to be goitred, as it secures exemption from military service. A goitre is a thing to be prized, exhibited, preserved —it is worth so much hard cash ; and it is an unquestionable fact that the perpetuation of the great goitrous family is assisted by this very circumstance.

When Savoy was annexed to France the administration took stock of the resources of its new territory, and soon discovered that although the acres were many the conscripts would be few. The government bestirred itself to amend this state of affairs, and after arriving at the conclusion that goitre was produced by drinking bad water (and that its production was promoted by sottish and bestial habits), took measures to cleanse the villages, to analyze the waters (in order to point out those which should not be drunk), and to give to children who came to school lozenges containing small doses of iodine. It is said that out of five thousand goitrous children who were so treated in the course of eight years, two thousand were cured, and the condition of two thousand others was improved ; and that the number of cures would have been greater if the parents "had not opposed the care of the government, *in order to preserve the priv-*

ilege of exemption from military service." These benighted creatures refused the marshal's bâton and preferred their "wallets of flesh !"

No wonder that the préfet for Haute-Savoie proposes that goitrous persons shall no longer be privileged. Let him go farther, and obtain a decree that all of them capable of bearing arms shall be immediately drafted into the army. Let them be formed into regiments by themselves, brigaded together and commanded by cretins. Think what *esprit de corps* they would have ! Who could stand against them ? Who would understand their tactics ? He would save his iodine and would render an act of justice to the non-goitred population. The subject is worthy of serious attention. If goitre is really an ally of cretinism, the sooner it is eradicated the better.

De Saussure substituted heat and stagnation of air as the cause of cretinism, in the place of badness of water. But this was only giving up one unsatisfactory explanation for another equally untenable ; and since there are places far hotter and with pernicious atmospheres where the disease is unknown, while, on the other hand, there are situations in which it is common where the heat is not excessive, and which enjoy a freely circulating atmosphere, his assumption may be set aside as insufficient to account for the cretinism of the valley of Aosta. And in regard to its particular case it may be questioned whether there is anything more than an imaginary stagnation of air. For my own part, I attribute the oppression which strangers say they feel in the middle of the valley not to stagnation of air, but to absence of shadow in consequence of the valley's course being east and west ; and believe that if the force of the wind were observed and estimated according to the methods in common use, it would be found that there is no deficiency of motion in the air throughout the entire year. Several towns and villages, moreover, where cretins are most numerous, are placed at the entrances of valleys and upon elevated slopes, with abundant natural facilities for drainage—free from malaria, which has been suggested as accounting for the cretinism of the Rhone valley.

Others have imagined that intemperance, poor living, foul habits and personal uncleanliness sow the seeds of cretinism ; and this opinion is entitled to full consideration. Intemperance of divers kinds is fruitful in the production of insanity, and herding together in filthy dwellings, with little or no ventilation, may possibly deteriorate *physique* as much as extreme indulgence may the mind. These ideas are popularly entertained, because cretins are more numerous among the lower orders than among the well-to-do classes. Yet they must, each and all, be regarded as inadequate to account for the disease, still less to explain its excess in the centre of the valley; for in these respects there is little or no distinction between it, the two extremities and the neighboring districts.

A conjecture remains to be considered regarding the origin of cretinism which is floating in the minds of many persons (although it is seldom expressed), which carries with it an air of probability that is wanting in the other explanations, and which is supported by admitted facts.

The fertility of the valley of Aosta is proverbial. It is covered with vineyards and cornfields, flocks and herds abound in it, and its mineral resources are great. There is enough and to spare both for man and beast. There are poor in the valley, as there are everywhere, but life is so far easy that they are not driven to seek for subsistence in other places, and remain from generation to generation rooted to their native soil. The large numbers of persons who are found in this valley having the same surnames is a proof of the well-known fact that there is little or no emigration from the valley, and that there is an indefinite amount of intermarriage between the natives. It is conjectured that the continuance of these conditions through a long period has rendered the population more or less consanguineous, and that we see in cretinism an example; upon a large scale, of the evil effects of alliances of kindred.

This explanation commends itself by reason of its general applicability to cretinism. The disease is commonly found in valleys, on islands or in other circumscribed areas in which circulation is restricted or the inhabitants are non-migratory ; and it is rare on plains, where communications are free. It will at once be asked, " Why, then, are not the tributary valleys of the valley of Aosta full of cretins ?" The answer is, that these lateral valleys are comparatively sterile, and are unable to support their population from their internal resources. Large numbers annually leave and do not return—some come back, having formed alliances elsewhere. There is a constant circulation and introduction of new blood. I am not aware that there are returns to show the extent to which this goes on, but the fact is notorious.

This conjecture explains, far better than the other guesses, why it is that cretinism has so strong a hold upon the lower classes, while it leaves the upper ones almost untouched ; for the former are most likely to intermarry with people of their own district, whilst the latter are under no sort of compulsion in this respect. It gives a clue, too, to the reason of the particular intensity in the centre of the valley. The inhabitants of the lower extremity communicate and mix with the untainted dwellers on the plains, whilst the conditions at the upper extremity approximate to those of the lateral valleys. Before this explanation will be generally received a closer connection will have to be established between the assumed cause and the presumed effect. Accepting it, nevertheless, as a probable and reasonable one, let us now consider what prospect there is of checking the progress of the disease.

It is, of course, impossible to change the habits of the natives of the valley of Aosta suddenly, and it would probably be very difficult to cause any large amount of emigration or immigration. In the present embarrassed condition of Italian finances there is very small chance of any measure of the sort being undertaken if it would involve a considerable expenditure. The opening of a railway from Ivrea to Aosta might possibly bring about, in a natural way, more movement than would be promoted by any legislation, and by this means the happiest effects might be produced.

There is little hope of practical results from attempts to cure cretins. Once a cretin, you are always one. The experiments of the late Dr. Guggenbühl demonstrated that some *half*-cretins may even become useful members of society if they are taken in hand early in life, but they did not show that the nature of the true or complete cretin could be altered. He essayed to modify some of the mildest forms of cretinism, but did not strike at the root of the evil. If fifty Guggenbühls were at work in the single valley of Aosta, they would take several generations to produce an appreciable effect, and they would never extirpate the disease so long as its sources were unassailed.

Nor will the house which has been built at Aosta to contain two hundred cretin beggars do much, unless the inmates are restrained from perpetuating their own degradation. Even the lowest types of cretins may be procreative, and it is said that the unlimited liberty which is allowed to them has caused infinite mischief. A large proportion of the cretins who will be born in the next generation will undoubtedly be offspring of cretin parents. It is strange that self-interest does not lead the natives of Aosta to place their cretins under such restrictions as would prevent their illicit intercourse; and it is still more surprising to find the Catholic Church actually legalizing their marriage. There is something horribly grotesque in the idea of *solemnizing* the union of a brace of idiots; and since it is well known that the disease is hereditary, and develops in successive generations, the fact that such marriages are sanctioned is scandalous and infamous.

The supply, therefore, is kept up from two sources. The first contingent is derived from apparently healthy parents;

the second, by inheritance from diseased persons. The origin of the first is obscure; and before its quota can be cut off, or even diminished, the mystery which envelops it must be dissipated. The remedy for the second is obvious, and is in the hands of the authorities, particularly in those of the clergy. Marriage must be prohibited to all who are affected, the most extreme cases must be placed under restraint, and cretins whose origin is illegitimate must be subject to disabilities. Nothing short of the adoption of these measures will meet the case. Useless it will be, so long as the primary sources of the disease are untouched, to build hospitals, to cleanse dwellings, to widen streets, or to attempt small ameliorations of the social circumstances of the natives. All of these things are good enough in themselves, but they are wholly impotent to effect a radical change.

No satisfactory conclusion will be arrived at regarding the origin of cretinism until the pedigrees of a large number of examples have been traced. The numerical test is the only one which is likely to discover the reality. The necessary inquiries are beyond the powers of private persons, and their pursuit will be found sufficiently difficult by official investigators. Great reluctance will be exhibited to disclose the information which should be sought, and the common cry will certainly be raised that such scrutiny is without general advantage and is painful to private feelings. But in matters which affect mankind in general, individual feelings must always be subordinated to the public interest; and if the truth is to be arrived at in regard to cretinism, the protests of the ignorant will have to be overridden.

Cretinism is the least agreeable feature of the valley of Aosta, but it is, at the same time, the most striking. It has been touched upon for the sake of its human interest, and on account of those unhappy beings who—punished by the errors of their fathers—are powerless to help themselves; the first sight of whom produced such an impression upon the most earnest of all Alpine writers that

THE GRANDES JORASSES AND THE DOIRE TORRENT, VAL FERRET (D'ITALIE).

Page 133.

he declared, in a twice-repeated expression, its recollection would never be effaced from his memory.

On the 23d of June, 1865, my guides and I were reposing upon the top of Mont Saxe, scanning the Grandes Jorasses with a view to ascending it. Five thousand feet of glacier-covered precipices rose above us, and up all that height we tracked a way to our satisfaction. Three thousand feet more of glacier and forest-covered slopes lay beneath, and *there*, there was only one point at which it was doubtful if we should find a path. The glaciers were shrinking, and were surrounded by bastions of rounded rock, far too polished to please the rough mountaineer. We could not track a way across them. However, at 4 A. M. the next day, under the dexterous leading of Michael Croz, we passed the doubtful spot. Thence it was all plain sailing, and at 1 P. M. we gained the summit. The weather was boisterous in the upper regions, and storm-clouds driven before the wind and wrecked against our heights enveloped us in misty spray, which danced around and fled away, which cut us off from the material universe, and caused us to be, as it were, suspended betwixt heaven and earth, seeing both occasionally, but seeming to belong to neither.

The mists lasted longer than my patience, and we descended without having attained the object for which the ascent was made. At first we followed the little ridge shown upon the accompanying engraving (The Grandes Jorasses from the Val Ferret), leading from our summit toward the spectator, and then took to the head of the corridor of glacier on its left, which in the view is left perfectly white. The slopes were steep and covered with new-fallen snow, flour-like and evil to tread upon. On the ascent we had reviled it, and had made our staircase with much caution, knowing full well that the disturbance of its base would bring down all that was above. In descending, the bolder spirits counseled trusting to luck and a glissade: the cautious ones advocated

avoiding the slopes and crossing to the rocks on their farther side. The advice of the latter prevailed, and we had half traversed the snow to gain the ridge when the crust slipped and we went along with it. "Halt!" broke from all four unanimously. The axe-heads flew round as we started on this involuntary glissade. It was useless—they slid over the underlying ice fruitlessly. "Halt!" thundered Croz, as he dashed his weapon in again with superhuman energy. No halt could be made, and we slid down slowly, but with accelerating motion, driving up waves of snow in front, with streams of the nasty stuff hissing all around. Luckily, the slope eased off at one place, the leading men cleverly jumped aside out of the moving snow, we others followed, and the young avalanche which we had started, continuing to pour down, fell into a yawning crevasse, and showed us where our grave would have been if we had remained in its company five seconds longer. The whole affair did not occupy half a minute. It was the solitary incident of a long day, and at nightfall we re-entered the excellent house kept by the courteous Bertolini, well satisfied that we had not met with more incidents of a similar description.

CHAPTER XVII.

THE COL DOLENT.

FREETHINKING mountaineers have been latterly in the habit of going up one side of an alp and coming down the other, and calling the route a pass. In this confusion of ideas may be recognized the result of the looseness of thought which arises from the absence of technical education. The true believer abhors such heresies, and observes with satisfaction that Providence oftentimes punishes the offenders for their greediness by causing them to be benighted. The faithful know that passes must be made between mountains, and not over their tops. Their creed declares that between any two mountains there *must* be a pass, and they believe that the end for which big peaks were created —the office they are especially designed to fulfill—is to point out the way one should go. This is the true faith, and there is no other.

We set out upon the 26th of June to endeavor to add one more to the passes which are strictly orthodox. We hoped, rather than expected, to discover a quicker route from Courmayeur to Chamounix than the Col du Géant, which was the easiest, quickest and most direct pass known at the time across the main chain of Mont Blanc. The misgivings which I had as to the result caused us to start at the unusual hour of 12.40 A. M. At 4.30 we passed the chalets of Pré du Bar, and thence, for some distance, followed the track which we had made upon the ascent of Mont Dolent, over the glacier of the same name. At a quarter-past eight we arrived at the head of the glacier, and at the foot of the only steep gradient upon the whole of the ascent.

It was the beau-ideal of a pass. There was a gap in the mountains, with a big peak on each side (Mont Dolent and the Aiguille de Triolet). A narrow thread of snow led up to the lowest point between those mountains, and the blue sky beyond said, Directly you arrive here you will begin to go down. We addressed ourselves to our task, and at 10.15 A. M. arrived at the top of the pass.

Had things gone as they ought, within six hours more we should have been at Chamounix. Upon the other side we knew that there was a couloir in correspondence with that up which we had just come. If it had been filled with snow, all would have been well: it turned out to be filled with ice. Croz, who led, passed over to the other side, and reported that we should get down somehow, but I knew from the sound of his axe how the *somehow* would be, and settled myself to sketch, well assured that *I* should not be wanted for an hour to come. What I saw is shown in the engraving—a sharp aiguille (nameless), perhaps the sharpest in the whole range, backed on the left by the Aiguille de Triolet; queer blocks of (probably) pro-

togine sticking out awkwardly through the snow; and a huge cornice from which big icicles depended, that broke away occasionally and went skiddling down the slope up which we had come. Of the Argentière side I could not see anything.

Croz was tied up with our good manila rope, and the whole two hundred feet were paid out gradually by Almer and Biener before he ceased working. After two hours' incessant toil, he was able to anchor himself to the rock on his right. He then untied himself, the rope was drawn in, Biener was attached to the end and went down to join his comrade. There was then room enough for me to stand by the side of Almer, and I got my first view of the other side. For the first and only time in my life I looked down a slope of more than a thousand feet long, set at an angle of about fifty degrees, which was a sheet of ice from top to bottom. It was unbroken by rock or crag, and anything thrown down it sped away unarrested until the level of the Glacier d'Argentière was reached. The entire basin of that noble glacier was spread out at our feet, and the ridge beyond, culminating in the Aiguille d'Argentiere, was seen to the greatest advantage. I confess, however, that I paid very little attention to the view, for there was no time to indulge in such luxuries. I descended the icy staircase and joined the others, and then we three drew in the rope tenderly as Almer came down. His was not an enviable position, but he descended with as much steadiness as if his whole life had been passed on ice-slopes of fifty degrees. The process was repeated, Croz again going to the front, and availing himself very skillfully of the rocks which projected from the cliff on our right. Our two hundred feet of rope again came to an end, and we again descended one by one. From this point we were able to clamber down by the rocks alone for about three hundred feet. They then became sheer cliff, and we stopped for dinner, about 2.30 P. M., at the last place upon which we could sit. Four hours' incessant work had brought

THE SUMMIT OF THE COL DOLENT.

Page 134.

us rather more than halfway down the gully. We were now approaching, although we were still high above, the schrunds at its base, and the guides made out, in some way unknown to me, that Nature had perversely placed the only snow-bridge across the topmost one toward the centre of the gully. It was decided to cut diagonally across the gully to the point where the snow-bridge was supposed to be. Almer and Biener undertook the work, leaving Croz and

MY ICE-AXE.

myself firmly planted on the rocks to pay out rope to them as they advanced.

It is generally admitted that veritable ice-slopes (understanding by *ice* something more than a crust of hard snow over soft snow) are only rarely met with in the Alps. They are frequently spoken of, but such as that to which I refer are *very* rarely seen, and still more seldom traversed. It is, however, always possible that they may be encountered, and on this account, if for no other, it is necessary for men who go mountaineering to be armed with ice-axes, and with

good ones. The form is of more importance than might be supposed. Of course, if you intend to act as a simple amateur and let others do the work, and only follow in their steps, it is not of much importance what kind of ice-axe you carry, so long as its head does not fall off or otherwise behave itself improperly. There is no better weapon for cutting steps in ice than a common pick-axe, and the form of ice-axe which is now usually employed by the best guides is very like a miniature pick. My own axe is copied from Melchior Anderegg's. It is of wrought iron, with point and edge steeled. Its weight, including spiked handle, is four pounds. For cutting steps in ice the pointed end of the head is almost exclusively employed: the adze-end is handy for polishing them up, but is principally used for cutting in hard snow. Apart from its value as a cutting weapon, it is invaluable as a grapnel. It is naturally a rather awkward implement when it is not being employed for its legitimate purpose, and is likely to give rise to much strong language in crushes at railway termini, unless its head is protected with a leathern cap or in some other way. Many attempts have been made, for the sake of convenience, to fashion an ice-axe with a movable head, but it seems difficult or impossible to produce one except at the expense of cutting qualities and by increasing the weight.

Mr. T. S. Kennedy (of the firm of Fairbairn & Co.), whose practical acquaintance with mountaineering and with the use and manufacture of tools makes his opinion particularly valuable, has contrived the best that I have seen; but even it seems to me to be deficient in rigidity, and not to be so powerful a weapon as the more common kind with the fixed head. The simple instrument which is shown in the annexed diagram is the invention of Mr. Leslie Stephen, and it answers the purposes for which he devised it—namely, for giving better

KENNEDY ICE-AXE.

hold upon snow and ice than can be obtained from the common alpenstock, and for cutting an occasional step. The amateur scarcely requires anything more imposing, but for serious ice-work a heavier weapon is indispensable.

To persons armed with the proper tools, ice-slopes are not so dangerous as many places which appeal less to the imagination. Their ascent or descent is necessarily laborious (to those who do the work), and they may therefore be termed difficult. They *ought* not to be dangerous. Yet they always seem dangerous, for one is profoundly convinced that if he slips he will certainly go to the bottom. Hence, any man who is not a fool takes particular care to preserve his balance, and in consequence we have the noteworthy fact that accidents have seldom or never taken place upon ice-slopes.

The same slopes covered with snow are much less impressive, and *may* be much more dangerous. They may be less slippery, the balance may be more easily preserved, and if one man slips he may be stopped by his own personal efforts, provided the snow which overlies the ice is consolidated and of a reasonable depth. But if, as is more likely to be the case upon an angle of fifty degrees (or anything approaching that angle), there is only a thin stratum of snow which is not consolidated, the occurrence of a slip will most likely take the entire party as low as possible, and, in addition to the chance of broken necks, there will be a strong probability that some, at least, will be smothered by the dislodged snow. Such accidents are far too common, and their occurrence,

as a rule, may be traced to the want of caution which is induced by the apparent absence of danger.

I do not believe that the use of the rope, in the ordinary way, affords the least *real* security upon ice-slopes. Nor do I think that any benefit is derived from the employment of crampons.

Mr. Kennedy was good enough to present me with a pair some time ago, and one of these has been engraved.

STEPHEN ICE-AXE

They are the best variety I have seen of the species, but I only feel comfortable with them on my feet in places where they are not of the slightest use—that is, in situations where there is no possibility of slipping—and would not wear them

CRAMPONS.

upon an ice-slope for any consideration whatever. All such adventitious aids are useless if you have not a good step in the ice to stand upon, and if you have got that nothing more is wanted except a few nails in the boots.

Almer and Biener got to the end of their tether: the rope no longer assured their safety, and they stopped work as we advanced and coiled it up. Shortly afterward they struck a streak of snow that proved to be just above the bridge of which they were in search. The slope steepened, and for thirty feet or so we descended face to the wall, making steps by kicking with the toes and thrusting the arms well into the holes above, just as if they had been rounds in a ladder. At this time we were crossing the uppermost of the schrunds. Needless to say that the snow was of an admirable quality: this performance would otherwise have been impossible. It was soon over, and we then found ourselves upon a huge rhomboidal mass of ice, and still separated from the Argentière glacier by a gigantic crevasse. The only bridge over this lower schrund was at its eastern end, and we were obliged to double back to get to it. Cutting continued for half an hour after it was passed, and it was 5.35 P. M. before the axes stopped work, and we could at last turn back and look comfortably at the formidable slope upon which seven hours had been spent.*

The Col Dolent is not likely to compete with the Col du Géant, and I would recommend any person who starts to cross it to allow himself plenty of time, plenty of rope and ample guide-power. There is no difficulty whatever upon any part of the route, excepting upon the steep slopes immediately below the summit on each side. When we arrived upon the Glacier d'Argentière our work was as good as over. We drove a straight track to the chalets of Lognan, and thence the way led over familiar ground. Soon after dusk we got into the high-road at Les Tines, and at 10 P. M. arrived at Chamounix. Our labors were duly rewarded. Houris brought us champagne and the other drinks which are reserved for the faithful, but before my share was consumed I fell asleep in an arm-chair. I slept soundly until daybreak, and then turned into bed and went to sleep again.

*I estimate its height at 1200 feet. The triangulation of Captain Mieulet places the summit of the pass 11,624 feet above the sea. This, I think, is too high.

CHAPTER XVIII.
ASCENT OF THE AIGUILLE VERTE.

MICHEL CROZ now parted from us. His new employer had not arrived at Chamounix, but Croz considered that he was bound by honor to wait for him, and thus Christian Almer of Grindelwald became my leading guide.

Almer displayed aptitude for mountaineering at an early age. Whilst still a very young man he was known as a crack chamois-hunter, and he soon developed into an accomplished guide. Those who have read Mr. Wills' graphic account of the first ascent of the Wetterhorn * will remember that when his

CHRISTIAN ALMER.

party was approaching the top of the mountain two stranger men were seen climbing by a slightly different route, one of whom carried upon his back a young fir tree, branches, leaves and all. Mr. Wills' guides were extremely indignant with these two strangers (who were evidently determined to be the first at the summit), and talked of giving them blows. Eventually they gave them a cake of chocolate instead, and declared that they were good fellows. "Thus the pipe of peace was smoked, and tranquillity reigned between the rival forces." Christian Almer was one of these two men.

* *Wanderings among the High Alps*, 1858.

This was in 1854. In 1858-'59 he made the first ascents of the Eigher and the Mönch, the former with a Mr. Harrington (?), and the latter with Dr. Porges. Since then he has wandered far and near, from Dauphiné to the Tyrol. With the exception of Melchior Anderegg, there is not, perhaps, another guide of such wide experience, or one who has been so invariably successful; and his numerous employers concur in saying that there is not a truer heart or a surer foot to be found amongst the Alps.

Before recrossing the chain to Courmayeur we ascended the Aiguille Verte. In company with Mr. Reilly I inspected this mountain from every direction in 1864, and came to the conclusion that an ascent could more easily be made from the south than upon any other side. We set out upon the 28th from Chamounix to attack it, minus Croz, and plus

ON THE MER DE GLACE.

a porter (of whom I will speak more particularly presently), leaving our comrade very downcast at having to kick his heels in idleness, whilst we were about to scale the most celebrated of his native aiguilles.

Our course led us over the old Mer de Glace, the glacier made famous by De Saussure and Forbes. The heat of the day was over, but the little rills and rivulets were still flowing along the surface of the ice; cutting deep troughs where the gradients were small, leaving ripple-marks where the water was with more difficulty confined to one channel, and falling over the precipitous walls of the great crevasses, sometimes in bounding cascades, and sometimes in diffused streams, which marked the perpendicular faces with graceful sinuosities.* As night came on, their music died away, the rivulets dwindled down to rills, the rills ceased to murmur, and the spark-

---

* Admirably rendered in the accompanying drawing by Mr. Cyrus Johnson. The "ripple-marks" are seen in the engraving upon p. 139.

ling drops, caught by the hand of frost, were bound to the ice, coating it with an enameled film which lasted until the sun struck the glacier once more.

The weathering of the walls of crevasses, which *obscures* the internal structure of the glacier, has led some to conclude that the stratification which is seen in the higher glacier-regions is *obliterated* in the lower ones. Others—Agassiz and Mr. John Ball, for example—have disputed this opinion, and my own experiences accord with those of these accu-

ON THE MER DE GLACE.

rate observers. It is, undoubtedly, very difficult to trace stratification in the lower ends of the Alpine glaciers, but we are not, upon that account, entitled to conclude that the original structure of the ice has been obliterated. There are thousands of crevasses in the upper regions upon whose walls no traces of bedding are apparent, and we might say, with equal unreasonableness, that it was obliterated there also. Take an axe and clear away the ice which has formed from water trickling down the faces and the weathered ice beneath, and you will expose sections of the min-

gled strata of pure and of imperfect ice, and see clearly enough that the primitive structure of the glacier has not been effaced, although it has been obscured.

We camped on the Couvercle (seventy-eight hundred feet) under a great rock, and at 3.15 the next morning started for our aiguille, leaving the porter in charge of the tent and of the food. Two hours' walking over crisp snow brought us up more than four thousand feet, and within about sixteen hundred feet of the summit. From no other direction can it be approached so closely with equal facility. Thence the mountain steepens. After his late severe piece of ice-work, Almer had a natural inclination for rocks; but the lower rocks of the final peak of the Verte were not inviting, and he went on and on, looking for a way up them, until we arrived in front of a great snow-couloir that led from the Glacier de Talèfre right up to the crest of the ridge connecting the summit of the Verte with the mountain called Les Droites. This was the route which I intended to be taken, but Almer pointed out that the gully narrowed at the lower part, and that if stones fell we should stand some chance of getting our heads broken; and so we went on still more to the east of the summit, to another and smaller couloir which ran up side by side with the great one. At 5.30 we crossed the schrund which protected the final peak, and a few minutes afterward saw the summit and the whole of the intervening route. "Oh, Aiguille Verte!" said my guide, stopping as he said it, "you are dead, you are dead!" which, being translated into plain English, meant that he was cock-sure we should make its ascent.

Almer is a quiet man at all times.

When climbing he is taciturn, and this is one of his great merits. A garrulous man is always a nuisance, and upon the mountain-side he may be a danger, for actual climbing requires a man's whole attention. Added to this, talkative men are hindrances : they are usually thirsty, and a thirsty man is a drag.

Guide-books recommend mountain-walkers to suck pebbles to prevent their throats from becoming parched. There is not much goodness to be got out of the pebbles, but you cannot suck them and keep the mouth open at the same time, and hence the throat does not become dry. It answers just as well to keep the mouth shut, without any pebbles inside—indeed, I think, better ; for if you have occasion to open your mouth you can do so without swallowing any pebbles.* As a rule, amateurs, and particularly novices, *will not* keep their mouths shut. They attempt to "force the pace ;" they go faster than they can go without being compelled to open their mouths to breathe, they pant, their throats and tongues become parched ; they drink and perspire copiously, and, becoming exhausted, declare that the dryness of the air or the rarefaction of the air (everything is laid upon the air) is in fault. On several accounts, therefore, a mountain-climber does well to hold his tongue when he is at his work.

At the top of the small gully we crossed over the intervening rocks into the large one, and followed it so long as it was filled with snow. At last ice replaced snow, and we turned over to the rocks upon its left. Charming rocks they were—granitic in texture, gritty, holding the nails well. At 9.45 we parted from them, and completed the ascent by a little ridge of snow which descended in the direction of the Aiguille du Moine. At 10.15 we stood on the summit (13,540 feet), and devoured our bread and cheese with a good appetite.

I have already spoken of the disappointing nature of purely panoramic views. That seen from Mont Blanc itself is notoriously unsatisfactory. When you are upon that summit you look down upon all the rest of Europe. There is nothing to look up to—all is below : there is no one point for the eye to rest upon. The man who is there is somewhat in the position of one who has attained all that he desires—he has nothing to aspire to : his position must needs be unsatisfactory. Upon the summit of the Verte there is not this objection. You see valleys, villages, fields ; you see mountains interminable rolling away, lakes resting in their hollows ; you hear the tinkling of the sheep-bells as it rises through the clear mountain air, and the roar of the avalanches as they descend to the valleys ; but above all there is the great white dome, with its shining crest high above ; with its sparkling glaciers, that descend between buttresses which support them ; with its brilliant snows, purer and yet purer the farther they are removed from this unclean world.

Even upon this mountain-top it was impossible to forget the world, for some vile wretch came to the Jardin and made hideous sounds by blowing upon a horn. Whilst we were denouncing him a change came over the weather : cumulous clouds gathered in all directions, and we started off in hot haste. Snow began to fall heavily before we were off the summit-rocks, our track was obscured and frequently lost, and everything became so sloppy and slippery that the descent took as long as the ascent. The schrund was recrossed at 3.15 P. M., and thence we raced down to the Couvercle, intending to have a carouse there ; but as we rounded our rock a howl broke simultaneously from all three of us, for the porter had taken down the tent, and was in the act of moving off with it. "Stop, there ! what are you doing ?" He observed that he had thought we were killed, or at least lost, and was going to Chamounix to communicate his ideas to the *guide chef*. "Unfasten the tent and get out the food." But instead of doing so, the porter fumbled in his pockets. "Get out the food," we roared, losing all patience. "Here it is," said our worthy

---

* I heard lately of two well-known mountaineers who, under the influence of sudden alarm, *swallowed their crystals*. I am happy to say that they were able to cough them up again.

friend, producing a dirty piece of bread about as big as a half-penny roll. We three looked solemnly at the fluff-covered morsel. It was past a joke—he had devoured everything. Mutton, loaves, cheese, wine, eggs, sausages—all was gone past recovery. It was idle to grumble and useless to wait. We were light, and could move quickly—the porter was laden inside and out. We went our hardest—he had to shuffle and trot. He streamed with perspiration; the mutton and cheese oozed out in big drops; he larded the glacier. We had our revenge, and dried our clothes at the same time, but when we arrived at the Montanvert the porter was as wet as we had been upon our arrival at the Couvercle. We halted at the inn to get a little food, and at a quarter-past eight re-entered Chamounix amidst firing of cannon and other demonstrations of satisfaction on the part of the hotel-keepers.

One would have thought that the ascent of this mountain, which had been frequently assailed before without success, would have afforded some gratification to a population whose chief support is derived from tourists, and that the prospect of the perennial flow of francs which might be expected to result from it would have stifled the jealousy consequent on the success of foreigners.*

It was not so. Chamounix stood on its rights. A stranger had ignored their regulations, had imported two foreign guides, and furthermore he had added injury to that insult—he had not taken a single Chamounix guide. Chamounix would be revenged! It would bully the foreign guides: it would tell them they had lied—they had not made the ascent! Where were their proofs? Where was the flag upon the summit?

Poor Almer and Biener were accordingly chivied from pillar to post, from one inn to another, and at length complained to me. Peter Perrn, the Zermatt guide, said on the night that we returned that this was to happen, but the story seemed too absurd to be true. I now bade my men go out again, and follow-

ed them myself to see the sport. Chamounix was greatly excited. The bureau of the *guide chef* was thronged with clamoring men. Their ringleader—one Zacharie Cachat, a well-known guide, of no particular merit, but not a bad fellow—was haranguing the multitude. He met with more than his match. My friend Kennedy, who was on the spot, heard of the disturbance and rushed into the fray, confronted the burly guide and thrust back his absurdities into his teeth.

There were the materials for a very pretty riot, but they manage these things better in France than we do, and the gensdarmes—three strong—came down and dispersed the crowd. The guides quailed before the cocked hats, and retired to cabarets to take little glasses of absinthe and other liquors more or less injurious to the human frame. Under the influence of these stimulants they conceived an idea which combined revenge with profit. "You have ascended the Aiguille Verte, you say. *We* say we don't believe it. *We* say, Do it again! Take three of us with you, and we will bet you two thousand francs to one thousand that you won't make the ascent!"

This proposition was formally notified to me, but I declined it with thanks, and recommended Kennedy to go in and win. I accepted, however, a hundred-franc share in the bet, and calculated upon getting two hundred per cent. on my investment. Alas! how vain are human expectations! Zacharie Cachat was put into confinement, and although Kennedy actually ascended the aiguille a week later with two Chamounix guides and Peter Perrn, the bet came to nothing.†

The weather arranged itself just as this storm in a teapot blew over, and we left at once for the Montanvert, in order to show the Chamouniards the easiest way over the chain of Mont Blanc, in return for the civilities which we had received from them during the past three days.

† It should be said that we received the most polite apologies for this affair from the chief of the gensdarmes, and an invitation to lodge a complaint against the ringleaders. We accepted his apologies and declined his invitation. Needless to add, Michel Croz took no part in the demonstration.

* The Chamounix tariff price for the ascent of the aiguille is now placed at four pounds *per guide.*

PART X.

WESTERN SIDE OF THE COL DE TALÈFRE.

CHAPTER XIX.

THE COL DE TALÈFRE.

THE person who discovered the Col du Géant must have been a shrewd mo ntaineer. The pass was in use before any other was known across the main chain of Mont Blanc, and down to the present time it remains the easiest and quickest route from Chamounix to Courmayeur, with the single exception of the pass that we crossed upon the 3d of July for the first time, which lies about midway between the Aiguille de Triolet and the Aiguille de Talèfre, and which,

142

for want of a better name, I have called the Col de Talèfre.

When one looks toward the upper end of the Glacier de Talèfre from the direction of the Jardin or of the Couvercle, the ridge that bounds the view seems to be of little elevation. It is overpowered by the colossal Grandes Jorasses and by the almost equally magnificent Aiguille Verte. The ridge, notwithstanding, is by no means despicable. At no point is its elevation less than eleven thousand six hundred feet. It does not look anything like this height. The Glacier de Talèfre mounts with a steady incline, and the eye is completely deceived.

In 1864, when prowling about with Mr. Reilly, I instinctively fixed upon a bent couloir which led up from the glacier to the lowest part of the ridge ; and when, after crossing the Col de Triolet, I saw that the other side presented no particular difficulty, it seemed to me that this was the *one* point in the whole of the range which would afford an easier passage than the Col du Géant.

We set out from the Montanvert at 4 A. M. upon July 3, to see whether this opinion was correct, and it fortunately happened that the Rev. A. G. Girdlestone and a friend, with two Chamounix guides, left the inn at the same hour as ourselves, to cross the Col du Géant. We kept in company as far as our routes lay together, and at 9.35 we arrived at the top of our pass, having taken the route to the south of the Jardin. Description is unnecessary, as our track is laid down very clearly on the engraving at the head of this chapter.

Much snow had fallen during the late bad weather, and as we reposed upon the top of our pass (which was about eleven thousand six hundred and fifty feet above the level of the sea, and six hundred feet above the Col du Géant), we saw that the descent of the rocks which intervened between us and the Glacier de Triolet would require some caution, for the sun's rays poured down directly upon them, and the snow slipped away every now and then from ledge to ledge just as if it had been water—in cascades not large enough to be imposing, but sufficient to knock us over if we got in their way. This little bit of cliff consequently took a longer time than it should have done, for when we heard the indescribable swishing, hissing sound which announced a coming fall, we of necessity huddled under the lee of the rocks until the snow ceased to shoot over us.

We got to the level of the Glacier de Triolet without misadventure, then steered for its left bank to avoid the upper of its two formidable ice-falls, and after descending the requisite distance by some old snow lying between the glacier and the cliffs which border it, crossed directly to the right bank over the level ice between the two ice-falls. The right bank was gained without any trouble, and we found there numerous beds of hard snow (avalanche débris), down which we could run or glissade as fast as we liked.

Glissading is a very pleasant employment when it is accomplished successfully, and I have never seen a place where it can be more safely indulged in than the snowy valley on the right bank of the Glacier de Triolet. In my dreams I glissade delightfully, but in practice I

find that somehow the snow will not behave properly, and that my alpenstock *will* get between my legs. Then my legs go where my head should be, and I

see the sky revolving at a rapid pace: the snow rises up and smites me, and runs away, and when it is at last overtaken it suddenly stops, and we come into violent collision. Those who are with me say that I tumble head over heels, and there may be some truth in what they say. Streaks of ice are apt to make the heels shoot away, and stray stones cause one to pitch headlong down. Somehow, these things always seem to come in the way, so it is as well to glissade only when there is something soft to tumble into.*

Near the termination of the glacier we could not avoid traversing a portion of its abominable moraine, but at 1.30 P. M. we were clear of it, and threw ourselves upon some springy turf, conscious that our day's work was over. An hour afterward we resumed the march, crossed the Doire torrent by a bridge a little below Gruetta, and at five o'clock entered Courmayeur, having occupied somewhat less than ten hours on the way. Mr. Girdlestone's party came in, I believe, about four hours afterward, so there was no doubt that we made a shorter pass than the Col du Géant; and I believe we dis-

---

* In glissading an erect position should be maintained, and the point of the alpenstock allowed to trail over the snow. If it is necessary to stop or to slacken speed, the point is pressed against the slope, as shown in the illustration.

covered a quicker way of getting from Chamounix to Courmayeur, or *vice versâ*, than will be found elsewhere so long as the chain of Mont Blanc remains in its present condition.

CHAPTER XX.
ASCENT OF THE RUINETTE—THE MATTER-HORN.

ALL of the excursions that were set down in my programme had been carried out, with the exception of the ascent of the Matterhorn, and we now turned our faces in its direction, but instead of returning *viâ* the Val Tournanche, we took a route across country, and bagged upon our way the summit of the Ruinette.

We passed the night of July 4 at Aosta, under the roof of the genial Tairraz, and on the 5th went by the Val d'Ollomont and the Col de la Fenêtre (9140 feet) to Chermontane. We slept that night at the chalets of Chanrion (a foul spot, which should be avoided), left them at 3.50 the next morning, and after a short scramble over the slope above, and a half-mile tramp on the Glacier de Breney, we crossed directly to the Ruinette, and went almost straight up it. There is not, I suppose, another mountain in the Alps of the same height that can be ascended so easily. You have only to go ahead : upon its southern side one can walk about almost anywhere.

Though I speak thus slightingly of a very respectable peak, I will not do anything of the kind in regard to the view which it gives. It is happily placed in respect to the rest of the Pennine Alps, and as a stand-point it has not many superiors. You see mountains, and nothing but mountains. It is a solemn —some would say a dreary—view, but it is very grand. The great Combin (14,164 feet), with its noble background of the whole range of Mont Blanc, never looks so big as it does from here. In the contrary direction the Matterhorn overpowers all besides. The Dent d'Hérens, although closer, looks a mere outlier of its great neighbor, and the snows of Monte Rosa behind seem intended for no other purpose than to give relief to the crags in front. To the south there is an endless array of Becs and Beccas, backed by the great Italian peaks, whilst to the north Mont Pleureur (12,159 feet) holds its own against the more distant Wildstrubel.

We gained the summit at 9.15, and stayed there an hour and a half. My faithful guides then admonished me that Prerayen, whither we were bound, was still far away, and that we had yet to cross two lofty ridges. So we resumed our harness and departed ; not, however, before a huge cairn had been built out of the blocks of gneiss with which the summit is bestrewn. Then we trotted down the slopes of the Ruinette, over the Glacier de Breney, and across a pass which (if it deserves a name) may be called the Col des Portons, after the neighboring peaks. From thence we proceeded across the great Otemma glacier toward the Col d'Olen.

The part of the glacier that we traversed was overspread with snow, which completely concealed its numerous pitfalls. We marched across it in single file, and of course roped together. All at once Almer dropped into a crevasse up to his shoulders. I pulled in the rope immediately, but the snow gave way as it was being done, and I had to spread out my arms to stop my descent. Biener held fast, but said afterward that his feet went through as well, so, for a moment, all three were in the jaws of the crevasse. We now altered our course, so as to take the fissures transversely, and after the centre of the glacier was passed, changed it again and made directly for the summit of the Col d'Olen.

It is scarcely necessary to observe, after what has been before said, that it is my invariable practice to employ a rope when traversing a snow-covered glacier. Many guides, even the best ones, object to be roped, more especially early in the morning, when the snow is hard. They object sometimes because they think it is unnecessary. Crevasses that are bridged by snow are almost always more or less perceptible by undulations on the surface : the snow droops down, and hollows mark the course of the chasms beneath. An experienced guide usually notices these almost imperceptible wrinkles, steps one side or the other, as the case may require, and rarely breaks through unawares. Guides think there is no occasion to employ a rope, because they think that they will *not* be taken by surprise. Michel Croz used to be of this opinion. He used to say that only imbeciles and children required to be tied up in the morning. I told him that in this particular matter I was a child to him. "You see these things, my good Croz, and avoid them. I do not, except you point them out to me, and so that which is not a danger to you *is* a danger to me." The sharper one's eyes get by use, the less is a rope required as a protective against these hidden pitfalls, but according to my experience the sight never becomes so keen that they can be avoided with unvarying certainty, and I mentioned what occurred upon the Otemma glacier to show that this is so.

I well remember my first passage of the Col Théodule, the easiest of the higher Alpine glacier passes. We had a rope, but my guide said it was not necessary—he knew all the crevasses. However, we did not go a quarter of a mile before he dropped through the snow into a crevasse up to his neck. He was a heavy man, and would scarcely have extricated himself alone; anyhow, he was very glad of my assistance. When he got on to his legs again, he said, "Well, I had no idea that there was a crevasse there." He no longer objected to use the rope, and we proceeded— upon my part with greater peace of mind than before. I have crossed the pass thirteen times since then, and have invariably insisted upon being tied.

Guides object to the use of the rope upon snow-covered glacier, because they are afraid of being laughed at by their comrades; and this, perhaps, is the more common reason. To illustrate this, here is another Théodule experience. We arrived at the edge of the ice, and I required to be tied. My guide (a Zermatt man of repute) said that no one used a

rope going across that pass. I declined to argue the matter, and we put on the rope, though very much against the wish of my man, who protested that he should have to submit to perpetual ridicule if we met any of his acquaintances. We had not gone very far before we saw a train coming in the contrary direction. "Ah!" cried my man, "there is R——" (mentioning a guide who used to be kept at the Riffel hotel for the ascent of Monte Rosa): "it will be as I said—I shall never hear the end of this." The guide we met was followed by a string of tomfools, none of whom were tied together, and had his face covered by a mask to prevent it becoming blistered. After we had passed, I said, "Now, should R—— make any observations to you, ask him why he takes such extraordinary care to preserve the skin of his face, which will grow again in a week, when he neglects such an obvious precaution in regard to his life, which he can only lose once." This was quite a new idea to my guide, and he said nothing more against the use of the rope so long as we were together.

I believe that the unwillingness to use a rope upon snow-covered glacier which born mountaineers not unfrequently exhibit, arises—first, on the part of expert men from the consciousness that they themselves incur little risk; secondly, on the part of inferior men from fear of ridicule, and from aping the ways of their superiors; and thirdly, from pure ignorance or laziness. Whatever may be the reason, I raise my voice against the neglect of a precaution so simple and so effectual. In my opinion, the very first thing a glacier-traveler requires is plenty of good rope.

A committee of the English Alpine Club was appointed in 1864 to test, and to report upon, the most suitable ropes for mountaineering purposes, and those which were approved are probably as good as can be found. One is made of Manila and another of Italian hemp. The former is the heavier, and weighs a little more than an ounce per foot (103 ounces to 100 feet). The latter weighs 79 ounces per 100 feet, but I prefer the Manila rope, because it is more easy

10

to handle. Both of these ropes will sustain 168 pounds falling 10 feet, or 196 pounds falling 8 feet, and they break with a dead weight of two tons. In 1865 we carried two 100-feet lengths of the Manila rope, and the inconvenience arising from its weight was more than made up for by the security which it afforded. Upon several occasions it was worth more than an extra guide.

Now, touching the *use* of the rope. There is a right way and there are wrong ways of using it. I often meet, upon glacier-passes, elegantly got-up persons, who are clearly out of their element, with a guide stalking along in front, who pays no attention to the innocents in his charge. They are tied together as a matter of form, but they evidently have no idea *why* they are tied up, for they walk side by side or close together, with the rope trailing on the snow. If one tumbles into a crevasse, the rest stare and say, "La! what is the matter with Smith?" unless, as is more likely, they all tumble in together. This is the wrong way to use a rope. It is abuse of the rope.

It is of the first importance to keep the rope taut from man to man. There is no real security if this is not done, and your risks may be considerably magnified. There is little or no difficulty in extricating one man who breaks through a bridged crevasse if the rope is taut, but the case may be very awkward if two break through at the same moment, close together, and there are only two others to aid, or perhaps only one other. Further, the rope ought not upon any account to graze over snow, ice or rocks, otherwise the strands suffer and the lives of the whole party may be endangered.

THE WRONG WAY TO USE THE ROPE.

Apart from this, it is extremely annoying to have a rope knocking about one's heels. If circumstances render it im-

THE RIGHT WAY TO USE THE ROPE.

possible for the rope to be kept taut by itself, the men behind should gather it up round their hands,* and not allow it to incommode those in advance. A man must either be incompetent, careless or selfish if he permits the rope to dangle about the heels of the person in front of him.

The distance from man to man must be neither too great nor too small. About

* For example, when the leader suspects crevasses, and *sounds* for them in the manner shown in the engraving, he usually loses half a step or more. The second man should take a turn of the rope around his hand to draw it back in case the leader goes through.

twelve feet is sufficient. If there are only two or three persons, it is prudent to allow a little more — say fifteen feet. More than this is unnecessary, and less than nine or ten feet is not much good.

It is essential to examine your rope from time to time to see that it is in good condition. If you are wise you will do this yourself every day. Latterly, I have examined every inch of my rope overnight, and upon more than one occasion have found the strands of the Manila rope nearly half severed through accidental grazes.

Thus far the rope has been supposed to be employed upon level, snow-covered glacier, to prevent any risk from concealed crevasses. On rocks and on slopes it is used for a different purpose (namely, to guard against slips), and in these cases it is equally important to keep it taut and to preserve a reasonable distance one from the other. It is much more troublesome to keep the rope taut upon slopes than upon the level, and upon difficult rocks it is all but impossible, except by adopting the plan of moving only one at a time.

From the Col d'Olen we proceeded down the combe of the same name to the chalets of Prerayen, and passed the night of the 6th under the roof of our old acquaintance, the wealthy herdsman. On the 7th we crossed the Va Cornère Pass, *en route* for Breuil. My thoughts were fixed on the Matterhorn, and my guides knew that I wished them to accompany me. They had an aversion to the mountain, and repeatedly expressed their belief that it was useless to try to ascend it. "*Anything* but Matterhorn, dear sir!" said Almer—"*anything* but Matterhorn." He did not speak of difficulty or of danger, nor was he shirking *work*. He offered to go *anywhere*, but he entreated that the Matterhorn should be abandoned. Both men spoke fairly enough. They did not think that an ascent could be made, and for their own credit, as well as for my sake, they did not wish to undertake a business which in their opinion would only lead to loss of time and money. I sent them by the short cut to Breuil, and walked down to Val Tournanche to look for Jean-Antoine Carrel. He was not there. The villagers said that he and three others had started on the 6th to try the Matterhorn by the old way, on their own account. They will have no luck, I thought, for the clouds were low down on the mountains; and I walked up to Breuil, fully expecting to meet them. Nor was I disappointed. About halfway up I saw a group of men clustered around a chalet upon the other side of the torrent, and crossing over

found that the party had returned. Jean-Antoine and Cæsar were there, C. E. Gorret and J. J. Maquignaz. They had had no success. The weather, they said, had been horrible, and they had scarcely reached the Glacier du Lion.

I explained the situation to Carrel, and proposed that we, with Cæsar and another man, should cross the Théodule by moonlight on the 9th, and that upon the 10th we should pitch the tent as high as possible upon the east face. He was unwilling to abandon the old route, and urged me to try it again. I promised to do so provided the new route failed. This satisfied him, and he agreed to my proposal. I then went up to Breuil, and discharged Almer and Biener — with much regret, for no two men ever served me more faithfully or more willingly.* On the next day they crossed to Zermatt.

The 8th was occupied with preparations. The weather was stormy, and black, rainy vapors obscured the mountains. Toward evening a young man came from Val Tournanche, and reported that an Englishman was lying there extremely ill. Now was the time for the performance of my vow, and on the morning of Sunday, the 9th, I went down the valley to look after the sick man. On my way I passed a foreign gentleman, with a mule and several porters laden with baggage. Amongst these men were Jean-Antoine and Cæsar, carrying some barometers. "Hullo!" I said, "what are you doing?" They explained that the foreigner had arrived just as they were setting out, and that they were assisting his porters. "Very well: go on to Breuil, and await me there —we start at midnight, as agreed." Jean-Antoine then said that he should not be able to serve me after Tuesday, the 11th, as he was engaged to travel "with a family of distinction" in the valley of Aosta. "And Cæsar?" "And Cæsar also." "Why did you not say this before?" "Because," said he, "it was not settled. The engagement is of long

---

* During the preceding eighteen days (I exclude Sundays and other non-working days) we ascended more than one hundred thousand feet, and descended ninety-eight thousand feet.

standing, but *the day* was not fixed. When I got back to Val Tournanche on Friday night, after leaving you, I found a letter naming the day." I could not object to the answer, but the prospect of being left guideless was provoking. They went up, and I down, the valley.

The sick man declared that he was better, though the exertion of saying as much tumbled him over on to the floor in a fainting-fit. He was badly in want of medicine, and I tramped down to Chatillon to get it. It was late before I returned to Val Tournanche, for the weather was tempestuous and rain fell in torrents. A figure passed me under the church-porch. " *Qui vive ?*" "Jean-Antoine." "I thought you were at Breuil." "No, sir: when the storm came on I knew we should not start to-night, and so came down to sleep here." "Ha, Carrel," I said, "this is a great bore. If to-morrow is not fine, we shall not be able to do anything together. I have sent away my guides, relying on you, and now you are going to leave me to travel with a party of ladies. That work is not fit for *you*" (he smiled, I supposed at the implied compliment): "can't you send some one else instead ?" "No, monsieur. I am sorry, but my word is pledged. I should like to accompany you, but I can't break my engagement." By this time we had arrived at the inn door. "Well, it is no fault of yours. Come presently with Cæsar, and have some wine." They came, and we sat up till midnight, recounting our old adventures, in the inn of Val Tournanche.

The weather continued bad upon the 10th, and I returned to Breuil. The two Carrels were again hovering about the above-mentioned chalet, and I bade them adieu. In the evening the sick man crawled up, a good deal better, but his was the only arrival. The Monday crowd * did not cross the Théodule, on account of the continued storms. The inn was lonely. I went to bed early, and was awoke the next morning by the invalid inquiring if I had heard the news.

"No—what news ?" "Why," said he, "a large party of guides went off this morning to try the Matterhorn, taking with them a mule laden with provisions."

I went to the door, and with a telescope saw the party upon the lower slopes of the mountain. Favre, the landlord, stood by. "What is all this about ?" I inquired: "who is the leader of this party ?" "Carrel." "What! Jean-Antoine ?" "Yes, Jean-Antoine." "Is Cæsar there too ?" "Yes, he is there." Then I saw in a moment that I had been bamboozled and humbugged, and learned, bit by bit, that the affair had been arranged long beforehand. The start on the 6th had been for a preliminary reconnaissance ; the mule that I passed was conveying stores for the attack ; the "family of distinction" was Signor F. Giordano, who had just despatched the party to facilitate the way to the summit, and who, when the facilitation was completed, was to be taken to the top along with Signor Sella ! †

I was greatly mortified. My plans were upset: the Italians had clearly stolen a march upon me, and I saw that the astute Favre chuckled over my discomfiture, because the route by the eastern face, if successful, would not benefit his inn. What was to be done ? I retired to my room, and, soothed by tobacco, re-studied my plans, to see if it was not possible to outmanœuvre the Italians. "They have taken a mule-load of provisions." That is *one* point in my favor, for they will take two or three days to get through the food, and until that is done no work will be accomplished." "How is the weather ?" I went to the window. The mountain was smothered up in mist—another point in my favor. "They are to facilitate the way. Well, if they do that to any purpose, it will be a long job." Altogether, I reckoned that they could not possibly ascend the mountain and come back to Breuil in less than seven days. I got cooler, for it was evident that the wily ones might be outwitted after all. There was time enough to go to Zermatt, to try

---

* Tourists usually congregate at Zermatt upon Sundays, and large gangs and droves cross the Théodule pass on Mondays.

† The Italian minister. Signor Giordano had undertaken the business arrangements for Signor Sella.

the eastern face, and, should it prove impracticable, to come back to Breuil before the men returned ; and then it seemed to me, as the mountain was not padlocked, one might start at the same time as the messieurs, and yet get to the top before them.

The first thing to do was to go to Zermatt. Easier said than done. The seven guides upon the mountain included the ablest men in the valley, and none of the ordinary muleteer-guides were at Breuil. Two men, at least, were wanted for my baggage, but not a soul could be found. I ran about and sent about in all directions, but not a single porter could be obtained. One was with Carrel, another was ill, another was at Chatillon, and so forth. Even Meynet the hunchback could not be induced to come : he was in the thick of some important cheese - making operations. I was in the position of a general without an army : it was all very well to make plans, but there was no one to execute them. This did not much trouble me, for it was evident that so long as the weather stopped traffic over the Théodule, it would hinder the men equally upon the Matterhorn ; and I knew that directly it improved company would certainly arrive.

About midday on Tuesday, the 11th, a large party hove in sight from Zermatt, preceded by a nimble young Englishman and one of old Peter Taugwalder's sons.* I went at once to this gentleman to learn if he could dispense with Taugwalder. He said that he could not, as they were going to recross to Zermatt on the morrow, but that the young man should assist in transporting my baggage, as he had nothing to carry. We naturally got into conversation. I told my story, and learned that the young Englishman was Lord Francis Douglas,† whose recent exploit—the ascent of the Gabelhorn—had excited my wonder and admiration. He brought good news. Old Peter had lately been beyond the Hörnli, and had reported that he thought

an ascent of the Matterhorn was possible upon that side. Almer had left Zermatt, and could not be recovered, so I determined to seek for old Peter. Lord Francis Douglas expressed a warm desire to ascend the mountain, and before long it was determined that he should take part in the expedition.

Favre could no longer hinder our departure, and lent us one of his men. We crossed the Col Théodule on Wednesday morning, the 12th of July, rounded the foot of the Ober Théodulgletscher, crossed the Furggengletscher, and deposited tent, blankets, ropes and other things in the little chapel at the Schwarzsee. All four were heavily laden, for we brought across the whole of my stores from Breuil. Of rope alone there were about six hundred feet. There were three kinds : first, two hundred feet of Manila rope ; second, one hundred and fifty feet of a stouter and probably stronger rope than the first ; and third, more than two hundred feet of a lighter and weaker rope than the first, of a kind that I used formerly (stout sash-line).

We descended to Zermatt, sought and engaged old Peter, and gave him permission to choose another guide. When we returned to the Monte Rosa hotel, whom should we see sitting upon the wall in front but my old *guide-chef*, Michel Croz! I supposed that he had come with Mr. B——, but I learned that that gentleman had arrived in ill health at Chamounix, and had returned to England. Croz, thus left free, had been immediately engaged by the Rev. Charles Hudson, and they had come to Zermatt with the same object as ourselves — namely, to attempt the ascent of the Matterhorn !

Lord Francis Douglas and I dined at the Monte Rosa, and had just finished when Mr. Hudson and a friend entered the *salle à manger*. They had returned from inspecting the mountain, and some idlers in the room demanded their intentions. We heard a confirmation of Croz's statement, and learned that Mr. Hudson intended to set out on the morrow at the same hour as ourselves. We left the room to consult, and agreed it

---

* Peter Taugwalder, the father, is called *old* Peter, to distinguish him from his eldest son, *young* Peter. In 1865 the father's age was about forty-five.

† Brother of the present marquis of Queensbury.

was undesirable that two independent parties should be on the mountain at the same time with the same object. Mr. Hudson was therefore invited to join us, and he accepted our proposal. Before admitting his friend, Mr. Hadow, I took the precaution to inquire what he had done in the Alps, and, as well as I remember, Mr. Hudson's reply was, "Mr. Hadow has done Mont Blanc in less time than most men." He then mentioned several other excursions, that were unknown to me, and added, in answer to a further question, "I consider he is a sufficiently good man to go with us." Mr. Hadow was admitted without any further question, and we then went into the matter of guides. Hudson thought that Croz and old Peter would be sufficient. The question was referred to the men themselves, and they made no objection.

So Croz and I became comrades once more, and as I threw myself on my bed and tried to go to sleep, I wondered at the strange series of chances which had first separated us and then brought us together again. I thought of the mistake through which he had accepted the engagement to Mr. B——; of his unwillingness to adopt my route; of his recommendation to transfer our energies to the chain of Mont Blanc; of the retirement of Almer and Biener; of the desertion of Carrel; of the arrival of Lord Francis Douglas; and lastly of our accidental meeting at Zermatt; and as I pondered over these things I could not help asking, "What next?" If any one of the links of this fatal chain of circumstances had been omitted, what a different story I should have to tell!

CHAPTER XXI.

THE ASCENT OF THE MATTERHORN.

WE started from Zermatt on the 13th of July at half-past five, on a brilliant and perfectly cloudless morning. We were eight in number—Croz, old Peter and his two sons,* Lord Francis Doug-

---

* The two young Taugwalders were taken as porters by desire of their father, and carried provisions amply sufficient for three days, in case the ascent should prove more troublesome than we anticipated.

las, Hadow, Hudson† and I. To ensure steady motion, one tourist and one native walked together. The youngest Taugwalder fell to my share, and the lad marched well, proud to be on the expedition and happy to show his powers. The wine-bags also fell to my lot to carry, and throughout the day, after

---

† I remember speaking about pedestrianism to a well-known mountaineer some years ago, and venturing to remark that a man who averaged thirty miles a day might be considered a good walker. "A fair walker," he said—"a *fair* walker." "What, then, would you consider *good* walking?" "Well," he replied, "I will tell you. Some time back a friend and I agreed to go to Switzerland, but a short time afterward he wrote to say he ought to let me know that a young and delicate lad was going with him who would not be equal to great things—in fact, he would not be able to do more than fifty miles a day!" "What became of the young and delicate lad?" "He lives." "And who was your extraordinary friend?" "Charles Hudson." I have every reason to believe that the gentlemen referred to *were* equal to walking more than fifty miles a day, but they were exceptional, not *good* pedestrians.

Charles Hudson, vicar of Skillington in Lincolnshire, was considered by the mountaineering fraternity to be the best amateur of his time. He was the organizer and leader of the party of Englishmen who ascended Mont Blanc by the Aiguille du Goûter, and descended by the Grands Mulets route, without guides, in 1855. His long practice made him surefooted, and in that respect he was not greatly inferior to a born mountaineer. I remember him as a well-made man of middle height and age, neither stout nor thin, with face pleasant though grave, and with quiet, unassuming manners. Although an athletic man, he would have been overlooked in a crowd; and although he had done the greatest mountaineering feats which have been done, he was the last man to speak of his own doings. His friend, Mr. Hadow, was a young man of nineteen, who had the looks and manners of a greater age. He was a rapid walker, but 1865 was his first season in the Alps. Lord Francis Douglas was about the same age as Mr. Hadow. He had had the advantage of several seasons in the Alps. He was nimble as a deer, and was becoming an expert mountaineer. Just before our meeting he had ascended the Ober Gabelhorn (with old Peter and Joseph Viennin), and this gave me a high opinion of his powers, for I had examined that mountain all round a few weeks before, and had declined its ascent on account of its apparent difficulty.

My personal acquaintance with Mr. Hudson was very slight; still, I should have been content to have placed myself under his orders if he had chosen to claim the position to which he was entitled. Those who knew him will not be surprised to learn that, so far from doing this, he lost no opportunity in consulting the wishes and opinions of those around him. We deliberated together whenever there was occasion, and our authority was recognized by the others. Whatever responsibility there was devolved upon us. I recollect with satisfaction that there was no difference of opinion between us as to what should be done, and that the most perfect harmony existed between all of us so long as we were together.

each drink, I replenished them secretly with water, so that at the next halt they were found fuller than before! This was considered a good omen, and little short of miraculous.

On the first day we did not intend to ascend to any great height, and we mounted, accordingly, very leisurely, picked up the things which were left in the chapel at the Schwarzsee at 8.20, and proceeded thence along the ridge connecting the Hörnli with the Matterhorn. At half-past eleven we arrived at the base of the actual peak, then quitted the ridge and clambered round some ledges on to the eastern face. We were now fairly upon the mountain, and were astonished to find that places which from the Riffel, or even from the Furggengletscher, looked entirely impracticable, were so easy that we could *run about*.

Before twelve o'clock we had found a good position for the tent, at a height of eleven thousand feet.* Croz and young Peter went on to see what was above, in order to save time on the following morning. They cut across the heads of the snow-slopes which descended toward the Furggengletscher, and disappeared round a corner, but shortly afterward we saw them high up on the face, moving quickly. We others made a solid platform for the tent in a well-protected spot, and then watched eagerly for the return of the men. The stones which they upset told that they were very high, and we supposed that the way must be easy. At length, just before 3 P. M., we saw them coming down, evidently much excited. "What are they saying, Peter?" "Gentlemen, they say it is no good." But when they came near we heard a different story: "Nothing but what was good—not a difficulty, not a single difficulty! We could have gone to the summit and returned to-day easily!"

We passed the remaining hours of daylight—some basking in the sunshine, some sketching or collecting—and when the sun went down, giving, as it departed, a glorious promise for the morrow, we returned to the tent to arrange for the night. Hudson made tea, I coffee, and we then retired each one to his blanket-bag, the Taugwalders, Lord Francis Douglas and myself occupying the tent, the others remaining, by preference, outside. Long after dusk the cliffs above echoed with our laughter and with the songs of the guides, for we were happy that night in camp, and feared no evil.

We assembled together outside the tent before dawn on the morning of the 14th, and started directly it was light enough to move. Young Peter came on with us as a guide, and his brother returned to Zermatt. We followed the route which had been taken on the previous day, and in a few minutes turned the rib which had intercepted the view of the eastern face from our tent platform. The whole of this great slope was now revealed, rising for three thousand feet like a huge natural staircase. Some parts were more and others were less easy, but we were not once brought to a halt by any serious impediment, for when an obstruction was met in front it could always be turned to the right or to the left. For the greater part of the way there was indeed no occasion for the rope, and sometimes Hudson led, sometimes myself. At 6.20 we had attained a height of twelve thousand eight hundred feet, and halted for half an hour: we then continued the ascent without a break until 9.55, when we stopped for fifty minutes at a height of fourteen thousand feet. Twice we struck the north-eastern ridge, and followed it for some little distance—to no advantage, for it was usually more rotten and steep, and always more difficult, than the face. Still, we kept near to it, lest stones perchance might fall.

We had now arrived at the foot of that part which, from the Riffelberg or from Zermatt, seems perpendicular or overhanging, and could no longer continue upon the eastern side. For a little distance we ascended by snow upon the arête—that is, the ridge—descending

* Thus far the guides did not once go to the front. Hudson or I led, and when any cutting was required we did it ourselves. This was done to spare the guides, and to show them that we were thoroughly in earnest. The spot at which we camped was just four hours' walking from Zermatt.

toward Zermatt, and then by common consent turned over to the right, or to the northern side. Before doing so we made a change in the order of ascent. Croz went first, I followed, Hudson came third: Hadow and old Peter were last. "Now," said Croz as he led off—"now for something altogether different." The work became difficult, and required caution. In some places there was little to hold, and it was desirable that those should be in front who were least likely to slip. The general slope of the mountain at this part was *less* than forty degrees, and snow had accumulated in, and had filled up, the interstices of the rock-face, leaving only occasional fragments projecting here and there. These were at times covered with a thin film of ice, produced from the melting and refreezing of the snow. It was the counterpart, on a small scale, of the upper seven hundred feet of the Pointe des Écrins; only there was this material difference—the face of the Écrins was about, or exceeded, an angle of fifty degrees, and the Matterhorn face was less than forty degrees. It was a place over which any fair mountaineer might pass in safety, and Mr. Hudson ascended this part, and, as far as I know, the entire mountain, without having the slightest assistance rendered to him upon any occasion. Sometimes, after I had taken a hand from Croz or received a pull, I turned to offer the same to Hudson, but he invariably declined, saying it was not necessary. Mr. Hadow, however, was not accustomed to this kind of work, and required continual assistance. It is only fair to say that the difficulty which he found at this part arose simply and entirely from want of experience.

This solitary difficult part was of no great extent. We bore away over it at first nearly horizontally, for a distance of about four hundred feet, then ascended directly toward the summit for about sixty feet, and then doubled back to the ridge which descends toward Zermatt. A long stride round a rather awkward corner brought us to snow once more. The last doubt vanished! The Matterhorn was ours! Nothing but two hundred feet of easy snow remained to be surmounted!

You must now carry your thoughts back to the seven Italians who started from Breuil on the 11th of July. Four days had passed since their departure, and we were tormented with anxiety lest they should arrive on the top before us. All the way up we had talked of them, and many false alarms of "men on the summit" had been raised. The higher we rose the more intense became the excitement. What if we should be beaten at the last moment? The slope eased off, at length we could be detached, and Croz and I, dashing away, ran a neck-and-neck race which ended in a dead heat. At 1.40 P. M. the world was at our feet and the Matterhorn was conquered! Hurrah! Not a footstep could be seen.

It was not yet certain that we had not been beaten. The summit of the Matterhorn was formed of a rudely level ridge, about three hundred and fifty feet long,* and the Italians might have been at its farther extremity. I hastened to the southern end, scanning the snow right and left eagerly. Hurrah again! it was untrodden. "Where were the men?" I peered over the cliff, half doubting, half expectant. I saw them immediately, mere dots on the ridge, at an immense distance below. Up went my arms and my hat. "Croz! Croz! come here!" "Where are they, monsieur?" "There—don't you see them down there?" "Ah! the *coquins!* they are low down." "Croz, we must make those fellows hear us." We yelled until we were hoarse. The Italians seemed to regard us—we could not be certain. "Croz, we *must* make them hear us— they *shall* hear us!" I seized a block of rock and hurled it down, and called upon my companion, in the name of

* The highest points are toward the two ends. In 1865 the northern end was slightly higher than the southern one. In bygone years Carrel and I often suggested to each other that we might one day arrive upon the top, and find ourselves cut off from the very highest point by a notch in the summit-ridge which is seen from the Théodule and from Breuil. This notch is very conspicuous from below, but when one is actually upon the summit it is hardly noticed, and it can be passed without the least difficulty.

friendship, to do the same. We drove our sticks in and prized away the crags, and soon a torrent of stones poured down the cliffs. There was no mistake about it this time. The Italians turned and fled.*

Still, I would that the leader of that party could have stood with us at that moment, for our victorious shouts conveyed to him the disappointment of the ambition of a lifetime. He was *the* man,

for the honor of his native valley. For a time he had the game in his hands: he played it as he thought best, but he made a false move, and lost it. Times have changed with Carrel. His supremacy is questioned in the Val Tournanche; new men have arisen, and he is no longer recognized as *the* chasseur above all others; but so long as he remains the man that he is to-day it will not be easy to find his superior.

The others had arrived, so we went back to the northern end of the ridge. Croz now took the tent-pole† and planted it in the highest snow. "Yes," we said, "there is the flag-staff, but where is the flag?" "Here it is," he answered, pulling off his blouse and fixing it to the stick. It made a poor flag, and there was no wind to float it out, yet it was seen all around. They saw it at Zermatt, at the Riffel, in the Val Tournanche. At Breuil the watchers cried, "Victory is ours!" They raised "bravos" for Carrel and "vivas" for Italy, and hastened to put themselves *en fête*. On the morrow they were undeceived. All was changed: the explorers returned sad —cast down—disheartened—confounded—gloomy. "It is true," said the men. "We saw them ourselves —they hurled stones at us! The old traditions *are* true—there are spirits on the top of the Matterhorn!" ‡

"CROZ! CROZ! COME HERE!"

of all those who attempted the ascent of the Matterhorn, who most deserved to be the first upon its summit. He was the first to doubt its inaccessibility, and he was the only man who persisted in believing that its ascent would be accomplished. It was the aim of his life to make the ascent from the side of Italy

* I have learned since from J.-A. Carrel that they heard our first cries. They were then upon the southwest ridge, close to the " Cravate," and *twelve hundred and fifty feet* below us, or, as the crow flies, at a distance of about one-third of a mile.

† At our departure the men were confident that the ascent would be made, and took one of the poles out of the tent. I protested that it was tempting Providence: they took the pole, nevertheless.

‡ Signor Giordano was naturally disappointed at the result, and wished the men to start again. *They all refused to do so, with the exception of Jean-Antoine.* Upon the 16th of July he set out again with three others, and upon the 17th gained the summit by passing (at first) up the south-west ridge, and (afterward) by turning over to the Z'Mutt, or north-western side. On the 18th he returned to Breuil.

Whilst we were upon the southern end of the sum-

We returned to the southern end of the ridge to build a cairn, and then paid homage to the view.*   The day was one of those superlatively calm and clear

THE SUMMIT OF THE MATTERHORN IN 1865 (NORTHERN END).

ones which usually precede bad weather. The atmosphere was perfectly still and free from all clouds or vapors. Mountains fifty — nay, a hundred — miles off looked sharp and near. All their details—ridge and crag, snow and glacier — stood out with faultless definition. Pleasant thoughts of happy days in bygone years came up unbidden as we recognized the old, familiar forms. All were revealed—not one of the principal peaks of the Alps was hidden.†   I see them clearly now — the great inner cir

mit-ridge we paid some attention to the portion of the mountain which intervened between ourselves and the Italian guides.   It seemed as if there would not be the least chance for them if they should attempt to storm the final peak directly from the end of the "shoulder." In that direction cliffs fell sheer down from the summit, and we were unable to see beyond a certain distance.   There remained the route about which Carrel and I had often talked—namely, to ascend directly at first from the end of the "shoulder," and afterward to swerve to the left (that is, to the Z'Mutt side), and to complete the ascent from the north-west.   When we were upon the summit we laughed at this idea. The part of the mountain that I have described upon page 619 was not easy, although its inclination was moderate.   If that slope were made only ten degrees steeper its difficulty would be enormously increased. To double its inclination would be to make it impracticable.   The slope at the southern end of the summit-ridge, falling toward the north-west, was *much* steeper than that over which we passed, and we ridiculed the idea that any person should attempt to as-

cend in that direction when the northern route was so easy.   Nevertheless, the summit was reached by that route by the undaunted Carrel.   From knowing the final slope over which he passed, and from the account of Mr. F. C. Grove—who is the only traveler by whom it has been traversed—I do not hesitate to term the ascent of Carrel and Bich in 1865 the most desperate piece of mountain-scrambling upon record. In 1869 I asked Carrel if he had ever done anything more difficult.   His reply was, "Man cannot do anything much more difficult than that."

* The summit-ridge was much shattered, although not so extensively as the south-west and north-east ridges.   The highest rock in 1865 was a block of mica-schist, and the fragment I broke off it not only possesses in a remarkable degree the *character* of the peak, but mimics in an astonishing manner the details of its form.   (See illustration on page 622.)

† It is most unusual to see the southern half of the panorama unclouded.   A hundred ascents may be made before this will be the case again.

cles of giants, backed by the ranges, chains and *massifs.* First came the Dent Blanche, hoary and grand ; the Gabelhorn and pointed Rothhorn, and then the peerless Weisshorn ; the towering Mischabelhörner, flanked by the Allaleinhorn, Strahlhorn and Rimpfischhorn ; then Monte Rosa—with its many Spitzes—the Lyskamm and the Breithorn. Behind were the Bernese Oberland, governed by the Finsteraarhorn, the Simplon and St. Gothard groups, the Disgrazia and the Orteler. Toward the

THE ACTUAL SUMMIT OF THE MATTERHORN.

south we looked down to Chivasso on the plain of Piedmont, and far beyond. The Viso—one hundred miles away— seemed close upon us ; the Maritime Alps—one hundred and thirty miles distant—were free from haze. Then came my first love—the Pelvoux ; the Écrins and the Meije ; the clusters of the Graians ; and lastly, in the west, gorgeous in the full sunlight, rose the monarch of all—Mont Blanc. Ten thousand feet beneath us were the green fields of Zermatt, dotted with chalets, from which blue smoke rose lazily. Eight thousand feet below, on the other side, were the pastures of Breuil. There were forests black and gloomy, and meadows bright and lively ; bounding waterfalls and tranquil lakes ; fertile lands and savage wastes ;

sunny plains and frigid plateaux. There were the most rugged forms and the most graceful outlines—bold, perpendicular cliffs and gentle, undulating slopes ; rocky mountains and snowy mountains, sombre and solemn or glittering and white, with walls, turrets, pinnacles, pyramids, domes, cones and spires ! There was every combination that the world can give, and every contrast that the heart could desire.

We remained on the summit for one hour—

> One crowded hour of glorious life.

It passed away too quickly, and we began to prepare for the descent.

CHAPTER XXII.

DESCENT OF THE MATTERHORN.

HUDSON and I again consulted as to the best and safest arrangement of the party. We agreed that it would be best for Croz to go first,* and Hadow second ; Hudson, who was almost equal to a guide in sureness of foot, wished to be third ; Lord F. Douglas was placed next, and old Peter, the strongest of the remainder, after him. I suggested to Hudson that we should attach a rope to the rocks on our arrival at the difficult bit, and hold it as we descended, as an additional protection. He approved the idea, but it was not definitely settled that it should be done. The party was being arranged in the above order whilst I was sketching the summit, and they had finished, and were waiting for me to be tied in line, when some one remembered that our names had not been left in a bottle. They requested me to write them down, and moved off while it was being done.

A few minutes afterward I tied myself to young Peter, ran down after the others, and caught them just as they were commencing the descent of the dif-

* If the members of the party had been more equally efficient, Croz would have been placed *last.*

ficult part.* Great care was being taken. Only one man was moving at a time : when he was firmly planted, the next advanced, and so on. They had not, however, attached the additional rope to rocks, and nothing was said about it. The suggestion was not made for my own sake, and I am not sure that it even occurred to me again. For some little distance we two followed the others, detached from them, and should have continued so had not Lord F. Douglas asked me, about 3 P. M., to tie on to old Peter, as he feared, he said, that Taugwalder would not be able to hold his ground if a slip occurred.

A few minutes later a sharp-eyed lad ran into the Monte Rosa hotel to Seiler, saying that he had seen an avalanche fall from the summit of the Matterhorn on to the Matterhorngletscher. The boy was reproved for telling idle stories : he was right, nevertheless, and this was what he saw.

Michel Croz had laid aside his axe, and in order to give Mr. Hadow greater security was absolutely taking hold of his legs and putting his feet, one by one, into their proper positions.† As far as I know, no one was actually descending. I cannot speak with certainty, because the two leading men were partially hidden from my sight by an intervening mass of rock, but it is my belief, from the movements of their shoulders, that Croz, having done as I have said, was in the act of turning round to go down a step or two himself : at this moment Mr. Hadow slipped, fell against him, and knocked him over. I heard one startled exclamation from Croz, then saw him and Mr. Hadow flying downward : in another moment Hudson was dragged from his steps, and Lord F. Douglas immediately after him.‡ All this was the

work of a moment. Immediately we heard Croz's exclamation, old Peter and I planted ourselves as firmly as the rocks would permit : § the rope was taut between us, and the jerk came on us both as on one man. We held, but the rope broke midway between Taugwalder and Lord Francis Douglas. For a few seconds we saw our unfortunate companions sliding downward on their backs, and spreading out their hands, endeavoring to save themselves. They passed from our sight uninjured, disappeared one by one, and fell from precipice to precipice on to the Matterhorngletscher below, a distance of nearly four thousand feet in height. From the moment the rope broke it was impossible to help them.

So perished our comrades ! For the space of half an hour we remained on the spot without moving a single step. The two men, paralyzed by terror, cried like infants, and trembled in such a manner as to threaten us with the fate of the others. Old Peter rent the air with exclamations of "Chamounix !—oh, what will Chamounix say ?" He meant, Who would believe that Croz could fall ?

ed good hold, and if he had been aware or had suspected that anything was about to occur, he might and would have gripped it, and would have prevented any mischief. He was taken totally by surprise. Mr. Hadow slipped off his feet on to his back, his feet struck Croz in the small of the back and knocked him right over, head first. Croz's axe was out of his reach, and without it he managed to get his head uppermost before he disappeared from our sight. If it had been in his hand I have no doubt that he would have stopped himself and Mr. Hadow.

Mr. Hadow, at the moment of the slip, was not occupying a bad position. He could have moved either up or down, and could touch with his hand the rock of which I have spoken. Hudson was not so well placed, but he had liberty of motion. The rope was not taut from him to Hadow, and the two men fell ten or twelve feet before the jerk came upon him. Lord F. Douglas was not favorably placed, and could move neither up nor down. Old Peter was firmly planted, and stood just beneath a large rock which he hugged with both arms. I enter into these details to make it more apparent that the position occupied by the party at the moment of the accident was not by any means excessively trying. We were compelled to pass over the exact spot where the slip occurred, and we found—even with shaken nerves—that *it* was not a difficult place to pass. I have described the *slope generally* as difficult, and it is so undoubtedly to most persons, but it must be distinctly understood that Mr. Hadow slipped at an easy part.

§ Or, more correctly, we held on as tightly as possible. There was no time to change our position.

---

* Described upon p. 619.

† Not at all an unusual proceeding, even between born mountaineers. I wish to convey the impression that Croz was using all pains, rather than to indicate extreme inability on the part of Mr. Hadow.

‡ At the moment of the accident, Croz, Hadow and Hudson were all close together. Between Hudson and Lord F. Douglas the rope was all but taut, and the same between all the others who were *above.* Croz was standing by the side of a rock which afford-

FOG-BOW SEEN FROM THE MATTERHORN ON JULY 14, 1865.

"THE TAUGWALDERS THOUGHT THAT IT HAD SOME CONNECTION WITH THE ACCIDENT."

Page 157.

The young man did nothing but scream or sob, "We are lost! we are lost!" Fixed between the two, I could move neither up nor down. I begged young Peter to descend, but he dared not. Unless he did, we could not advance. Old Peter became alive to the danger, and

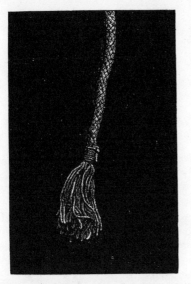

ROPE BROKEN ON THE MATTERHORN.

swelled the cry, "We are lost! we are lost!" The father's fear was natural— he trembled for his son; the young man's fear was cowardly—he thought of self alone. At last old Peter summoned up courage, and changed his position to a rock to which he could fix the rope: the young man then descended, and we all stood together. Immediately we did so, I asked for the rope which had given way, and found, to my surprise—indeed, to my horror—that it was the weakest of the three ropes. It was not brought, and should not have been employed, for the purpose for which it was used. It was old rope, and, compared with the others, was feeble. It was intended as a reserve, in case we had to leave much rope behind attached to rocks. I saw at once that a serious question was involved, and made them give me the end. It had broken in mid-air, and it did not appear to have sustained previous injury.

For more than two hours afterward I

thought almost every moment that the next would be my last, for the Taugwalders, utterly unnerved, were not only incapable of giving assistance, but were in such a state that a slip might have been expected from them at any moment. After a time we were able to do that which should have been done at first, and fixed rope to firm rocks, in addition to being tied together. These ropes were cut from time to time, and were left behind.* Even with their assurance the men were afraid to proceed, and several times old Peter turned with ashy face and faltering limbs, and said with terrible emphasis, "*I cannot !*"

About 6 P. M. we arrived at the snow upon the ridge descending toward Zermatt, and all peril was over. We frequently looked, but in vain, for traces of our unfortunate companions: we bent over the ridge and cried to them, but no sound returned. Convinced at last that they were within neither sight nor hearing, we ceased from our useless efforts, and, too cast down for speech, silently gathered up our things and the little effects of those who were lost, preparatory to continuing the descent. When lo! a mighty arch appeared, rising above the Lyskamm high into the sky. Pale, colorless and noiseless, but perfectly sharp and defined, except where it was lost in the clouds, this unearthly apparition seemed like a vision from another world, and almost appalled we watched with amazement the gradual development of two vast crosses, one on either side. If the Taugwalders had not been the first to perceive it, I should have doubted my senses. They thought it had some connection with the accident, and I, after a while, that it might bear some relation to ourselves. But our movements had no effect upon it. The spectral forms remained motionless. It was a fearful and wonderful sight, unique in my experience, and impressive beyond description, coming at such a moment.†

* These ends, I believe, are still attached to the rocks, and mark our line of ascent and descent.

† See Illustration. I paid very little attention to this remarkable phenomenon, and was glad when it disappeared, as it distracted our attention. Under ordinary circumstances I should have felt vexed after-

I was ready to leave, and waiting for the others. They had recovered their appetites and the use of their tongues. They spoke in patois, which I did not understand. At length the son said in French, "Monsieur." "Yes." "We are poor men; we have lost our Herr; we shall not get paid; we can ill afford this."* "Stop!" I said, interrupting him —"that is nonsense: I shall pay you, of course, just as if your Herr were here." They talked together in their patois for a short time, and then the son spoke again: "We don't wish you to pay us. We wish you to write in the hotel-book at Zermatt and to your journals that we have not been paid." "What nonsense are you talking? I don't understand you. What do you mean?" He proceeded: "Why, next year there will be many travelers at Zermatt, and we shall get more *voyageurs*."

Who would answer such a proposition? I made them no reply in words,† but they knew very well the indignation that I felt.

ward at not having observed with greater precision an occurrence so rare and so wonderful. I can add very little about it to that which is said above. The sun was directly at our backs—that is to say, the fog-bow was opposite to the sun. The time was 6.30 P. M. The forms were at once tender and sharp, neutral in tone, were developed gradually, and disappeared suddenly. The mists were light (that is, not dense), and were dissipated in the course of the evening.

It has been suggested that the crosses are incorrectly figured in the Illustration, and that they were probably formed by the intersection of other circles or

ellipses, as shown in the annexed diagram. I think this suggestion is very likely correct, but I have preferred to follow my original memorandum.

In Parry's *Narrative of an Attempt to Reach the North Pole*, 4to, 1828, there is, at pp. 99, 100, an account of the occurrence of a phenomenon analogous to the above-mentioned one: "At half-past 5 P. M. we witnessed a very beautiful natural phenomenon. A broad white fog-bow first appeared opposite to the sun, as was very commonly the case," etc. I follow Parry in using the term fog-bow.

* They had been traveling with, and had been engaged by, Lord F. Douglas, and so considered him their employer, and responsible to them.

† Nor did I speak to them afterward, unless it was absolutely necessary, so long as we were together.

They filled the cup of bitterness to overflowing, and I tore down the cliff madly and recklessly, in a way that caused them, more than once, to inquire if I wished to kill them. Night fell, and for an hour the descent was continued in the darkness. At half-past nine a rest-

MONSIEUR ALEX. SEILER.

ing-place was found, and upon a wretched slab, barely large enough to hold the three, we passed six miserable hours. At daybreak the descent was resumed, and from the Hörnli ridge we ran down to the chalets of Buhl and on to Zermatt. Seiler met me at his door, and followed in silence to my room: "What is the matter?" "The Taugwalders and I have returned." He did not need more, but burst into tears, but lost no time in useless lamentations, and set to work to arouse the village. Ere long a score of men had started to ascend the Hohlicht heights, above Kalbermatt and Z'Mutt, which commanded the plateau of the Matterhorngletscher. They returned after six hours, and reported that they had seen the bodies lying motionless on the snow. This was on Saturday, and they proposed that we should leave on Sunday evening, so as to arrive upon the plateau at daybreak on Monday. Unwilling to lose the slightest chance, the Rev. J. M'Cormick and I resolved to start on Sunday morning. The Zermatt men, threatened with excommunication by their priests if they failed to attend the early mass, were unable to accompany us. To several of them, at least, this was a severe trial, and Peter Perrn declared with tears that nothing else would have prevented him from joining in the search for his old comrades. Englishmen came to our aid. The Rev. J. Robertson and Mr. J. Phillpotts offered themselves and their guide, Franz Andermatten : another Englishman lent us Joseph Marie and Alexandre Lochmatter. Frédéric Payot and Jean Tairraz of Chamounix also volunteered.

THE MANILA ROPE.*

We started at 2 A. M. on Sunday, the 16th, and followed the route that we had taken on the previous Thursday as far as the Hörnli. From thence we went down to the right of the ridge, and mounted through the *séracs* of the Matterhorngletscher. By 8.30 we had got to the plateau at the top of the glacier, and within sight of the corner in which we knew my companions must be. As we saw one weather-beaten man after

another raise the telescope, turn deadly pale and pass it on without a word to the next, we knew that all hope was gone. We approached. They had fallen below as they had fallen above— Croz a little in advance, Hadow near him, and Hudson some distance behind, but of Lord F. Douglas we could see nothing.† We left them where they fell, buried in snow at the base of the grandest cliff of the most majestic mountain of the Alps.

All those who had fallen had been tied with the Manila, or with the second and equally strong rope, and consequently there had been only one link — that between old Peter and Lord F. Douglas — where the weaker rope had been used. This had a very ugly look for Taugwalder, for it was not possible to suppose that the others would have sanctioned the employment of a rope so greatly inferior in strength when there were more than two hundred and fifty feet of the better qualities still out of use.‡ For the sake of the old guide (who bore a good reputation), and upon all other accounts, it was desirable that this matter should be cleared up; and after my examination before the court of inquiry which was instituted by the government was over, I handed in a number of questions which were framed so as to afford old Peter an opportunity of exculpating himself from the grave suspicions which at once fell upon him. The questions, I was told, were put and answered, but the answers, although promised, have never reached me.§

---

* The three ropes have been reduced by photography to the same scale.

† A pair of gloves, a belt and boot that had belonged to him were found. This, somehow, became publicly known, and gave rise to wild notions, which would not have been entertained had it been also known that the boots of *all* those who had fallen *were off*, and were lying upon the snow near the bodies.

‡ I was one hundred feet or more from the others whilst they were being tied up, and am unable to throw any light on the matter. Croz and old Peter no doubt tied up the others.

§ This is not the only occasion upon which M. Clemenz (who presided over the inquiry) has failed to give up answers that he has promised. It is greatly to be regretted that he does not feel that the suppression of the truth is equally against the interests of travelers

Meanwhile, the administration sent strict injunctions to recover the bodies, and upon the 19th of July twenty-one men of Zermatt accomplished that sad and dangerous task. Of the body of Lord Francis Douglas they too saw nothing: it is probably still arrested on the rocks above.* The remains of Hudson and Hadow were interred upon the north side of the Zermatt church, in the presence of a reverent crowd of sympathizing friends. The body of Michel Croz lies upon the other side, under a simpler tomb, whose inscription bears honorable testimony to his rectitude, to his courage and to his devotion.†

and of the guides. If the men are untrustworthy, the public should be warned of the fact, but if they are blameless, why allow them to remain under unmerited suspicion?

Old Peter Taugwalder is a man who is laboring under an unjust accusation. Notwithstanding repeated denials, even his comrades and neighbors at Zermatt persist in asserting or insinuating that he *cut* the rope which led from him to Lord F. Douglas. In regard to this infamous charge, I say that he *could* not do so at the moment of the slip, and that the end of the rope in my possession shows that he did not do so beforehand. There remains, however, the suspicious fact that the rope which broke was the thinnest and weakest one that we had. It is suspicious, because it is unlikely that any of the four men in front would have selected an old and weak rope when there was abundance of new and much stronger rope to spare; and on the other hand, because if Taugwalder thought that an accident was likely to happen, it was to his interest to have the weaker rope where it was placed.

I should rejoice to learn that his answers to the questions which were put to him were satisfactory. Not only was his act at the critical moment wonderful as a feat of strength, but it was admirable in its performance at the right time. I am told that he is now nearly incapable of work—not absolutely mad, but with intellect gone and almost crazy; which is not to be wondered at, whether we regard him as a man who contemplated a scoundrelly meanness, or as an injured man suffering under an unjust accusation.

In respect to young Peter, it is not possible to speak in the same manner. The odious idea that he propounded (which I believe emanated from *him*) he has endeavored to trade upon, in spite of the fact that his father was paid (for both) in the presence of witnesses. Whatever may be his abilities as a guide, he is not one to whom I would ever trust my life or afford any countenance.

* This or a subsequent party discovered a sleeve. No other traces have been found.

† At the instance of Mr. Alfred Wills, a subscription-list was opened for the benefit of the sisters of Michel Croz, who had been partly dependent upon his earnings. In a short time more than two hundred and eighty pounds were raised. This was considered sufficient, and the list closed. The proceeds were invested in French Rentes (by Mr. William Mathews), at the recommendation of M. Dupui, at that time maire of Chamounix.

So the traditional inaccessibility of the Matterhorn was vanquished, and was replaced by legends of a more real character. Others will essay to scale its proud cliffs, but to none will it be the

THE SECOND ROPE.

mountain that it was to its early explorers. Others may tread its summit-snows, but none will ever know the feelings of those who first gazed upon its marvelous panorama, and none, I trust, will ever be compelled to tell of joy turned into grief, and of laughter into mourning. It proved to be a stubborn foe; it resisted long and gave many a hard blow; it was defeated at last with an ease that none could have anticipated, but, like a relentless enemy conquered but not crushed, it took terrible vengeance. The time may come when the Matterhorn shall have passed away, and nothing save a heap of shapeless fragments will mark the spot where the great mountain stood, for, atom by atom, inch by inch, and yard by yard, it yields to forces which nothing can withstand. That time is far distant, and ages hence generations unborn will gaze upon its awful precipices and wonder at its unique form. However exalted may be their ideas and however exaggerated their expectations, none will come to return disappointed !

The play is over, and the curtain is about to fall. Before we part, a word upon the graver teachings of the mountains. See yonder height! 'Tis far away—unbidden comes the word "Impossible!" "Not so," says the mountaineer. "The way is long, I know: it's difficult—it may be dangerous. It's possible, I'm sure : I'll seek the way, take counsel of my brother mountaineers, and find how they have gained similar heights and learned to avoid the dangers." He starts (all slumbering down below): the path is slippery—maybe laborious too. Caution and perseverance gain the day —the height is reached ! and those beneath cry, "Incredible! 'tis superhuman !"

We who go mountain-scrambling have constantly set before us the superiority of fixed purpose or perseverance to brute force. We know that each height, each step, must be gained by patient, laborious toil, and that wishing cannot take the place of working : we know the benefits of mutual aid—that many a difficulty must-be encountered, and many an obstacle must be grappled with or turned ; but we know that where there's a will there's a way ; and we come back to our daily occupations better fitted to fight the battle of life and to overcome the impediments which obstruct our paths, strengthened and cheered by the recollection of past labors and by the memories of victories gained in other fields.

I have not made myself an advocate or an apologist for mountaineering, nor do I now intend to usurp the functions of a moralist, but my task would have been ill performed if it had been concluded without one reference to the

more serious lessons of the mountaineer. We glory in the physical regeneration which is the product of our exertions ; we exult over the grandeur of the scenes that are brought before our eyes, the splendors of sunrise and sunset, and the beauties of hill, dale, lake, wood and waterfall ; but we value more highly the development of manliness, and the evolution, under combat with difficulties, of those noble qualities of human nature— courage, patience, endurance and fortitude.

Some hold these virtues in less estimation, and assign base and contemptible motives to those who indulge in our innocent sport.

Be thou chaste as ice, as pure as snow, thou shalt not escape calumny.

Others, again, who are not detractors, find mountaineering, as a sport, to be wholly unintelligible. It is not greatly to be wondered at—we are not all constituted alike. Mountaineering is a pursuit essentially adapted to the young or vigorous, and not to the old or feeble. To the latter toil may be no pleasure, and it is often said by such persons, "This man is making a toil of pleasure." Toil he must who goes mountaineering, but out of the toil comes strength (not merely muscular energy — more than that, an awakening of all the faculties), and from the strength arises pleasure. Then, again, it is often asked, in tones which seem to imply that the answer must at least be doubtful, "But does it repay you ?" Well, we cannot estimate our enjoyment as you measure your wine or weigh your lead : it is real, nevertheless. If I could blot out every reminiscence or erase every memory, still I should say that my scrambles amongst the Alps have repaid me, for they have given me two of the best things a man can possess—health and friends.

The recollections of past pleasures cannot be effaced. Even now as I write they crowd up before me. First comes an endless series of pictures, magnificent in form, effect and color. I see the great peaks with clouded tops, seeming to mount up for ever and ever ; I hear the music of the distant herds, the peasant's jodel and the solemn church-bells; and I scent the fragrant breath of the pines: and after these have passed away another train of thoughts succeeds—of those who have been upright, brave and true; of kind hearts and bold deeds; and of courtesies received at stranger hands, trifles in themselves, but expressive of that good-will toward men which is the essence of charity.

Still, the last sad memory hovers round, and sometimes drifts across like floating mist, cutting off sunshine and chilling the remembrance of happier times. There have been joys too great to be described in words, and there have been griefs upon which I have not dared to dwell; and with these in mind I say, Climb if you will, but remember that courage and strength are naught without prudence, and that a momentary negligence may destroy the happiness of a lifetime. Do nothing in haste, look well to each step, and from the beginning think what may be the end.

APPENDIX.

A. SUBSEQUENT ASCENTS OF THE MATTERHORN.

Mr. Craufurd Grove was the first traveler who ascended the Matterhorn after the accident. This was in August, 1867. He took with him as guides three mountaineers of the Val Tournanche—J.-A. Carrel, J. Bich and S. Meynet, Carrel being the leader. The natives of Val Tournanche were, of course, greatly delighted that his ascent was made upon their side. Some of them, however, were by no means well pleased that J.-A. Carrel was so much regarded. They feared, perhaps, that he would acquire the monopoly of the mountain. Just a month after Mr. Grove's ascent, six Val Tournanchians set out to see whether they could not learn the route, and so come in for a share of the good things which were expected to arrive. They were three Maquignazes, Cæsar Carrel (my old guide), J.-B. Carrel, and a daughter of the last named! They left Breuil at 5 A. M. on September 12, and at 3 P. M. arrived at the hut, where they passed the night. At 7 A. M the next day they started again (leaving J.-B. Carrel behind), and proceeded along the "shoulder" to the final peak; passed the cleft which had stopped Bennen,

and clambered up the comparatively easy rocks on the other side until they arrived at the base of the last precipice, down which we had hurled stones on July 14, 1865. They (young woman and all) were then about three hundred and fifty feet from the summit! Then, instead of turning to the left, as Carrel and Mr. Grove had done, Joseph and J.-Pierre Maquignaz paid attention to the cliff in front of them, and managed to find a means of passing up, by clefts, ledges and gullies, to the summit. This was a shorter (and it appears to be an easier) route than that taken by Carrel and Grove, and it has been followed by all those who have since then ascended the mountain from the side of Breuil. Subsequently, a rope was fixed over the most difficult portions of the final climb.

In the mean time they had not been idle upon the other side. A hut was constructed upon the eastern face at a height of 12,526 feet above the sea, near to the crest of the ridge which descends toward Zermatt (north-east ridge). This was done at the expense of Monsieur Seiler and of the Swiss Alpine Club. Mons. Seiler placed the execution of the work under the direction of the Knubels, of the village of St. Nicholas, in the Zermatt valley ; and Peter Knubel, along with Joseph Marie Lochmatter of the same village, had the honor of making the second ascent of the mountain upon the northern side with Mr. Elliott. This took

PINNACLES NEAR SACHAS IN THE VALLEY OF THE DURANCE, FORMED FROM AN OLD MORAINE.

place on July 24 and 25, 1868. Since then numerous ascents have been made, and of these the only one which calls for mention is' that by Signor Giordano, on September 3–5, 1868. This gentleman came to

Breuil several times after his famous visit in 1865, with the intention of making the ascent, but he was always baffled by weather. In July, 1866, he got as high as the "cravate" (with J.-A. Carrel and other men), and *was detained there five days and nights, unable to move either up or down!* At last, upon the above-named date, he was able to gratify his desires, and accomplished the feat of ascending the mountain upon one side and descending it upon the other. Signor Giordano is, I believe, the only geologist who has ascended the Matterhorn. He spent a considerable time in the examination of its structure, and became benighted on its eastern face in consequence.

B. DENUDATION IN THE VALLEY OF THE DURANCE.

In the summer of 1869, whilst walking up the valley of the Durance from Mont Dauphin to Briançon, I noticed, when about five kilomètres from the latter place, some pinnacles on the mountain-slopes to the west of the road. I scrambled up, and found the remarkable natural pillars which are represented in the annexed engraving. They were formed out of an unstratified conglomerate of gritty earth, boulders and stones. Some of them were more thickly studded with stones than a plum-pudding usually is with plums, whilst from others the stones projected like the spines from an echinoderm. The earth (or mud) was extremely hard and tenacious, and the stones embedded in it were extricated with considerable difficulty. The mud adhered very firmly to the stones that were got out, but it was readily washed away in a little stream near at hand. In a few minutes I extracted fragments of syenite, mica-schist, several kinds of limestone and conglomerate, and some fossil plants characteristic of carboniferous strata. Most of the fragments were covered with scratches, which told that they had traveled underneath a glacier. The mud had all the character of glacier-mud, and the hillside was covered with drift. From these indications, and from the situation of the pinnacles, I concluded that they had been formed out of an old moraine. The greatest of them were sixty to seventy feet high, and the moraine had therefore been at least

that height. I judged from appearances that the moraine was a frontal-terminal one of a glacier which had been an affluent of the great glacier that formerly occupied the valley of the Durance, and which during retrogression had made a stand upon this hillside near Sachas. This lateral glacier had flowed down a nameless *vallon* which descends toward the east-south-east from the mountain called upon the French government map Sommet de l'Eychouda (8740 feet).

Only one of all the pinnacles that I saw was *capped* by a stone (a small one), and I did not notice any boulders lying in their immediate vicinity of a size sufficient to account for their production in the manner of the celebrated pillars near Botzen. The readers of Sir Charles Lyell's *Principles* (10th ed., vol. i., p. 338) will remember that he attributes the formation of the Botzen pillars chiefly to the protection which boulders have afforded to the underlying matter from the direct action of rain. This is no doubt correct: the Botzen pinnacles are mostly capped by boulders of considerable dimensions. In the present instance this does not appear to have been exactly the case. Running water has cut the moraine into ridges (shown upon the right hand of the engraving), and has evidently assisted in the work of denudation. The group of pinnacles here figured belonged, in all probability, to a ridge which had been formed in this way, whose crest, in course of time, became sharp, perhaps attenuated. In such a condition very small stones upon the crest of the ridge would originate little pinnacles: whether these would develop into larger ones would depend upon the quantity of stones embedded in the surrounding moraine-matter. I imagine that the largest of the Sachas pinnacles owe their existence to the portions of the moraine out of which they are formed having been studded with a greater quantity of stones and small boulders than the portions of the moraine which formerly filled the gaps between them; and, of course, primarily, to the facts that glacier-mud is extremely tenacious when dry, and is readily washed away. Thus, the present form of the pinnacles is chiefly due to the direct action of rain, but their production was assisted, in the first instance, by the action of running water.